THE POLITICS OF GLOBAL
HEALTH GOVERNANCE

Mark Zacher: Publications

Dag Hammarskjold's United Nations (New York: Columbia University Press, 1970).

Canadian Foreign Policy and the Law of the Sea (Vancouver: University of British Columbia Press, 1977) (coeditor with Barbara Johnson).

International Conflicts and Collective Security, 1946–77: The United Nations, Organization of American States, Organization of African Unity, and Arab League (New York: Praeger, 1979).

Pollution, Politics and International Law: Tankers at Sea (Berkeley: University of California Press, 1979) (with R. Michael M'Gonigle).

"The GATT and the Regulation of Trade Barriers: Regime Dynamics and Functions," *International Organization* 35 (Autumn 1981): 561–602. [Reprinted in Stephen Krasner, ed., *International Regimes* (Ithaca, NY: Cornell University Press, 1983), pp 273–314] (with Jock A. Finlayson).

"Trade Gaps, Analytical Gaps: Regime Analysis and International Commodity Trade Regulations," *International Organization* 41 (Spring 1987): 173–202.

"The United Nations and Collective Security: Retrospect and Prospect," in T.B. Gati, ed., *The US, the UN, and the Management of Global Change* (New York: New York University Press, 1983), pp. 162–83 (with Jock A. Finlayson).

Managing International Markets: Developing Countries and the Commodity Trade Regime (New York: Columbia University Press, 1988) (with Jock A. Finlayson).

"Down to the Sea with Stakes: The Evolving Law of the Sea and the Future of the Deep Seabed Regime," *Ocean Development and International Law* 21 (1990): 71–103 (first author; with James McConnell).

"The Decaying Pillars of the Westphalian Temple: Implications for International Order and Governance," in James Rosenau, ed., *Governance without Government* (Cambridge: Cambridge University Press, 1992), pp. 58–101.

Canadian Foreign Policy and International Economic Regimes (Vancouver: UBC Press, 1992) (coeditor with Claire Cutler).

The International Political Economy of Natural Resources (2 vols.) (London: Edward Elgar, 1992) (editor). "Multilateral Organizations and the Institution of Multilateralism: The International Regimes for Non-terrestrial Spaces," in John G. Ruggie, ed., *Multilateralism Matters: The Theory and Praxis of an Institutional Form* (New York: Columbia University Press, 1993), pp. 399–442.

"Liberal International Theory: Common Threads, Divergent Strands," in Charles Kegley, ed., *Controversies in International Relations Theory: Realism and the Neoliberal Challenge* (New York: St. Martin's, 1995), pp. 107–149 (first author; with Richard A. Matthew).

Governing Global Networks: International Regimes for Transportation and Communications (Cambridge University Press, 1996) (first author; with Brent Sutton).

"Mutual Interests, Normative Continuities, and Regime Theory: Cooperation in International Transportation and Communications Industries," *European Journal of International Relations* 2 (Spring 1996): 5–46 (with Brent Sutton).

"The Global Economy and the International Political Order: Some Diverse and Pardoxical Relationships," in Thomas Courchene, ed., *The Nation State in a Global/Information Era: Policy Challenges* (Kingston, ON: John Deutsch Institute for the Study of Economic Policy, 1997), pp. 67–82.

"Epidemiological Surveillance: International Cooperation to Monitor Infectious Diseases," in Inge Kaul, Marc Stern, and Isabelle Grunberg, eds., *Global Public Goods* (Oxford: Oxford University Press, 1999), pp. 268–85.

"Uniting Nations: Global Regimes and the UN System," in Raimo Vayrynen, ed., *Global Governance* (Lanham, MD: Rowman and Littlefield, 1999), pp. 47–66.

The United Nations and Global Commerce (New York: United Nations, 1999).

"The Territorial Integrity Norm: International Boundaries and the Use of Force," *International Organization* 55 (Spring 2001): 215–50.

"Capitalism, Technology, and Liberalization: The International Telecommunications Regime, 1865–1998," in James N. Rosenau and J.P. Singh, eds., *Information Technologies and Global Politics: The Changing Scope of Power and Governance* (State University of New York Press, 2002), pp. 189–210.

"The International Health Regulations in Historical Perspective," in Andrew Price-Smith, *Plagues and Politics: Infectious Diseases and International Policy* (New York: Palgrave/St. Martin's, 2002) (second author; with Simon Carvalho).

"The Conundrums of Power Sharing: The Politics of Security Council Reform" (Ottawa: Canadian Centre for Foreign Policy Development, Department of Foreign Affairs and International Trade, March 28, 2003) (www.dfait-maeci, gc.ca/cfp-pec/library/Zacher-en.asp).

"International Health Governance—Surveillance, Regulation, and Material Assistance: Trends and Lessons for the Future" (Ottawa: External Advisory Committee on Smart Regulation, Privy Council Office, November 2003) (www.smartregulation.gc.ca/en/06/01/su-12.asp).

The United Nations and Global Security (New York: Palgrave, 2004) (coedited with Richard Price).

"The Conundrums of Power Sharing: The Politics of UN Security Council Reform," in Price and Zacher, eds., *The United Nations and Global Security* (New York: Palgrave Macmillan, 2004), pp. 211–226.

"Human Security and International Collaboration: Lessons from Public Goods Theory," in Lincoln Chen, Sakido Fukuda-Parr and Ellen Seidenbsticker, eds., *Human Insecurity in a Global World* (Cambridge, MA: Global Equity Initiative, Asia Center, Harvard University, 2003) (coauthored with Fen Hampson).

"Human Security and Global Governance," in Chantal de Jonge Andraat, ed., *Transatlantic Relations and Global Governance* (Washington, DC: Johns Hopkins School of Advanced International Studies, 2006) (with Brian Job).

"The Transformation of Global Health Collaboration since the 1990s," in Andrew F. Cooper, John J. Kirton, and Ted Schrecker, eds., *Governing Global Health: Challenge, Response, Innovation* (Aldershot, UK: Ashgate, 2007), p. 1528.

THE POLITICS OF GLOBAL HEALTH GOVERNANCE

UNITED BY CONTAGION

Mark W. Zacher

and

Tania J. Keefe

First published in 2008 by
PALGRAVE MACMILLAN™
175 Fifth Avenue, New York, N.Y. 10010 and
Houndmills, Basingstoke, Hampshire, England RG21 6XS
Companies and representatives throughout the world.

PALGRAVE MACMILLAN is the global academic imprint of the Palgrave Macmillan division of St. Martin's Press, LLC and of Palgrave Macmillan Ltd. Macmillan® is a registered trademark in the United States, United Kingdom and other countries. Palgrave is a registered trademark in the European Union and other countries.

ISBN-13: 978–0–230–60589–3
ISBN-10: 0–230–60589–3

Library of Congress Cataloging-in-Publication Data

Zacher, Mark W.
    The politics of global health governance : united by contagion / by Mark W. Zacher, Tania J. Keefe.
        p. cm.
    Includes bibliographical references and index.
    ISBN-13: 978–0–230–60589–3
    ISBN-10: 0–230–60589–3
    1. Medical policy—International cooperation. 2. Communicable diseases—Congrol—International cooperation. 3. World health. I. Keefe, Tania J. II. Title.
    [DNLM: 1. Communicable Disease Control—methods. 2. Health Policy. 3. International Cooperation. 4. World Health. WA 110 Z16p 2008]

RA394.Z33 2008
362.1—dc22   2007047295

A catalogue record for this book is available from the British Library.

Design by Newgen Imaging Systems (P) Ltd., Chennai, India.

First edition: May 2008

10 9 8 7 6 5 4 3 2 1

Printed in the United States of America.

CONTENTS

TABLES

Appendix A

ACKNOWLEDGMENTS

We have benefited a great deal from the assistance of individuals and institutions during the course of researching and writing this study. In particular, we would like to thank the following people. Simon Carvalho, now a lawyer with Health Canada Legal Services, was especially helpful in researching and deciphering the early negotiations and agreements on global health collaboration. Both Hilla Aharon and Oana Papuc carried out excellent research on a variety of topics cheerfully and conscientiously. Finally, Nadya Repin provided invaluable assistance both in terms of the caliber of her research and in completing the unenviable yet critical tasks of organizing the extensive list of references and compiling the index.

We appreciate the valuable and insightful commentary on early drafts of the manuscript provided by Jillian Clare Cohen-Kohler, Christina Clark, Ronald St. John, and Devi Sridhar. Also, Toby Wahl, and Emily Hue of Palgrave Macmillan have been very helpful in providing assistance related to the publication of the book.

Financial support for the project was generously provided by the Humanities and Social Sciences Research Council of Canada, the Peter Wall Institute for Advanced Studies (University of British Columbia), the Center of International Relations (UBC), the Liu Institute for Global Issues (UBC), and the Munk Center for International Studies (including the Comparative Program on Health and Society, University of Toronto). Particular thanks are extended to Brian Job, Dianne Newell, Janice Stein, Jennifer Matheson, and Jennifer MacKay (especially for the fig newtons!).

Tania Keefe is very grateful to her partner Brad Zaytsoff for his support and willingness to listen to frequent diatribes on infectious diseases. Mark Zacher is likewise very grateful to his wife Carol for her constant support and tolerance of his prolonged involvement in this project.

ABBREVIATIONS

Acquired Immune Deficiency Syndrome (AIDS)
Agreement on Sanitary and Phytosanitary Measures (SPS)
Agreement on Technical Barriers to Trade (TBT)
Agreement on Trade Related Aspects of Intellectual Property (TRIPS)
Antiretroviral therapy (ART)
Bacille Calmette Guerin (BCG)
Centers for Disease Control and Prevention (CDC)
Consumer Project on Technology (CPTech)
Dengue Haemorrhagic Fever (DHF)
Dichloro diphenyltrichloroethane (DDT)
Direct Observation Treatment—Short-course (DOTS)
Disability Adjusted Life Years (DALYs)
Enterohaemorrhagic E.coli (EHEC)
Food and Agriculture Organization (FAO)
General Agreement on Tariffs and Trade (GATT)
General Agreement on Trade in Services (GATS)
Global Emerging Infections Surveillance and Response System (GEIS)
Global health partnerships (GHPs)
Global Outbreak Alert and Response Network (GOARN)
Global Public Health Intelligence Network (GPHIN)
Health Action International (HAI)
Human Immunodeficiency Virus (HIV)
Human Papillomavirus (HPV)
International Civil Aviation Organization (ICAO)
International Federation of Red Cross and Red Crescent Societies (IFRC)
International Health Regulations (IHR)
International Maritime Organization (IMO)
International Sanitary Regulations (ISR)
League of Nations Health Organization (LNHO)
List of Essential Medicines (EML)
Medecins Sans Frontieres (MSF)

Multidrug Therapy (MDT)
National Influenza Centers (NICs)
Office Internationale d'Hygiene Publique (OIHP)
Official Development Assistance (ODA)
Oral Rehydration Salts (ORS)
Organization for Economic Cooperation and Development (OECD)
Pan-American Health Organization (PAHO)
President's Emergency Plan for AIDS Relief (PEPFAR)
Program for Monitoring Emerging Diseases (ProMED)
Severe Acute Respiratory Syndrome (SARS)
Tuberculosis (TB)
U.S. Army Medical Research Institute of Infectious Diseases (USAMRIID)
UN Relief and Rehabilitation Administration (UNRRA)
United Nations Children's Fund (UNICEF)
United Nations Development Program (UNDP)
United Nations Population Fund (UNFPA)
United States Trade Representative (USTR)
Weekly Epidemiological Record (WER)
World Health Assembly (WHA)
World Health Organization (WHO)
World Intellectual Property Organization (WIPO)
World Organization for Animal Health (OIE)
World Trade Organization (WTO)

CHAPTER 1

OVERVIEW OF INFECTIOUS DISEASES
AND ANALYTICAL FRAMEWORK

Health, or the lack thereof, has shaped human civilizations for millennia, and it is undoubtedly going to be a predominant issue throughout the twenty-first century. Health is the ultimate unifying issue for humankind—the world is becoming an ever smaller place, and microbes that cause devastating diseases do not stop for border guards. More and more we are coming to understand that people with diseases located anywhere from down the street to the other side of the globe have important and varied impacts on our well-being. Health has become more than a medical issue; it is also a development issue, a commercial issue, a humanitarian issue, and a security issue.

In recent years, people from all walks of life have become involved in the health sphere. It seems that everyone—from billionaire philanthropists, to government bureaucrats, to world famous rock musicians—has something to say about the global health situation. The significance of health is recognized everywhere. Hollywood regularly releases blockbuster films about disease outbreaks that wipe out vast segments of the human race; novels that depict bioterrorist attacks of gruesome diseases consistently make the bestseller lists; and barely a newspaper gets printed that does not have some mention of AIDS, influenza, anthrax, or Ebola and the threats these diseases pose to humans around the globe. Although other aspects of health, including noncommunicable diseases and mental health, are certainly serious issues, this study specifically focuses on efforts to control the incidence and spread of infectious diseases because of the lessons that can be learned about cooperation and multilateralism within international relations.[1]

Throughout history, humans have been victims of disease-causing microbes, viruses, and parasites. Indeed, for the vast majority of our history, we had virtually no comprehension of the causes of diseases let alone how to cure them. In the past century and a half, however, knowledge regarding human health has increased at an entirely unprecedented rate. This knowledge has allowed us to prevent, treat, and cure diseases that used to decimate entire civilizations. In fact, medical knowledge has increased so dramatically that in the late 1960s and early 1970s many health officials genuinely believed that humans were on the verge of eradicating infectious diseases once and for all. Although the discovery of the HIV/AIDS virus in 1981 put a stop to this kind of naively optimistic thinking, there are measurable indicators such as increased life expectancy and the reduction of infectious diseases in developed countries that prove humans now have the capacity to significantly improve their own health. But improvements in health care have not been distributed equally, and there is now a global drive to improve health for all.

This book describes and explains how the fight to control infectious diseases has brought together state governments, intergovernmental organizations (IGOs) and nongovernmental organizations (NGOs), and private actors around the world to an unprecedented degree. It seeks to explain how and why this collaboration has occurred, what impact it has had on reducing the impact of disease on humanity, and what cooperation in the health sphere can teach us about cooperation in other spheres of international relations.

Global Impacts of Disease: Historical Overview

Microbes that cause infectious diseases (bacteria, viruses, parasites, and fungi) have long caused death, debilitation, and disfigurement for human beings. In fact, for much of human history since the emergence of stable agricultural communities, they have been the predominant cause of death. In the millennia before the first century AD, microbes that caused diseases largely circulated among humans in regional settings; there was little exchange of these microbes between continents.[2] Nevertheless, the destruction wrought by infectious diseases, in terms of both health and politics, had disastrous effects on most populated regions of the world. For example, an epidemic disease struck the Athenian Empire during the Peloponnesian wars in the fifth century BC that killed between one-third and two-thirds of the population.[3] Also, one half of the population of the Byzantine Empire was killed, probably by plague, in the sixth century AD.[4] The Roman Empire, between the second and sixth centuries AD, suffered recurrent large numbers of deaths from a variety of diseases—particularly smallpox, gonorrhea, bubonic plague, and malaria. The Mediterranean world was certainly not the only region that suffered major losses from the plague in this era; Asia regularly confronted large numbers of deaths from the spread of this disease.

Europe, during the Middle Ages, witnessed the spread of deadly infectious diseases from the Middle East and Asia. Smallpox and measles, which are thought to have originated in and around what is now Egypt and Iraq, arrived in Europe in the early Middle Ages and killed many.[5] The Crusaders played an important role in spreading diseases to Europe—notably leprosy.[6] The impact of disease on the Crusaders themselves while in the Middle East is highlighted by the comment of Hans Zinsser: "That the Crusades were turned back by epidemics much more effectively than they were by the armed power of the Saracens can hardly be questioned."[7]

In the latter Middle Ages diseases began to spread over greater distances owing to improvements in ship design and burgeoning maritime and overland trade. To quote William McNeill: "After 1300, contacts between the major civilizations of the Old World became closer and closer. Disease exchanges intensified correspondingly, with frequent disastrous, but never quite paralyzing, consequences."[8] In fact, the end of the Middle Ages in the fourteenth century witnessed a major health and societal disaster in the form of an epidemic of the plague—commonly referred to as the Black Death. The Black Death, which raged for just one year between 1348 and 1349, killed between 30 and 50 percent of the population of Western Europe. It was spread by traders who contracted it from Tartars who were besieging ports on the Black Sea. Most people ascribe the pandemic to bubonic and pneumonic plague; however, some argue that it acted in tandem with an outbreak of anthrax.[9] Regardless of its agent, the Black Death has been referred to as "the greatest bio-medical disaster in European and possibly world history."[10]

The Black Death acted as the catalyst for the first major attempts on the part of political authorities to control the movement of infected travelers and ships. For example, during this outbreak of plague, Venice and Milan for the first time prevented ships from infected regions from entering their ports. The Republic of Ragusa established the practice of isolating potentially infected travelers for a period of 40 days. In fact, the term "quarantine" is derived from the Latin and Italian words for 40. By 1403, Venice had established quarantine stations or lazarettos at the major marine entry points to the city to control the entry of infected voyagers.[11] In 1527, a practice of requiring bills of health (documents verifying that a ship was free of disease in its last port of call) was instituted by some countries, and by 1665 bills of health were accepted by most political entities.[12] By the nineteenth century, virtually all states had developed systems of quarantine control in ports and at borders, albeit quite varied ones.[13]

McNeill has written that "as ships began to ply the oceans they carried germs as well as goods."[14] And if there is one overpowering example of this evaluation, it was the spreading of diseases between Europe, Africa, and the Western Hemisphere following the entry of Spanish colonialists into the Western Hemisphere in the late fifteenth and early sixteenth centuries. The worst disasters befell natives of what we now know as Latin America and the Caribbean. In the sixteenth and seventeenth centuries, the introduction of European and African diseases led to the death of an appalling 90 percent of the native Indian population of Latin America. The most lethal diseases were smallpox, measles, influenza, typhus, and malaria; other very harmful diseases were diphtheria, mumps, pertussis (whooping cough), plague, and tuberculosis (TB).[15] It is highly doubtful whether the Spanish under Cortez in Mexico, or under Pizzaro in Peru, would have enjoyed the military successes that they did if it had not been for the huge number of indigenous people who died from European infectious diseases. Apart from the diseases that were spread from Europe to the Western Hemisphere, some other illnesses were introduced into the region by the 11 million African slaves who were forcibly brought to the Americas in the seventeenth and eighteenth centuries. These diseases included malaria, sleeping sickness, schistosomiasis, yellow fever, and elephantiasis.[16] Yellow fever was first transmitted from Africa to Mexico in the middle of the seventeenth century, and in the following two and a half centuries it killed millions of people in South and North America.[17]

The major disease that was probably transmitted from Europe to the Western Hemisphere is syphilis, but it spread to many other areas of the world as well.[18] At the same time, typhus was introduced into Europe by soldiers returning home from Cyprus. It was sometimes referred to as "a disease of dirt" because it thrived in poor and dirty living conditions such as those often inhabited by armies.[19]

Europeans spread diseases to many parts of the world in the sixteenth and seventeenth centuries and many of them also died at this time from endemic diseases—typhus, plague, dysentery, typhoid fever, measles, and smallpox. Diseases spread by armies between 1618 and 1648 during the Thirty Years War had particularly devastating effects on both soldiers and the general population—especially from typhus.[20] At the same time, by the end of the seventeenth century plague had largely disappeared from Europe.[21] One notable aspect of the seventeenth century, from the perspective of global health, is that for the first time the same pattern of diseases existed in almost all regions of the world. As McNeill explains, "after the sixteenth century, no really large human communities remained outside the disease-net European shipping had already woven across all the earth's oceans and coastlines."[22]

The early part of the nineteenth century witnessed developments that caused both optimism and pessimism regarding the international spread of infectious diseases. On the one hand, in 1796, William Jenner developed a vaccine for smallpox, which soon had a dramatic impact on most industrializing nations. On the other hand, diseases spread by the Napoleonic Wars (especially typhus and dysentery) from the late 1790s through 1815 took large tolls of human life among troops and civilians.[23] Also, in 1817, the first of six global cholera pandemics that occurred in the nineteenth century spread from the Indian subcontinent. Each of the cholera pandemics killed millions of people as it raced from Asia to different parts of the world.[24] Cholera was the major international health concern in the 1800s, although the spread of yellow fever was a very important issue in the Western Hemisphere. Controlling cholera was a particular concern in the Middle East, especially in the areas of Mecca and Medina in present-day Saudi Arabia, which attracted large numbers of Muslim pilgrims. Between the 1820s and 1840s, health councils were established in the Middle East—the most significant being located in Alexandria (1820), Constantinople (1839), and Tangiers (1840).[25] These councils generally included both local and European members, hence assuring the Europeans of some influence over both the possible spread of infectious diseases and the ways in which they were managed.[26] The creation of these regional bodies was followed by 10 international health conferences between 1851 and 1897. These conferences did not succeed in developing any important agreements until the 1890s, following some significant advances in medical science in the last decades of the nineteenth century.[27] The accords reached in the 1890s were eventually integrated into the first major global international health agreement–the International Sanitary Regulations (ISR) of 1903. In addition, the creation of the first major global health institution, Office International d'Hygiene Publique (OIHP), followed shortly in 1907. The OIHP, in fact, was given the task of monitoring and revising the ISR.[28]

Important changes in health conditions occurred in the late nineteenth and early twentieth centuries for two reasons. First, there were significant improvements in public health infrastructures—particularly about the disposal of sewage and the protection of clean water supplies. Second, there were major improvements in scientists' ability to understand pathogens and consequently to develop vaccines and medicines. In the 1870s and 1880s, Louis Pasteur of France and Robert Koch of Germany isolated three pathogens that caused important infectious diseases, namely, anthrax, TB, and cholera. A major factor behind these advances in medical science was the marked improvement in microscopes, which for the first time in history allowed researchers to see and study the miniscule organisms that cause diseases.[29] The explosion of knowledge within the field of medical science at this time constituted what Sheldon Watts has called "the start of modern medicine" and what Hans Zinsser has phrased "a turning point in the epidemic history of the Western World."[30] A by-product of the improvements in medical science and the treatments that emanated from this progress was a significant decline in the number of deaths from disease in war. Before this period, diseases killed more soldiers than actual warfare.[31] Thanks to the advancements in medical care made in the nineteenth century, the Prussian Army in the Franco-Prussian War (1870–1871) had the dubious distinction of being the first army to have fewer soldiers die of infectious disease than from combat-related wounds.[32]

The last decade of the nineteenth century saw increasing progress in the field of medical science. In 1891, a medicine for curing diphtheria was discovered.[33] Then, in 1896, a vaccine for typhoid fever was developed. Between 1898 and 1900, it was learned that both malaria and yellow fever were transmitted by mosquito bites, and major efforts were launched to eliminate mosquitoes in Cuba and the Panama Canal Zone.[34] Between 1910 and 1912, it was learned that typhoid fever was transmitted by lice, and this knowledge greatly reduced the number of deaths from typhoid fever during World War II. Although the advances in vaccines and medicines created increasing optimism regarding infectious diseases in the early decades of the twentieth century, there were significant epidemics in the final years of World War I and its immediate aftermath. For example, 3 million people died of typhus in eastern Europe and the Soviet Union between 1917 and 1921. Most significantly, the world's worst influenza pandemic, the Spanish Flu, which lasted 18 months between 1918 and 1919, is estimated to have killed between 20 and 100 million people—many times more people than were killed during World War I in less than half the time.[35]

The beginning of the modern era of international health collaboration is often dated to the acceptance of the ISR of 1903. The regulations were aimed in large part at preventing the spread of diseases from developing to industrialized countries and preventing national quarantine controls by nonindustrialized states from impeding the flow of commerce between countries. They had a number of notable features. First, the 1903 treaty included only regulations pertinent to cholera and plague, although yellow fever was added in 1912. In 1926, three diseases that were prevalent in both the developed and developing worlds—relapsing fever, typhus, and smallpox—were added to the ISR. However, the three original diseases that threatened the Western world (cholera, plague, and yellow fever) were given priority in most deliberations on the ISR. Second, the regulations largely concerned requirements that states report disease outbreaks on their territories and that they treat infected travelers and seafarers in accordance with specific standards. There was a strong injunction that port authorities could not impose stricter rules than those contained in the ISR—thus giving commercial interests protection from costly delays in international shipping.

The years between World Wars I and II witnessed significant progress in medical research on infectious diseases, and important steps were made in the development of new vaccines and remedial drugs. In the 1920s and 1930s, vaccines for diphtheria, pertussis, tetanus, and yellow fever were discovered. In the mid-1930s, a substitute for quinine as a malaria drug, namely chloroquine, was invented. Then in 1939, the powerful antibiotic penicillin was discovered, which, among other things, proved particularly important in curing syphilis and gonorrhea.[36] In the late 1930s and 1940s, sulpha drugs, which were useful against poliomyletis (polio), meningitis, and even TB, were developed.[37] In the realm of public health, improved access to clean water reduced the frequency of enteric fevers and the incidence of gastroenteritis during the interwar period.[38] A major advance during World War II was the development of the insecticide dichlorodiphenyltrichloroethane, more commonly known as DDT, which facilitated large-scale destruction of mosquitoes and lice, which by that time were known to transmit malaria, yellow fever, and typhus.[39]

It is also notable that during the years between World War I and II major breakthroughs in the aircraft industry occurred that opened the door to major changes in international travel. In the late 1930s, for the first time, planes were built that could carry recreational travelers[40] and could accomplish transatlantic flights. These developments were the first steps leading to an explosion in air travel starting in the last years of World War II—and consequently the international spread of diseases by aircraft.[41]

In the interwar decades there were some modest improvements in international health cooperation. Most notably, the League of Nations Health Organization (LNHO) was founded in 1923. Many health experts anticipated that it would be amalgamated with the OIHP, but this did not occur because the United States refused to join a LNHO. The LNHO focused on the gathering and sharing of information concerning diseases in nonindustrialized countries, and it also provided some technical assistance. During this period other modest improvements were the establishment of a convention concerning efforts to control venereal diseases in 1924 and a convention on aerial navigation in 1932.[42]

In 1948, the World Health Organization (WHO) was created as a successor to both the OIHP and the LNHO, and this involved its taking over the responsibilities of the OIHP for revising the ISR. These regulations were revised in 1951 and again in 1969 when they were retitled the International Health Regulations (IHR). In 1969 and 1981, relapsing fever, typhus, and smallpox were removed from the coverage of the regulations as they no longer posed major threats, particularly in the industrialized world.

The decades from the late 1940s through the 1970s were an era of increasing optimism regarding the elimination and control of infectious diseases. Some describe the last half of the twentieth century as an era of "epidemiological transformation," which refers to a marked reduction in the percentage of the population that died from disease before the age of five.[43] An indicator of the optimistic feeling at that time was a statement made by William H. Stewart, then U.S. surgeon general, in 1967 that "it was time to close the book on infectious diseases and shift all national attention (and dollars) to . . . chronic diseases."[44] The popular catch-phrase "there is a drug for every bug" epitomized the mind-set that humanity was on its way to conquering infectious diseases through science. A major development in spurring this trend was the invention of the Salk vaccine for polio in 1955. Then, between 1965 and 1970, vaccines were developed for measles, mumps, hepatitis, chicken-pox, and rubella. Finally there was the dramatic impact of the WHO-led Global Program on Smallpox Eradication that operated between 1966 and 1977, and led to the worldwide eradication of the disease.[45] This was the first, and to date the only, successful disease eradication program in human history. Progress during these postwar decades also resulted from the development of new antibiotics apart from penicillin that were utilized to control certain diseases as well as infections following operations.[46]

The 1980s witnessed some gradual medical progress concerning infectious diseases, such as the development of a vaccine for hepatitis B in 1981. However, the decade was dominated by the identification of HIV/AIDS in the same year. This signaled, more than any other development, that the optimism concerning the disappearance of infectious diseases was misguided. In fact, the 1990s and the early years of the twenty-first century have witnessed the emergence of several new diseases, the reemergence of many familiar diseases, as well as the proliferation of drug-resistant strains of still other diseases.

Over the past 15 years, there have been some significant developments in surveillance methods thanks to advances in information technology and the establishment of new health-oriented NGOs. In addition, WHO has become a much more effective actor regarding emergency outbreaks. Many of the changes in this area have been integrated into WHO's Global Outbreak Alert and Response Network (GOARN). Many new surveillance and control innovations have also been integrated into the 2005 version of the IHR. Significant expansions in disease-control guidelines and compliance measures have also occurred, and more importantly there have been marked increases in the forms and magnitude of financial and material assistance to improve health standards in developing countries. These latter changes indicate that the industrialized countries have been more concerned with improving intrastate health conditions rather than trying to control the transborder spread of diseases.

The world is presently in a remarkable situation where the average human life span in the industrialized world has increased from approximately 40 to 80 years in two centuries, and this has significantly been due to the declining impact of infectious diseases. As three *New York Times* reporters noted in 2001, "One by one, history's greatest killers and cripplers . . . have been vanquished or tamed."[47] Although this statement has a certain resonance in the rich countries of the West, it is certainly not the case for developing nations, and it is this disparity in the provision of good health care that makes the topic of infectious disease control so relevant today.

Global Impacts of Disease: Contemporary Overview

Approximately 57 million people died in 2001. An estimated third of this number—17 million—died unnecessarily from diseases for which we have the medical knowledge and capability to cure. Millions of children and adults die each year of preventable, treatable infectious diseases. Universal access to health care services, medicines, sufficient food, and clean water would drastically alter the current disease burden and spread.[48]

Again in 2002, there were approximately 57 million deaths. Of this number, 10.5 million were children under 5, and 98 percent of these child-deaths occurred in the developing world.[49] Many, if not the majority, of child-deaths could have been prevented with vaccines and drugs that are now commonplace in industrialized countries. In the words of the 1993 World Bank Report: "child mortality rates are about ten times higher than those in the established market economies. If death rates among children in poor countries were reduced to those prevailing in the rich countries, 11 million fewer children would die each year."[50] Thirty percent of the people living in the developing world die of infectious diseases, and in the case of sub-Saharan African countries the figure is fifty percent. This must be contrasted with the reality that only 1 percent of the people in developed countries die of infectious diseases. Disturbingly, the health situation in the developing world seems to be worsening. In fact, "35 percent of Africa's children are at higher risk of death than they were 10 years ago . . . those who do make it past childhood are confronted with adult death rates that exceed those of 30 years ago."[51]

On a global level, life expectancy has increased by nearly two decades in the last half of the twentieth century. Between 1950 and 1955 life expectancy was 46.5 years; in 2002, it was 65.2 years.[52] While this is undoubtedly a positive phenomenon, not every country has witnessed an improvement in health. The life expectancy range demonstrates a shocking disparity between rich and poor countries. While a Japanese woman can expect to live to 85 years of age, a woman in Sierra Leone can expect just 35 years of life. Recent studies have shown that life expectancy is actually decreasing in parts of Africa, predominantly owing to the AIDS epidemic.[53]

HIV/AIDS, TB, and malaria are the three most deadly diseases for mankind. Together they account for more than one-third—39 percent—of infectious disease deaths.[54] These and other diseases such as hepatitis, cholera, and influenza kill millions of people around the world each year. Examining the number of deaths alone, however, does not provide an accurate picture of the worldwide burden of disease because it does not account for the morbidity and lack of productivity caused by illness before death.

Recognizing this, the World Bank's World Development Report of 1993, *Investing in Health*, introduced the concept of Disability Adjusted Life Years or DALYs. DALYs are the years of healthy life lost owing to premature death and disability. Although the mathematical model behind DALYs has been criticized, the measure is important because it allows economists and public health workers to develop a deeper understanding of the costs of disease, particularly in developing countries. For example, TB kills approximately 2 million people each year; however, DALYs show us that the total range of disease burdens is even worse. Beyond the 2 million lives lost, TB causes the loss of more than 36 million healthy, productive years of work because its victims are weakened to the point of not being able to work for extended periods of time. Malaria, which kills approximately 1 million people per year, costs more than 42 million DALYs. Other diseases that cause extensive economic losses include lymphatic filariasis and onchocerciasis (River Blindness). As these diseases are debilitating rather than fatal, they are often deemed less important in comparison to diseases with high mortality rates. The DALYs measurement, however, tells us that more than 5 million and 1 million productive years are lost to these diseases respectively, resulting in serious economic losses for the individuals, families, and communities in the developing countries where these diseases are endemic.[55]

Working with a similar premise regarding the economic impact of disease, the WHO's Commission on Macroeconomics and Health produced a report in 2001 that detailed many of the links between improving health conditions and improving economic prospects. According to the report, "The linkages of health to poverty reduction and to long term economic growth are powerful, much stronger than is generally understood . . . Increased investments in health . . . would translate into hundreds of billions of dollars per year of increased income to the low income countries."[56]

It's a well-known fact that health and economic development are interdependent. Recently, the impact of another factor on health was highlighted, namely global security relations. Since the 9/11 terrorist attacks in the United States, a growing number of people have argued that there is an extremely important relationship between the health sphere and the security sphere. Health affects global security in two major ways. First, and most obvious, is the potential for a terrorist attack with a biological agent designed and deployed to cause illness. The two best known incidents of modern day bioterrorism are the 1996 sarin nerve gas attack on the Tokyo subway by the Aum Shinrikyo cult and the post-9/11 "letter campaign" to spread anthrax. The second way in which health is related to security is less direct, but is also very serious. Widespread disease can weaken a country's infrastructure and cause political destabilization and unrest. Many experts now view controlling the AIDS epidemic in Africa as a security issue in so far as it can cause the social and political destabilization of countries.[57]

As the earlier discussion demonstrates, many recent research studies of the early years of the new millennium have repeatedly reinforced the message that the developed countries have a vested interest in curbing the spread of infectious diseases around the globe. Unfortunately, however, disturbing trends of resurgence and resistance among well-known diseases are making the task of combating disease more difficult. In recent decades, the pathogens that cause many infectious diseases have developed resistance to traditional drugs, making many diseases harder to treat and cure. Furthermore, many breeds of mosquitoes, among the most common disease vectors, are developing resistance to existing pesticides, making it much harder to control the spread of diseases such as malaria, dengue, and West Nile encephalitis.

Not only are old diseases becoming more difficult to cure, but new diseases with no known effective drugs or vaccines have also been emerging at the disturbing rate of approximately one per year since the early 1980s.[58] A variety of factors are contributing to the emergence of new diseases. Population increases have meant further encroachment by humans into previously uninhabited areas. This increases human contact with wild animals, some of which are hosts to disease-causing pathogens that are dangerous to humans. Also, as population rates rise, especially in areas that have experienced significant socioeconomic progress, such as China, demand for meat products is increasing. Thus, the number of pigs and chickens raised for slaughter has grown exponentially, and with this the threat of zoonotic diseases, which are animal diseases that can be transmitted to humans, has increased.

Recently discovered diseases such as Ebola, SARS, and avian influenza, all of which can be fatal and none of which can be cured with available medicines, inevitably provoke fear of a Hollywood-style global pandemic. Such fears are not altogether unwarranted given recent developments in transportation technology, which have increased the likelihood of humans coming into contact with unknown and potentially deadly bacteria, viruses, and parasites, and then spreading disease-causing pathogens across the globe in a matter of days. Quick, long-distance travel has become so commonplace that the World Tourism Organization[59] estimated that in 2002 there were more than 700 million international travelers, with 1.4 million people traveling by air each day.[60] According to the U.S.-based Institute of Medicine, "the spatial mobility of the average human has increased more than 1000-fold since 1800. As the number of global travelers increases, so does the threat of the spread of infectious disease."[61] Phrased even more pessimistically,

> [T]he speed of travel has rendered most existing frontier or port medical assessments almost irrelevant in identifying travellers who may be ill with communicable infectious diseases of significant public health importance. High-speed air travel allows the international movement of individuals within the incubation period of virtually all of the contagious virulent infections.[62]

A prime example of the consequences of improved transportation technology was seen in Surat, India in 1994. In September of that year, a pneumonic plague epidemic broke out. It immediately caused widespread panic, resulting in more than half a million residents boarding buses and trains and any other available mode of transportation within 48 hours of the news being released.[63] These half million people, all potentially having come in contact with plague, had spread across the subcontinent and beyond before medical experts had even begun to control the city of Surat itself. Thankfully, the strain of plague found in Surat turned out to be relatively mild, with a comparatively low mortality rate—causing 56 deaths in total. However, this incident demonstrates the potential for a deadly disease to become a global problem in a very short space of time, and clearly elucidates the need for emergency preparedness plans.[64]

As the preceding texts suggest, the current global situation about infectious diseases is highly complex. To provide an easy-to-digest overview of the situation, the authors developed tables that rank and organize different aspects the global disease burden. These tables are found in Appendix A, but the below section provides some analysis of patterns that were detected based on the table data. The research for this study has encompassed a large number of infectious diseases, but the subsequent analysis only includes a representative crosssection of diseases that kill a significant number of humans, infect a significant number of humans, or kill infected humans very quickly.[65] The list of diseases examined in tables 1 through 5 is not intended to be a comprehensive review of all infectious diseases that cause illness among humans; rather the tables are designed to highlight information regarding a representative sample of diseases that provoke serious health concerns today.

Table 1 concerns the number of people who are infected with particular diseases. Table 2 presents information on the number of people who die annually from these diseases. Table 3 presents information on the geographic spread of the diseases—looking at whether the diseases are found globally, dominantly in developed countries, or dominantly in developing countries. (A disease is classified as having global spread if at least 2 percent of the infected people come from both the developed and developing world.) Table 4 classifies most of the serious infectious diseases and whether effective vaccines and drugs exist to combat the illness. Finally, table 5 provides data on the mortality rate of the diseases examined here.

Table 1 tells us that there are large numbers of people in the world who have infectious diseases. More than 1 billion people have contracted one of six major infectious diseases. Most people would expect to see TB and influenza in this list, but they would not expect Helicobacter Pylori (H. Pylori), hepatitis B, ascariasis, and hookworm. The three largest infectors, H. Pylori, TB, and hepatitis B, infect billions of people; however, only a small proportion actually develops symptoms of the disease. Also, there are seven diseases that are contracted by 100 million to 1billion individuals each year—malaria, E-coli, schistosomiasis, hepatitis C, shigella, rotavirus, and lymphatic filariasis. The next group of diseases that are contracted by between 1 million and 100 million people includes 14 diseases— one of which is HIV/AIDS. Interestingly of the 54 infectious diseases listed in the tables, 19 have less than 50,000 cases, and of these 17 cause less than 1,000 cases per year. It is also interesting to note that diseases with the highest number of cases have low mortality rates. In fact, none of the top 10 infectors kill more than 1 percent of their victims.

The figures on deaths in table 2 provide some interesting contrasts with table 1. The five top killers are HIV/AIDS, TB, shigella, malaria, and streptococcus pneumoniae. They each have annual mortality figures in the range of 1 to 3 million. It is interesting to note that, despite the public focus on newly emerging diseases such as Ebola and SARS, the most serious diseases in terms of fatality rates are these four well-known diseases. There are 11 diseases that cause between 100,000 and 1 million deaths per year and 7 that cause between 21,000 and 60,000 deaths. Interestingly there are 23 at less than 100 deaths per year, and many of these diseases cause death only in conjunction with other medical problems. The first four diseases account for 61 percent of total deaths, and the next nine diseases account for an additional 33 percent. An interesting and important conclusion that can be drawn from this is that the number of diseases that must be controlled to make a huge impact on mortality is rather small.

Table 3, which focuses on the geographical spread of the diseases between the developed and developing worlds, highlights the extent to which infectious diseases are significantly a problem for those living in nonindustrialized states. There are 30 diseases that exist just in the developing world, as compared to just one that exists only in the developed world, namely, Legionnaire's disease. Twenty-three diseases are present in both worlds. Of this group, however, the developed countries carry a very small percentage of the disease burden—2 percent or less. This means that even within the group of diseases that have spread globally, the developing nations are home to a vastly disproportionate number of cases and deaths. The exceptions are influenza, hepatitis C, and HIV/AIDS. Influenza is a truly global disease with relatively even case distribution around the globe; hepatitis C occurs predominantly in the Western Pacific and Africa, but approximately 15 percent of cases are found in developed countries; and 5 percent of all HIV/AIDS cases occur in developed countries.

Table 4 focuses on whether effective vaccines and drugs exist for the diseases examined here. Clear information on these issues is crucial in seeking to develop disease-control strategies. There are 10 diseases that have both effective vaccines and drugs, and there are another 4 that have just effective vaccines. In other words, vaccines exist for just 14 of the 54 diseases. In total, 41 diseases have effective drugs (10 also having effective vaccines). This means that there are just 13 diseases for which neither effective vaccines nor drugs exist. Unfortunately two of these are HIV/AIDS and hepatitis C that account for significant numbers of infections and deaths across the globe. This chart also demonstrates that the existence of a vaccine does not necessarily equate to effective control of the disease. For example, although recent efforts to combat measles has resulted in a drastic reduction of case numbers and deaths, this disease still infects approximately 20 million and kills nearly 350,000 people annually—the vast majority of whom are children in developing countries. This occurs despite the fact that an effective vaccine has been readily available in developed countries since 1963.

Table 5 displays some intriguing information regarding the mortality rates of the diseases in question. Of the group of diseases where there is a death rate of above 10 percent, there are only two that account for a significant number of deaths—HIV/AIDS and Noma, with 3 million and

450,000 deaths each year respectively. Of the 12 diseases with mortality rates between 1 percent and 10 percent, the only large killers are measles (750,000 deaths per year) and typhoid fever (600,000 deaths per year). Interestingly, the 18 diseases with mortality rates below one percent account for some of the largest annual killers. For example, despite very low mortality rates, TB kills 2 million people each year; shigella—1.1 million; malaria—1 million; rotavirus—740,000; hepatitis C—600,000; hepatitis B—500,000; and influenza—375,000. This means that despite the attention-grabbing headings produced by extremely fatal diseases such as Ebola, more mundane diseases such as TB and shigella need to be combated to bring about a decline in the number of worldwide deaths owing to infectious disease.

Analytical Framework of the Study

The third and final section of the chapter lays out the definitions and analytical approach of the study. The discussion of global health governance that concerns the impacts of infectious diseases analyzes the nature of cooperation among actors involved in combating such diseases and controlling their international spread. By global governance we are referring to collaborative activities among states, IGOs, and NGOs that seek to influence the character of particular international problems. The study addresses two major questions:

- How has global governance to control the emergence and spread of infectious diseases evolved; and how has the evolving governance system impacted global health conditions?
- What developments and conditions have particularly shaped international health governance?

Describing International Governance

The concept of governance as applied to cooperation among international actors was first introduced by James Rosenau in the volume *Governance without Government*. He wrote that,

[G]overnance is not synonymous with government. Both refer to purposive behavior, to goal-oriented activities, to systems of rule; but government suggests activities that are backed by formal authority, by police powers to insure the implementation of duly constituted policies, whereas governance refers to activities backed by shared goals that may or may not derive from legal and formally prescribed responsibilities that do not necessarily rely on police powers to overcome defiance and attain compliance.[66]

John Ruggie addressed the same definitional issue in a similar manner, stating that "governance, at whatever level of social organization it may take place, refers to conducting the public's business: to the constellation of authoritative rules, institutions and practices by means of which any collectivity manages its affairs."[67] He went on to stress something that is very important in this study—namely, the importance of governance participants that are transnational: "the 'public' involved in the business of global governance now routinely includes not only states but also social actors for which territoriality is not the cardinal organizing principle or national interests the core driver."[68] Robert Keohane and Joseph Nye approach the definition of governance from a slightly different perspective. They argue that governance is "the processes and institutions, both formal and informal that guide and restrain the collective activities of a group."[69] These authors have highlighted important and varied dimensions of governance, and their ideas form the definitional bases that we have used throughout this study. Therefore, integrating these insights into the concept of global governance, we would offer the following conception. Global governance includes formal and informal institutions and rules that are created to manage interdependencies among governmental and nongovernmental actors. A crucial feature of this concept of global governance is that it encompasses mutual constraints among public and private actors and that these state and non-state parties attach legitimacy to the network of decision-making institutions and rules.

This study identifies and explains the three predominant strategies used by participants in global health politics to control the incidence and spread of infectious diseases.[70] Strategies are activities that alter the character of an international problem, and that maximize the benefits and minimize the costs for different parties. In this study the key problem is the incidence of infectious diseases, the deaths they cause, and the impact they have on commerce, development, and security. Regarding health governance, the three key strategies are

- Promoting *surveillance* of infectious disease and disseminating knowledge of their impacts;
- Providing financial and material *assistance* for emergency interventions and long-term health improvement programs; and
- Adopting *rules* that prescribe and proscribe particular behaviors.

The first strategy of *surveillance*, or the promotion of transparency, is crucial for managing most international problems because political actors need in-depth knowledge of a problem to develop effective regulatory and collaborative arrangements. Surveillance entails the gathering of information on crucial activities and events in an issue area. With regard to this study, it involves the gathering of information on disease outbreaks and their consequences. A key issue in designing surveillance measures in the global health context is whether international institutions should rely on information solely from governments or from both governmental and nongovernmental sources. In the regime-controlling infectious diseases, states insisted for many years that surveillance should be limited to governmental reporting. In this, and many other issue areas, technological developments have had an important impact on international regulatory developments. For example, the Internet has permitted vast amounts of information to be quickly disseminated among countries. This has made it increasingly difficult for governments to control the flow of information from their states.

The second strategy used in this regime is the provision of *financial and material assistance* for emergency interventions and long-term remedial and preventive health care. Arguably, the most important change in the international health regime in the past half century has been the dramatic increase in multilateral financial assistance and the development of global health partnerships (GHPs).[71] GHPs have mixed memberships that can include any combination of states, IGOs, NGOs, philanthropic foundations, and private companies. These partnerships have had important impacts on the global health regime by increasing awareness of diseases and politicizing health issues, which have in many cases led to increased financial support for health providers in developing nations. Furthermore, GHPs have opened new channels for the provision of material and nonmaterial aid. The amount of funding now geared toward global health issues has, unsurprisingly, attracted controversy. Billions, if not trillions, of dollars are currently tied to global health programs, and many previously uninterested actors, have become vocal participants in the debate as to how aid money should be spent. Increasing aid effectiveness and ensuring that donors can achieve their governance goals are becoming an integral part of the regime.

Central to most international regimes is a third strategy of *rule-making*. In fact, many people associate governance with rule-making. Rules, after all, are behavioral prescriptions and proscriptions that state and nonstate actors adopt because they judge that they will benefit from their mutual compliance. A central issue within this strategy, especially at the international level, is whether the members of the community should adopt legally binding or recommendatory rules. These options are often referred to as hard and soft law, and the central issue between them concerns the degree to which the rules are legally binding. The key criteria that define the existence of hard and soft law are the clarity of a legal obligation, the delegation of dispute settlement to judicial or other legally binding bodies, and the precision of the rules.[72] Related to these criteria is the range of procedures that political actors adopt to promote compliance.

In the case of many international issue areas, state and nonstate actors do not exert pressure on other actors to enforce compliance because they will not suffer serious consequences owing to noncompliance of other actors. In some aspects of health governance the actor choosing not to comply with proscriptions is the one that is most damaged by noncompliance, and thus it is not deemed necessary to develop a system of strict penalties. However, in other areas, such as information sharing, compliance is an important issue and international organizations are currently experimenting with methods of encouraging compliance with rules that are not legally binding.

Explaining International Governance

The explanation of global health collaboration in this study rests on the influence of three factors:

- Patterns of interdependence that create international constellations of interest and power;
- The evolution and dissemination of knowledge that provides insight into how to manage particular problems; and
- The development of varied international institutions that facilitate collaboration and the realization of important policy interests.

The most important factor among the interconnected explanatory factors mentioned above is the pattern of interdependencies among states and nongovernmental groups and their resultant interests in collaborative arrangements. As noted by Oran Young,

> The demand for governance in world affairs has never been greater. Broadly speaking, this development is a product of rising interdependencies among the members of international society and . . . global civil societies, which make it increasingly difficult for states or other autonomous actors to isolate themselves from events occurring in other parts of the world, however much they might wish to do so.[73]

In the case of international health problems, as with many other contemporary international issues, one needs to focus on mutual dependencies or vulnerabilities between developed and developing countries—and the interests in collaboration that these interdependencies create. At times there have been common interests in collaboration between developed and

developing states, and at other times there have not been such commonal-
ities of interest. In fact, historically there have been periods when neither
grouping was particularly anxious to promote global health collaboration.
The contemporary period, however, is characterized by a clear desire to
collaborate on the part of both state and nonstate actors owing to recognition of the linkages between global health and development and security.

There are a number of key points concerning patterns of interest and
power that are highlighted in subsequent chapters. First, international
cooperation seldom rests simply on states' concern with a single interest
such as the promotion of health; rather, it rests on benefits and costs associated with a variety of interests. For example, in the case of international
cooperation concerning infectious diseases, it rests in varying degrees on
reducing the transnational spread of diseases, preventing interruptions in
the flow of commerce, enhancing the economic development of poor
countries, improving possibilities for trade and investment between developed and developing countries, promoting political stability in developing
states, and reducing security concerns regarding bioterrorism. Of course,
the importance of different interests for countries varies considerably over
time. Increased understanding of the multiple negative impacts of diseases
in the late twentieth century caused a reversal in policy on the part of
developed states.[74]

The second factor that helps to explain the development of global governance is the state of scientific and technological knowledge in an issue
area. Some international relations scholars believe that the growth of technology creates stronger international interdependencies and that these
interdependencies lead to broader and deeper international collaboration.[75]
For example, James Rosenau states that "[W]orld politics is increasingly
marked by interdependence, by new issues that cannot be addressed or
resolved through the threat or use of military capabilities and that instead
require cooperation among states if obstacles are to be diminished or eliminated," and "by their very nature interdependence issues tend to require
multilateral cooperation among governments for their amelioration."[76]
Similarly, Keohane and Nye have written concerning a liberal "economic
process model" of international politics that "technological change and
increases in economic interdependence will make existing international
regimes obsolete. They will be inadequate to cope with the increased volume of transactions . . ."[77] A related comment by a Canadian government
study on "smart regulation" is that "As new products are developed and
new risks emerge, more and more international institutions are being
formed to manage and mitigate harm."[78] What will be highlighted in subsequent parts of this study is that scientific and technological progress can
not only promote demands for international cooperation, but it can also

facilitate states' ability to control interdependencies on their own—and hence promote a lack of interest in cooperation. In other words, technological change is a double-edged sword when it comes to the growth of international cooperation.

Regarding international health interdependencies, progress in medical science gives states a better idea of what kinds of international regulations are effective in reducing the incidence of disease, but it also gives states better insights into how they can control infectious diseases contracted by their citizens within their own territories. In fact, throughout most of the twentieth century, progress in medical science mainly helped developed countries to control international health interdependencies on their own. Richard Cooper noted accurately that states' agreement on the ISR in 1903 rested on the surge in medical scientific knowledge at the end of the nineteenth century.[79] However, Cooper did not push his analysis of international health cooperation into the twentieth century, and if he had, he probably would have come to the conclusion that the growth of scientific knowledge from 1903 until at least the 1990s had just the opposite effect. Until the late 1990s, states were generally confident that they could control diseases among their own populations single-handedly.

Despite this double-edged sword impact of medical science, one aspect of technological progress that unequivocally promotes international cooperation is the dramatic improvement in information technology in recent decades. The development of fax, e-mail, the Internet, and other communications technologies has meant that medical professionals and the media have been able to report on many disease outbreaks throughout the world. The increase in transparency created by developments in information technology has transformed problems regarding adequate surveillance and monitoring in quite dramatic ways; and their impacts have had positive ramifications on international cooperation in many health areas.

The third and final explanatory factor underlying contemporary global health governance is the growth in the forms and resources of international institutions. There has been a modest expansion in traditional IGOs such as WHO and the World Bank, but there has been a much more dramatic growth in NGOs, and hybrid organizations often referred to as public-private partnerships (PPPs) or GHPs. NGOs include humanitarian groups, commercial organizations, and private foundations, and they have become key actors in the global health regime. "Civil society organizations have become the main international dispensers of direct assistance to people in developing countries, through foreign aid, humanitarian relief and a variety of other internationally supported services."[80] Although international aid organizations have their own international programs, increasingly they operate as part of larger collaborative entities, which demonstrates the varied and diverse composition of contemporary global health governance systems.

There are a variety of factors that have promoted and sustained the growth of civil society groups and GHPs. First, the multiplicity of public and private participants provides hybrid organizations with strong legitimacy in that they draw on the backing of both civil societies and governments. It is important to recognize that both governments and NGOs are important sources of legitimacy. Second, most of these diverse actors have significant financial, material, or human resources. Of particular importance in recent years is funding from foundations, which are backed by wealthy individuals such as Bill and Melinda Gates and Warren Buffett. There have been, throughout the centuries, rich donors to health projects such as John D. Rockefeller, but recent private donations are of a different magnitude than seen in the past. The contributions of these donors are often important because the required funds for many global and regional health projects are very large. This is especially true, as the publicity that surrounds generous contributions from philanthropic foundations can often induce state governments to increase their levels of foreign aid. Third, large and diverse international institutions, especially large IGOs and public-private bodies, are important because they facilitate international accords. The participants share valuable information concerning key issues, and some of their features reduce the time and resources required to negotiate accords. This process is often referred to as reducing transaction costs. These advantages are often underestimated, which is unfortunate as they are crucial in the politics of international collaboration.[81]

This study is written largely from the perspective of liberal functionalist theory although it does draw on some insights from the realist power-oriented tradition. Regarding the liberal perspective it stresses an increase in international interdependencies (influenced significantly by technological change), a growing mutuality of interests in collaboration, an increase in the number and resources of NGOs, and a growth in the number and size of international institutions that facilitate the development of global governance.

On the other hand, the study also stresses the importance in the evolution of perceived interests of wealthy state and nonstate actors and the need to accommodate their policy perspectives in the bargaining process. There is no doubt that the marked transformation in global health governance starting in the 1990s is attributable to the industrialized countries that determined that they would benefit on a number of levels from improvements in the health of developing country populations. In many instances, they used their economic and reputational leverage to shape international decision-making processes. Hence, developed country leverage is clearly used to bring about the transformation of those countries with serious

health problems. Liberal and realist perspectives each contribute to understanding the significant change in global health governance that has emerged
in recent decades.[82]

Framework of the Following Chapters

Chapter 2 provides a historical overview of global health governance since
the first international health conferences took place in the mid-nineteenth
century. It explores and explains how the nature of the regime evolved in
the different versions of the IHR that were negotiated and implemented
between 1903 and 1981. The chapter also discusses the increased activity
by international organizations in the twentieth century, particularly since
the creation of the WHO in 1948, which has been responsible for many
developments in global health collaboration.

Chapter 3 is concerned with the containment of and prevention of disease outbreaks, and in so doing it focuses on the strategies of surveillance,
emergency responses, behavioral rules, and standards for managing diseases,
and the promotion of compliance with these rules and standards. The
analysis is concerned in particular with the activities of the WHO and two
multifaceted programs that operate under it—the IHR and the GOARN.
The chapter analyzes the ways in which these entities have developed significantly since the 1990s.

Chapter 4 examines the most extensive and complicated sphere in contemporary health governance: the provision of health assistance. Health aid
programs are generally aimed at reducing the incidence of infectious diseases, and they have grown exponentially, both in numbers and in importance, in recent years. In exploring the nature of assistance initiatives and
the factors that have influenced their evolution the chapter provides an
overview of the actors involved in contemporary health assistance initiatives and a broad descriptive section on the ways in which aid is distributed.
The chapter also focuses on the marked increase in GHPs that are comprised of diverse groups of international health institutions.

The important issue of access to essential medicines is the theme of
chapter 5. Access to affordable drugs has long been a concern for global
health professionals; however, over the past decade it has become a major
issue for economic development specialists, trade experts, security analysts,
and human rights advocates as well. The chapter begins with a chronological breakdown of the major economic treaties that are relevant to the
pharmaceutical industry, particularly those concerning intellectual property
rights. It then provides a description of major political and legal events that
have occurred over the past decade that have influenced the debate over
access to essential medicines. The third section includes an analysis of the

role played by NGOs in this field. The final section consists of concluding comments and an assessment of the rationale behind the use of hard law (as opposed to soft law) treaties in laying out the rules regarding international trade in pharmaceutical products.

The sixth and final chapter provides conclusions regarding the utilization of different strategies and the factors that have shaped actors' preferences and the success of their initiatives. The chapter also draws out some insights concerning collaboration in a variety of global issue areas.

CHAPTER 2

GLOBAL HEALTH GOVERNANCE IN
THE TWENTIETH CENTURY

The nineteenth century was a remarkable period in terms of advances in transportation and telecommunications, expansion of international trade, and growth of migration. These developments both encouraged the spread of diseases and the incentives for preventing them. The middle decades of the century saw the introduction of steel-hulled steamships, railways, and telegraph—and increases in international commerce followed rapidly in the wake of these advances. The growth and impact of improvements in shipping were particularly notable. World shipping tonnage jumped from 700,000 tons in 1850 to 26,200,000 in 1910.[1] The demand for raw materials doubled every nine years, and the demand for tropical agricultural products also rose markedly as a result of advances in transportation. To quote one author, technological progress was "pro-trade biased."[2]

An important technological feat that promoted trade—particularly between Europe and Asia—was the building of the Suez Canal that opened in 1869. The Canal had a marked impact on the cost of transportation and hence the volume of goods. It also increased the movement of people— Western travelers, Muslim pilgrims, and migrants seeking better living and working conditions. Between 1815 and 1915, 46 million people left Europe for different parts of the world—predominantly North America.[3] Elsewhere, 50 million migrants left China and India in the nineteenth century— particularly for Latin America, Africa, and island colonies. Despite the efforts of immigration officials they often brought serious diseases into their new home countries.

A central fact concerning the international transmission of diseases is "the pathways of infection correspond to the system of human communication."[4] In the past, some of the key routes on which people and diseases traveled were between Asia and the Hejaz (the area surrounding Mecca and Medina), between Africa and the Hejaz, between Asia and Europe (via the Mediterranean and Russia), and between Europe and the Western Hemisphere. In Asia, major pandemic diseases such as cholera and plague were endemic in Bengal, the Ganges Valley, Hunan, Manchuria, and Mongolia. Diseases generally spread from these places. The most important source of secondary infection, especially for the European states, was Egypt since its population was frequently infected by travelers going between Asia and Europe or returning from the pilgrimage to Mecca.[5]

In the middle of the nineteenth century international trade was dominated by Europe, which accounted for 70 percent of global trade. The dominant trading country was Britain with 20 percent of total trade. Although Europeans and North Americans traded a great deal with each other, the most rapidly expanding trade route at this time was between Europe and Asia, where many serious communicable diseases were endemic. This increase in the flow of international travelers inevitably made international health an important policy issue for the European states.[6]

The formative years of the international health regime began in 1851 with the convening of the first International Sanitary Conference; 10 more conferences were to follow over the next 50 years. However, the most significant steps in establishing cooperation between states regarding international health occurred during the four International Sanitary Conferences that took place during the 1890s. The catalyst for these conferences was a series of seven cholera pandemics over the course of the century, each one causing millions of deaths throughout Asia and Europe.[7] The first cholera pandemic began in India in the late 1820s, reached Russia in 1829, and soon spread across Europe. The main pathways for the spread of the disease were the land route from South Asia through Russia into Western Europe, and the sea route linking India, the Red Sea, and Europe. Central to this sea route was the religious pilgrimage of Muslims to Mecca and Medina from both Asia and the Mediterranean region. Until the opening of the Suez Canal in 1869 the Asia-Europe and Mecca-Mediterranean voyages required land transportation between the northern end of the Red Sea and a Mediterranean port, and the travelers crossing Egypt often transmitted cholera and other diseases to the local population during this leg of the journey.

Before 1850, the dominant methods of controlling the spread of diseases were implemented unilaterally by states. The most important of these measures was the establishment of quarantines and embargoes on ships' passengers and goods. These regulations differed a great deal among states, and often imposed terrible suffering for passengers who were generally confined to isolated and primitive land stations or lazarettos. With the increase in trade via shipping routes in the nineteenth century, the financial losses suffered by shipowners, cargoowners, and passengers as a result of delays in port grew dramatically. Additional burdens for commercial shipping interests were caused by requirements of some states that ships entering their ports present bills of health providing information on inspections at ports of origin and on disease outbreaks during the voyage. The requirement for a bill of health was an important step forward in controlling the spread of infectious diseases; however, the system had a serious flaw in that bribery was a common practice. In fact, the bill of health shown at port often bore little resemblance to the actual situation of the ship in question.[8]

In the mid-nineteenth century there were some international efforts to curtail the spread of diseases through the establishment of regional sanitary councils composed of local and foreign authorities in Egypt (1843), Constantinople (1838), Tangiers (1840), and Tehran (1867). The councils were established largely at the behest of foreign states and were focused on preventing the spread of diseases from the Middle East to European countries, but for the most part they were not very effective because of tensions between the local and foreign members. Interestingly, in some cases the local authorities wanted highly flexible obligations that would avoid expensive public health programs, and in other cases the local officials preferred stringent measures to prevent the introduction of diseases.[9]

The Early International Sanitary
Conferences: 1851–1897

It is important to note that the impetus for instituting international health regulations (IHR) in the middle of the nineteenth century came not from the southern European or Middle Eastern states that were the major "importers" of diseases, but from a few industrialized states with strong maritime interests that were concerned with the delays imposed on ships by quarantines. Among the 12 states attending the first International Sanitary Conference in 1851, Britain was by far the strongest opponent of the right of states to impose quarantines, although there were also other opponents mainly from northern Europe. Most state representatives attending the conference on behalf of countries bordering the Mediterranean or Black Sea opposed the British position and supported the right of port authorities to maintain quarantines. Nevertheless, Middle Eastern and Mediterranean states were willing, in the interest of facilitating commerce, to accept limited restraints on quarantine procedures, as long as the basic principle of quarantining ships remained acceptable. The basic provisions approved in 1851 remained in subsequent draft conventions over the next 50 years, although the only convention that entered into force was the one adopted in 1892.[10] The key provisions were

• The obligation of ship owners to maintain ship sanitation standards;
• The obligation of ship officers to maintain a log on the health of crew and passengers;
• The obligation of port authorities to allow passengers to land if the ship possessed a clean bill of health;
• The obligation of port authorities to provide lazarettos with good facilities for diseased passengers;
• The right of inspection of ships in ports;
• The right to issue and inspect bills of health; and
• The right of port authorities to enforce quarantines for passengers from infected vessels for a specified number of days.

Although only three states ratified the 1851 convention and the major shipping power of the era—Britain—strongly opposed its legitimization of quarantines, the convention did lead to some alteration in state practices, and it served as a model for future attempts to design an international health regime.[11]

The central medical debate at the 1851 conference pitted "contagionists," who believed in the transmission of diseases between people, against the "anticontagionists," who believed that diseases were contracted from pathogens that emanated from the soil.[12] The argument on these issues remained very much the same for almost half a century until scientific advances in epidemiology broke the deadlock. The contagionists led by the countries of the eastern Mediterranean proclaimed that it was absolutely clear that the major diseases (particularly cholera) were transmitted from human to human and therefore strict quarantines were necessary. In fact, about two-thirds of the 12 states at the 1851 conference were of this opinion. The British position, on the other hand, was that there were no scientific grounds for believing that diseases could be transmitted between humans. Rather, they argued that diseases were spread owing to certain environmental conditions and that public health measures were the best remedial health strategy. As close to three-quarters of all vessels traveling between Asia and Europe were under the British flag, the British had a clear commercial interest in discouraging measures that would impede the movement of ships. A succinct summation of the British view was made by a leading health official who stated that the 1851 draft convention, which permitted quarantine measures, constituted an "irrational derangement of commerce."[13] The convention in question did not, in the end, receive the requisite number of ratifications to enter into force because of differences between the two groups of states. Nevertheless, the key provisions of the 1851 convention—although not binding—had some important effects on state practices.

A second health conference was convened in Paris in 1859, and it was basically a replica of the meeting held eight years previously.[14] Britain was even more fervent about the uselessness of quarantines, the value of medical inspections of ships in ports, and the treatment of diseased passengers. At the other end of the spectrum, the Ottoman Empire and Greece were adamant in maintaining states' authority to impose quarantine restrictions. The draft treaty produced after five months was very similar to the 1851 draft and had little influence.[15]

The fourth cholera pandemic began in 1864 and lasted until 1872. It originated in India and quickly spread to other regions. It had devastating effects throughout the Ottoman Empire and Egypt owing to infected pilgrims returning from the Hejaz. In direct response to the outbreak, the Ottoman Empire convened another International Sanitary Conference in 1865.[16] At the conference, there was almost unanimous acceptance of the fact that the cholera pandemic had started in India and had gradually been spread to other countries by infected travelers. The British, however, remained adamant that the disease was not spread from human to human. Although the epidemiology of cholera was hotly contested, the conference did recommend the adoption of a variety of medically sound measures such as the establishment of a quarantine station between the Hejaz region and Egypt. Of the 21 states at the conference, four (Britain, Russia, the Ottoman Empire, and Persia) opposed rules concerning quarantines, but their reasons differed. Britain and Russia (now concerned about restrictions on vessels trading through its Black Sea ports) did not want any interruptions of commerce, whereas the Ottoman Empire and Persia did not want to accept expensive medical programs in ports and constraints on quarantine restrictions during serious disease outbreaks. At the end of the conference, the participants could only agree on general principles that ships and port authorities should follow owing to differing perspectives on the relevant medical issues.[17]

The next international health conference took place in 1874. It was organized by Russia, but held in Vienna.[18] In Vienna, Russia, along with the majority of Northern European states, continued to oppose quarantine restrictions. They were confronted, however, by most of the Mediterranean states that were adamant protagonists on behalf of the effectiveness of quarantines and their right to take action against infected vessels in their ports. In the end, the conference recommended that states could employ either medical inspections or quarantines—hence legitimizing a very weak regulatory system. An interesting recommendation of the 1874 conference was that states create an International Commission on Epidemics to collect information on disease outbreaks around the world. The proposal for a monitoring commission was not implemented by states after the conference, but it was finally approved after 28 years in 1907.[19]

The next International Sanitary Conference, held in 1885, was also prompted by a cholera outbreak that began in 1883 in India, spread to Egypt and then onto Europe.[20] Unfortunately the etiology of cholera was discovered in Germany by scientist Robert Koch the year before the 1885 meeting, but this information was ignored at the conference. Koch's work showed that cholera was transmitted through oral ingestion of a pathogenic microbe that originated largely from human waste. Although the discovery was widely discussed in European scientific circles after its announcement, it took 10 years before it was accepted in intergovernmental conclaves, in part because this new knowledge about the mode of transmission of cholera contradicted the anticontagionist position held by Britain. Ironically, however, it was soon realized that the dominant British strategy of promoting sanitary drinking water and isolating cholera patients was the best strategy that could have been employed to control the spread of the disease. Essentially, the British were doing the right things for the wrong reasons.[21]

Despite this new knowledge about cholera, the 1885 Rome meeting debates were remarkably similar to those of earlier conferences. In fact, "no sooner did [delegates] touch upon the matter of quarantine on the Red Sea and in the Suez Canal than frank and open polemics started up between the delegates of Britain and France."[22] The hostile discussions were in large part owing to the fact that several European states were furious with Britain's failure to establish a good quarantine system between the Red Sea and the Mediterranean. In fact, by this time all states, except Britain, accepted the contagionist position that justified quarantines.

The next three conferences concerning cholera took place in 1892, 1893, and 1894 following serious outbreaks of the disease in South Asia, the Middle East, and eastern Europe. The etiology of the disease was still in dispute during the 1892 conference, but Koch's findings were generally accepted by the 1894 meeting. All three conferences produced conventions, and these were the first International Sanitary Conventions that were ratified by a significant number of states. The 1892 conference focused on preventing the spread of diseases by pilgrims who were returning from Mecca to their home countries around the Mediterranean.[23] The central dispute was whether ships with sick passengers should be required to disembark their passengers at a quarantine station before proceeding through the Suez Canal. The British, who then controlled Egypt, opposed disembarkations to quarantine stations as useless and costly. They preferred medical inspection and hospitalization of diseased passengers at ports of final disembarkation. In the end the British accepted disembarkation of sick passengers at quarantine stations on the Red Sea since the proposed regulations concerned solely pilgrims—and not European travelers. The convention accepted by the participating states required the quarantine of all ships with infected passengers at a Suez lazaretto. British officials requested that their ships heading for England be exempt from the 15-day quarantine at the El Tor quarantine station on the Red Sea. This was opposed by the other countries on the grounds that special rights for one state were unreasonable and, more practically, that it would be too difficult to monitor British ships at possible stops in Europe.[24]

In 1892, cholera spread to Europe owing to an outbreak that began in Russia. In an attempt to limit the spread of the outbreak, many states imposed a wide variety of expensive restrictions on international shipping and travel. In 1893, Germany called a conference to determine ways to reduce impediments to commerce in the case of future pandemics.[25] The deliberations at the 1893 meeting resulted in some significant changes to the common practices of the day. For example, land quarantines were forbidden, and stopping trains was only permitted if passengers had clear manifestations of cholera. Also, rights to impose maritime quarantines were circumscribed, and for the first time states were obligated to report outbreaks of cholera in their ports and territory. The participating states did not include any obligations about measures that should be taken in Asia where cholera commonly originated, steps whose costs would be borne by colonial powers (especially the United Kingdom). Interestingly, for the first time at an international conference Britain recognized that cholera could be spread from person to person, but it still continued to argue that quarantines were ineffective.[26]

Owing to another outbreak of cholera among pilgrims in Mecca, another International Sanitary Conference was convened in 1894.[27] Pressure was largely focused on Britain and the Ottoman Empire to implement various health measures since they controlled the areas from which most pilgrims came.[28] At the 1894 conference Britain agreed for the first time to undertake medical inspections of pilgrims in ports. The Ottoman Empire was most displeased with the convention because it contained a variety of rules concerning sanitary conditions around the Muslim holy sites and placed constraints on quarantine policies. Unlike the conventions approved in 1892 and 1893, the 1894 convention never entered into force because many states had reservations that prevented them from ratifying the agreement.[29]

As the earlier discussion makes clear, the predominant focus of the late nineteenth century conferences was cholera. However, two conferences were organized to deal with the other major pestilential diseases of the time—yellow fever and plague. The 1881 conference in Washington, which focused on yellow fever, was unique because the central issue was not the right of states to impose quarantine restrictions or sanitary conditions on vessels. Rather, it concerned the request of the United States that its consuls in foreign ports (as opposed to local government authorities) be allowed to issue the bills of health to all vessels going to the United States. This kind of extraterritorial jurisdiction was strongly resisted by other states, especially those in Latin America.[30]

The conference on plague occurred in 1897 after a serious outbreak of the disease, which originated in Bombay and then spread to certain parts of Europe.[31] The problems and conflicts that occurred during the plague conference mirrored those at the cholera conferences in 1892, 1893, and 1894; however, important progress was made and many guidelines in the plague convention were integrated into future conventions. Knowledge about plague actually lagged behind that of cholera at this time. Scientists knew of the plague bacillus by 1894 and even correlated its presence with the existence of rats. What was not yet understood was the nature of the flea vector that transmitted the infection from rats to humans.[32] In reaction to the 1897 outbreak, many countries imposed very stringent quarantine measures that were much harsher than the standards they had recently accepted in international conventions on cholera. For example, many countries prevented Muslims from making the pilgrimage to Mecca, and they erected quarantine shields around themselves in uncoordinated attempts to keep plague out of their countries. The key European trading states were appalled at what was occurring, and at the 1897 conference they sought to develop more effective regulations to deal with plague. The outcome was an accord that states interpreted and judged differently. The regulations in the convention imposed obligations on states of embarkation to inspect vessels and passengers and provided rules relating to quarantines and medical inspection in ports of disembarkation. However, central to the regulations was the concern of maritime interests to "emancipate trade and shipping from excessive restrictions."[33] The 1897 treaty for plague also followed the conventions concerning cholera in that states were obligated to telegraph information on outbreaks of disease to other states. Improved information was viewed as central to effective and nonexcessive international health measures.[34]

The latter half of the nineteenth century witnessed the birth of a new health regime. Although the regime was designed to govern global health issues, the earlier discussion explains that it was a combination of health and trade concerns—not solely health concerns—that acted as an instigator for the first cautious attempts at multilateral control of infectious diseases.

Although reducing the number and severity of cholera, plague, and yellow fever outbreaks, was undoubtedly a concern for states at the time, the predominant catalyst for collaboration was the belief that uncoordinated responses to disease outbreaks were hindering global trade by delaying ships and passengers in ports—and not reducing the incidence of diseases. The complexity of the issues, and the deeply entrenched conflicting opinions held by states made negotiating global health conventions a monumental task. In any case, it took nearly four decades for the international community to produce a convention that entered into force. This occurred in 1892. Another factor that made it difficult to establish a regime was the lack of knowledge regarding the etiology of the bacteria and viruses that caused diseases. It is important to stress that an even stronger force that undermined the attempts at concluding legal accords was the divergent economic and health interests between the industrialized and nonindustrialized countries.

The Formative Years of the Health Regime: 1900–1990

The following discussion of the development of the global health regime is organized in the first instance in chronological categories—1900–1919, 1920–1945, and 1946–1980s. Within each of these chronological periods there are analyses of developments regarding three spheres of international collaboration—surveillance, the provision of material and financial assistance, and rule-making.

Developments between 1900 and 1945

The contemporary global health regime was launched at the beginning of the twentieth century with the creation of International Sanitary Regulations (ISR) in 1903. It was built on the conferences of the nineteenth century and more particularly, the four conferences (three on cholera and one on plague) that were held during the 1890s. One of the most important areas of international health collaboration in the early twentieth century concerned surveillance or what was often referred to as "notification." A central issue in the 1903 ISR, as well as subsequent versions of the treaty, concerned the reporting of disease outbreaks. The importance of cholera and plague in the regulations was highlighted by a cholera epidemic in the Philippines and a plague epidemic in Kenya in 1902.[35] The interest of states in a broader and stronger regulatory regime was heightened by significant progress in epidemiology in the last two decades of the nineteenth century.[36] The 1903 convention required that only cholera and plague, be reported. However, yellow fever was added in

1912, and typhus, relapsing fever, and smallpox were included in 1926. It is significant that the first three diseases, which attracted the most political attention, were largely developing country diseases, whereas the latter three occurred in both the industrialized and nonindustrialized states. Typhus and relapsing fever attracted the political attention of states particularly because of their destructive impacts in eastern Europe during and immediately after World War I. It is also noteworthy that all diseases that could be spread by Muslim pilgrims and people with whom they came in contact were also designated as deserving specific regulatory responses.

The participants in the 1903 International Sanitary Conference requested that France sponsor a subsequent meeting that would focus on the creation of an international organization that could facilitate the sharing of information on disease outbreaks. This led to the creation of the Office International d'Hygiene Publique (OIHP) in 1907. It was provided with a permanent secretariat in Paris (the Paris Office) as well as a central decision-making body—the Permanent Committee—that was composed of all signatory states.[37] An addition to the surveillance arrangements outlined in the regulations was the assigning of certain responsibilities to promote greater disease awareness by the four regional health councils in the Middle East and the Mediterranean. Particular responsibilities were assigned to the Egyptian Quarantine Council because of its strategic location in relation to the Muslim pilgrimage to the holy sites of Mecca and Medina.[38] One of the most important features of the OIHP was that it assumed responsibility for collecting data on a number of diseases other than just the three listed in the original regulations. To quote an article on international health institutions: "the OIHP functioned chiefly as an international clearing house, and by World War I was systematizing the latest findings on malaria, typhoid, hookworm, tuberculosis and other health threats."[39] Although the OIHP undoubtedly disseminated important knowledge, this statement connotes that there was more collaboration than actually occurred since only 15 states had ratified the ISR at the outbreak of World War I.

The first stage of rule-making for the ISR in 1903 focused on the integration of the health conventions that were adopted in the 1890s. Thus, the 1903 IHR included regulations on a broad range of issues including sanitary standards on ships and in ports, inspection of ships, certificates of inspection, quarantines of infected ships and travelers, and bills of health of people on board ship. Most of these issues had particular resonance for developing countries. In fact, David Fidler has noted that 71 percent of the articles in the 1903 regulations focused particularly on the developing countries of the Middle East, Asia, and Africa. The central concerns of the participants were the prevention of the spread of diseases from the developing world to the industrialized world and the harmonization of quarantine practices, which itself concerned the prevention of financial losses for Western maritime interests.[40] A significant number of the regulations also dealt with the contributions of the regional health councils in controlling the spread of diseases by pilgrims.[41] Pertinent to these points, an important writer on IHR, N. Howard-Jones, noted that the OIHP was "firmly rooted in the ideas of the past. Fundamentally, it was a club of . . . health administrators, most European, whose main preoccupation was to protect their countries from importation of exotic diseases without imposing too drastic restrictions on international commerce."[42] Well-known health epidemiologists such as Robert Koch as well as other scientists have adopted a different critical perspective on the ISR in that the scientists deemed them ineffective in controlling the spread of infectious diseases. Their view was that the spread of diseases could be better controlled by focusing on their source within the nonindustrialized countries rather than at borders.[43]

The most contentious issues in the international health conferences in both the nineteenth and twentieth centuries concerned whether states should be allowed to adopt regulations that imposed more stringent measures than those in the ISR. The developed countries were adamantly opposed to the ability of states to impose more stringent measures than those in the regulations. They also opposed allowing states to have broad escape clauses, which they often referred to as "excessive measures." In fact, to secure political support from the developing countries for the regulations, they were allowed to adopt more stringent measures regarding the movement of pilgrims and national emergencies.[44]

The notion of providing assistance to poor countries to limit the impact of infectious diseases is not a new one. Health assistance as a governance strategy began to be employed, albeit in a very limited fashion, in the early years of the health regime. Initially it was provided by colonial powers to developing nations through bilateral accords; however, some multilateral and nongovernmental efforts were in existence very early in the twentieth century. For example, the International Sanitary Bureau (renamed the Pan-American Sanitary Bureau in 1923, and again renamed the Pan-American Health Organization in 1958) was created in 1902 as an intergovernmental organization designed to provide assistance and medical advice to states throughout the Western Hemisphere.

Alongside the International Sanitary Bureau, the influential Rockefeller Foundation was very active in improving health conditions in Latin America from the date of its inception in 1913. The foundation's most notable achievement was the clearing of malaria from the Canal Zone, but it also made major accomplishments with other diseases including hookworm and yellow fever. Its greatest contributions were in Mexico where it influenced not only the control of certain diseases but health legislation as well.[45] The Rockefeller Foundation's work reflected the economic and political concerns of the U.S. government and business in the region, and it supported the sorts of programs that were established by colonial governments in Asia and Africa.

The Pasteur Institute, which is probably the oldest health organization still providing assistance, was founded in 1887 and inaugurated in 1888. In many ways, it was a Francophone-world equivalent of the Rockefeller Foundation as most of the institutes were in French colonies. It was active in conducting health research and providing advice, but it also sponsored local health projects. A Pasteur official provided a positive picture of the health programs when he stated that "if Europeans can live safely in hostile Africa and the Far East, if morbidity and mortality decrease in a striking way for native populations, all these transformations must be attributed to colonial medicine."[46]

In looking back at the governmental and private health assistance programs, it is important to recognize the economic and political incentives underlying their activities. However, it is equally important to understand that these health assistance activities were rooted in the recognition that attempts to stem the spread of diseases at ports and at land boundaries were unlikely to succeed. More likely to be influential were programs designed to curtail the incidence of diseases within state borders.

There was a significant change in the obligations for surveillance in the next major version of the ISR in 1926. Three more diseases were added to the list of diseases that had to be reported to the OIHP—typhus, relapsing fever, and smallpox. There was also a change in the general surveillance system in that the OIHP, from 1926 onwards was obligated to notify signatory states of outbreaks, expanding its role from merely being a receiver of information to being a disseminator of information.[47] Another important innovation that occurred in the mid-1920s was the publication launch of the Weekly Epidemiological Review (WER). It has been published weekly since 1926 and is an important source of information on outbreaks occurring around the globe although its reports were often written sometime after outbreaks occurred.

There were also a number of developments regarding surveillance outside of the structure of the OIHP and the ISR. In 1923 the League of Nations Health Organization (LNHO) was created, and under it there were two important bodies—the Epidemic Commission (which reported on select outbreaks, especially in eastern Europe) and the Singapore Bureau (which gathered and circulated information on disease outbreaks in Asia). The Singapore Bureau in many ways mirrored the Pan-American Sanitary Bureau, which operated under a slightly different title from 1902 through

1923 when it acquired its new title. The Pan-American Sanitary Bureau reported developments on 10 different diseases and sometimes facilitated material assistance to countries with infectious disease problems. A different type of institution—the Office Internationale des Epizooties (OIE)—was created in 1924 to gather and circulate information on disease outbreaks among animals. Then another OIHP legislative product in the form of the Sanitary Convention on Aerial Navigation was adopted in 1933.[48]

The 1926 ISR contained a variety of new rules, but substantively they did not diverge significantly from the 1912 version. It is noteworthy that the regulations focused on ship standards, certificates of compliance, and states' responsibilities with regard to pilgrims.[49] The most important provision in the 1926 regulations related to the obligations of states to avoid more stringent measures than those depicted in the regulations. For the first time, the ISR accepted a provision stating that "measures as laid out in this chapter constitute a maximum."[50]

During the interwar decades, states became increasingly supportive of international health assistance. In fact, the president of the OIHP stated in 1919 that the organization should alter its focus from trying to prevent the spread of disease across borders to improving health conditions inside states by enhancing national public health systems.[51] An interesting example of the recognition of the need for remedial treatment to cure diseases (as opposed to merely preventing their spread) occurred in 1924 with the adoption of the Agreement Respecting Facilities to be given to Merchant Seaman for Treatment of Venereal Diseases. This agreement required that states provide medical faculties at ports to treat infected seafarers.[52]

There was, in fact, limited collaboration to provide health assistance at this time, and the reason was significantly because much of the developing world was controlled by colonial powers, meaning that financial and material aid was given bilaterally from the colonial powers to developing states.[53] Apart from the colonial powers, the major providers of international health assistance were nongovernmental organizations such as the Rockefeller Foundation, the Pasteur Institute, and the League of Red Cross Societies. The Rockefeller Foundation established a clear policy of seeking to improve economic standards in the developing world.[54] One commentator on health assistance programs noted: "Where mass diseases are brought under control, productivity tends to increase . . . through augmenting their strength and ambition to work."[55]

The newly created LNHO also played a significant role in providing health assistance. The LNHO's most notable work was in the early 1920s when its Epidemic Commission actively helped states to manage serious typhus and smallpox problems in eastern Europe. Millions died of typhus before it was brought under control. The Epidemic Commission was successful by introducing clinics and medicines and creating a "zone *sanitaire*" that blocked the spread of the disease to the West.[56] An important demonstration of the League's commitment to health was the creation, in 1920, of the Epidemic Commission. The Epidemic Commission was formed to combat the postwar outbreak of typhus fever in eastern Europe, most seriously in Poland and Soviet Russia. A major motivation behind the formation of this body was the fear that the typhus epidemic would spread into western Europe, causing a medical and even political, disaster. The commission assisted afflicted states by providing material goods, such as soap, medicines, medical equipment, ambulances, and other such tangible goods necessary to combat the disease.[57] Despite insufficient funding for the project, the commission was largely successful. It remains a significant achievement as this was one of the first examples of an international body providing material goods to treat and cure an infectious disease rather than merely provide advice or recommendations to limit the spread of disease.

During World War II, the most important international health body was the UN Relief and Rehabilitation Administration (UNRRA).[58] It took over responsibilities for the OIHP in 1943, and it also revised the ISR in 1944. It is actually better known for the assistance work that it carried out in war-torn areas. It provided pesticides such as DDT to fight typhus and malaria and vaccines to fight cholera and yellow fever. The assistance activities of UNRRA were good precursors of the range of activities of the World Health Organization (WHO), which were approved in 1946.

Developments between 1946 and 1990

Some scholars have noted that the industrialized countries gradually lost interest in global health issues after World War II because of the medical progress achieved in the early twentieth century.[59] In 1969, typhus and relapsing fever were removed from the list of reportable and quarantinable diseases from the IHR due to successful campaigns to reduce incidents of the diseases. Just over a decade later, in 1981, smallpox was not only removed from the regulations, but also declared officially eradicated after a hugely successful WHO campaign to eliminate the disease.[60] These developments created a mindset among the developed country leaders that infectious diseases could be brought under control through advancements in medical technology. This belief in turn led to a complacent attitude toward infectious diseases and a concomitant reduction in interest in global health matters.

Another reduction in the responsibilities and activities of WHO concerned the removal of most provisions relating to the movement of Muslim pilgrims throughout the Hejaz region. This occurred largely in the 1956 revision of the ISR. From this point on, most provisions relating to these pilgrims pertained solely to sanitary standards on ships.[61] There were, however, some additional provisions as per Article 103, which permitted states to apply more stringent measures regarding the movement of pilgrims when there were serious outbreaks.

Apart from the provisions regarding the Muslim pilgrims, there were no dramatic changes in the ISR between 1951 and 1956. There were, however, extensive deliberations on certain regulatory issues during the meetings on the revision of the 1951 and 1956 regulations and in the meetings of the Committee on International Quarantines (retitled the Committee on the Surveillance of Communicable Diseases in 1969). The issue that attracted the most political interest was the right of states to adopt measures that were more stringent than those in the texts of the ISR. The Western or industrialized countries were adamantly opposed to the right to adopt "excessive measures" since this could lead to interruptions in maritime commerce. In fact, during the revision of the 1951 regulations France was the most adamant opponent of the right to employ more stringent measures.[62] The developing countries, on the other hand, spoke just as vehemently in favor of the right to adopt more stringent measures since they did not have the national health systems that could control the spread of diseases. There were, however, provisions in all of the drafts of the ISR (and the IHR) that allowed more stringent measures in the case of health crises that concerned migrants and seasonal workers.[63] There was another issue that provoked important political dialogues, and this was the question of whether the regulations should focus more on health conditions within states as opposed to the spread of diseases between states. In fact, this issue arose from the early years of the ISR (see reference to Robert Koch earlier). There was one discussion during the 1970s where some experts strongly criticized the use of border controls and recommended improved disease surveillance and stronger national public health systems.[64]

An issue that permeates the deliberations on global health is states' compliance with different rules. Over the last half of the twentieth century there were numerous complaints about the failures of countries to report outbreaks—often because they feared that a public report would bring about retaliation in the form of embargos on their goods and citizens.[65] One WHO committee commented on the ubiquitous "gross under-reporting of cholera."[66] The regulation that was frequently discussed and often violated was the obligation of countries to provide yearly reports on outbreaks within their borders and their responses to these outbreaks. Many countries never provided these yearly reports and others reported them infrequently. There were also many statements by public and private officials that ships and aircraft violated sanitary standards and their obligations to carry certifi-cates of inspection.[67] Despite the range and number of violations of rules, David Leive has reported that the IHR have been "useful" in promoting global health improvements.[68] One strategy of promoting compliance with rules is the appointment of mediators to settle disputes. The IHR had a provision that the WHO director general could be asked to mediate a con-flict. This formal procedure was only used on one occasion in a conflict between Turkey, on the one side, and Romania and Bulgaria on the other.[69] Although this formal procedure was seldom used, WHO member states did adopt an informal system of asking the director general to inter-vene in conflicts and assist the disputing parties in finding a solution to their conflict. In fact an informal jurisprudence developed from the periodic interventions of the director general and his staff.

A final strategic approach to the promotion of global health is the pro-vision of material and financial assistance. The major approach to such assis-tance is the creation of expert groups that assist countries with managing outbreaks. The WHO was very active in bringing together medical experts who could provide advice to states and nongovernmental actors confronted with health problems. To this end, WHO promoted formal affiliations with nongovernmental organizations (NGOs), groups of medical experts, and scientists affiliated with national laboratories (titled WHO Collaborating Centers). In addition, the WHO created six regional com-missions that are to this day conduits for the provision of assistance to countries in need, as well as being important sources of information. The WHO also not only utilized approximately half of its annual budget to assist countries in need, but also mobilized funds that were equivalent to approximately one and a half times its regular budget for extra-budgetary programs.[70] It is notable that some WHO officials were active in promot-ing global health assistance as opposed to remedial strategies of preventing the transborder spread of diseases. An example was a comment by the assis-tant director general in 1963 that WHO should turn its attention from attempting to control the transborder spread of disease to providing resources to control diseases at their source.

The Strategic Development of
Global Health Governance

The growth of global health governance was quite modest in the century and a half from the mid-1800s through the 1980s. No significant progress occurred in the last half of the nineteenth century except for a greater understanding among states of each other's divergent interests and diverse understandings of diseases. These learning processes should not be entirely dismissed because they did pave the way to certain collaborative efforts in the twentieth century; however, the progress was more educational than it was substantive.

Substantive health collaboration commenced with the 1903 ISR, but the scope of the cooperation through the 1980s must be viewed as quite modest when seen from the perspective of the magnitude and significance of the problems. These comments are not meant to dismiss the importance of the progress in international health governance, but they are meant to stress that the scope of cooperation has to be interpreted as very limited when seen against what was happening in some other international issue areas.

Turning first to what happened regarding the very important sphere of surveillance, it is noteworthy that states only accepted responsibility for reporting on a mere handful of diseases (between three and six) that did not even pose significant crises after 1920. Tragically, there was a widespread ignoring of most of the diseases that wreaked havoc on developing countries. A central reason for the weakness of the surveillance system was that states where outbreaks occurred has a veto over whether the OIHP or WHO could publicize the outbreaks to the outside world. States often refused to allow international organizations to disseminate information on outbreaks since they feared that other countries would impose embargoes on the entry of their citizens and goods. States with disease outbreaks were generally able to block the flow of information on disease to international institutions.

With regard to rule-making, some interesting developments occurred but they predominantly fell within the confines of what has been called "soft law." That is to say, the decisions of international bodies were only recommendatory or they were treated as recommendatory even if they were legally binding. This evaluation was corroborated by the decisions of the WHO. The World Health Assembly had the power to approve legally binding international conventions, and the IHR was the one example of such a convention before 2000.[71] However, it was clear over most of the twentieth century that states did not regard these rules as legally binding. In reality, the ISR (after 1969 referred to as the IHR) was generally seen as no more binding than the decisions of the WHO World Health Assembly, Executive Board, and various expert committees that formally had recommendatory powers. Although such decisions did not have great legal significance, they had modest influence on global health collaboration.[72] The states, health professionals, and NGOs to whom prescriptions and proscriptions were directed, often did not regard them as legally binding, but they frequently viewed them as practical professional guidelines and as such they were respected.

The last of the three spheres of strategic collaboration is financial and material assistance. It is clear from some of the health policies of states and NGOs that such assistance was gradually recognized as the best approach to curtailing the international spread of disease. Such programs also had the marked advantage of promoting both health and economic standards in the third world. It has been the tying of improved health conditions not just to human health but also to a broad range of conditions that enhance human betterment. As noted earlier, health experts gradually concluded since the late nineteenth century that the best strategy for controlling the spread of diseases was to reduce their incidence within countries. Attempts to control the cross-border spread of disease through guidelines for ship standards and controls over port authorities proved to have little effect in an era of growing commercial shipping and migration. The best approach to reducing the spread of disease increasingly appeared to be improved health systems within countries.

CHAPTER 3

DISEASE CONTAINMENT: SURVEILLANCE SYSTEMS, EMERGENCY RESPONSES, AND TRANSBORDER REGULATIONS

The cliché that the world is becoming a smaller place has a particular resonance in the field of global health. Outbreaks of virulent diseases can occur anywhere at anytime, and given how interconnected the world is nowadays, a disease can spread around the globe in a matter of days. Therefore, it is imperative that outbreaks of infectious diseases are contained rapidly to prevent them from becoming global threats. To accomplish this feat, three things are necessary: sophisticated surveillance systems to discover outbreaks in a timely fashion; efficient emergency response programs for medical experts to contain disease outbreaks before they spread; and finally effective transborder regulations to prevent or slow the propagation of diseases. This chapter examines how all three of these strategies of disease containment have evolved and thus how they have helped to create a stronger coordinated global health regime.

Human health is a dynamic field of study. New and improved medical knowledge continuously enhances our ability to prevent, diagnose, treat, and cure diseases. However, as quickly as we learn new ways to protect ourselves, new threats emerge. There are three contemporary challenges to disease containment: emerging (or new) diseases, reemerging diseases (often owing to the development of antimicrobial resistance), and threat of bioterrorism, which has garnered significant attention in recent years. New diseases, which have never before been encountered by humans, have been emerging at a consistent rate of one per year for the past 30 years.[1] Probably the best-known example of such a disease is Ebola, which was first discovered in 1976. It can have a mortality rate of more than 90 percent, gruesomely killing its victims within 48 hours, and to date it is neither treatable nor curable (although it can be controlled through effective hospital measures). New diseases pose an obvious threat to humankind because treatment options are often unknown, as are prevention and containment methods. Moreover, according to the Institute of Medicine, diseases are going to play an increasingly important role in global health in the future as "[w]e will inevitably see more emerging infections in the future as the factors that lead to emergence become more prevalent and converge with increased frequency."[2]

Reemerging diseases are known illnesses that have been brought under control by medical science, but have undergone some kind of change that makes them a significant threat once again. The most common contemporary reason for disease reemergence is antimicrobial resistance. As the 2003 Institute of Medicine report states, "The world is facing an imminent crisis in the control of infectious diseases as the result of a gradual but steady increase in the resistance of a number of microbial agents to available therapeutic drugs."[3]

One of the best examples of this phenomenon is tuberculosis (TB). TB was largely brought under control owing to advances in living standards in the post–Industrial Revolution era; however, due to a variety of factors (but especially improper treatment) TB bacilli have developed resistance to many first-line drugs, and there is even a strain called XDR TB (Extreme Drug Resistant Tuberculosis) that has developed resistance to almost all known drugs and is therefore virtually untreatable. Thus, TB, which was thought to be under control a decade ago, is now reemerging as a serious threat. Influenza is also an important example of a reemerging disease because the influenza microbe has the ability to mutate. It does this approximately every 12 months, rendering previous vaccines useless. Therefore, medical experts continuously have to develop new ways to prevent and treat this familiar disease. Numerous influenza experts are concerned that one day influenza will mutate in such a way that it becomes highly pathogenic and impossible to treat.[4]

The third contemporary challenge to disease containment is bioterrorism, which can be defined as the deliberate release of viruses, bacteria, or other germs used to cause illness or death in people, animals, or plants to advance the political, social, or religious aims of the group.[5] Most people have heard of the Aum Shinrikyo sarin nerve gas attack on the Tokyo subway in 1995 that killed 12 people and injured hundreds of others. Most people, however, are not aware of the fact that Aum Shinrikyo

. . . dabbled in many different biological agents. They cultured and experimented with botulin toxin, anthrax, cholera, and Q fever. In 1993, [the cult leader] led a group of 16 cult doctors and nurses to Zaire, on a supposed medical mission. The actual purpose of the trip to Central Africa was to learn as much as possible about and . . . to bring back samples of Ebola virus. In early 1994, cult doctors were quoted on Russian radio as discussing the possibility of using Ebola as a biological weapon.[6]

The subway sarin gas attack was not notable in its lethality; indeed, in biological terms the attack was largely unsuccessful. However, it is immensely significant because the attack and the active research into other diseases demonstrated unequivocally for the first time that nonexperts could gain access to and manipulate biological weapons. Nowadays, "[t]he knowledge needed for developing biological weapons is accessible to individuals through the open literature and the Internet; the technology is readily available and affordable; and, perhaps most alarming, as the field of molecular genetics advances, an increased capability exits to bioengineer vaccine- or antimicrobial-resistant strains of biological agents."[7] Thus, since 1995, security specialists have been clamoring for more research funding and surveillance to combat the threat of bioterrorism.

The anthrax letter campaign, which followed the 9/11 terrorist attacks on the United States in the fall of 2001, greatly exacerbated the perceived need to fund bioterrorism defense systems. Since late 2001, spending on bioterrorism has increased exponentially. In the United States alone, spending has increased from $424 million in 2001 to $7.6 billion in 2006, and other countries have augmented biodefense programs significantly as well.[8] Anthrax, smallpox, plague, tularemia, and botulinum toxin have been identified as high priority threats that could be used in a bioterrorist attack, and as such significant research grants have been allocated to developing treatment and response options to these diseases. The development of emergency plans to counter a biological attack has been deemed a priority as "[n]umerous commissions have . . . uniformly concluded that the United States is vulnerable to a bioterrorist attack and that the likelihood of such an event is high."[9]

These three factors—emerging diseases, reemerging diseases, and bioterrorism—have increased the likelihood of disease outbreaks and the likelihood that an outbreak will have a severe global impact. When combined with other nonmedical factors such as advances in transportation technology, it becomes even more apparent that outbreaks can impact people around the globe, wherever they occur. This chapter deals with attempts to combat emergency disease outbreaks, and in doing so it has three main sections. The first examines the significant changes to global health surveillance since 1990. The second section reviews several important multilateral interventions intended to control infectious disease outbreaks. These interventions have shaped the ongoing political dialogue regarding international controls concerning infectious diseases. The third section focuses on the development of international controls on the spread of infectious diseases—largely owing to the revision of the International Health Regulations (IHR). Efforts to revise the Regulations formally commenced in 1995, and they came to fruition in 2005. As the third section of the chapter explains, the 2005 Regulations provided some significant changes in global health governance, but they included some marked continuities between the pre- and post-1995 regimes.

Advances in Global Surveillance Capabilities

The period from the early 1990s to the present has unquestionably been the most innovative and interesting period in the development and politics of global health collaboration. One of the most important developments about controlling the transnational spread of diseases has been improved surveillance. As recently as 15 years ago, a study from the U.S. Institute of Medicine noted that "[T]here is insufficient awareness and appreciation for the value of comprehensive surveillance programs."[10] Before the mid-1990s, countries were obligated by the IHR to report outbreaks of only three diseases to World Health Organization (WHO)—plague, cholera, and yellow fever—that occurred on their territories and on ships and aircraft arriving in their ports/airports.[11] Even though this was an established requirement of the Regulations, states frequently chose not to report disease outbreaks for fear of the imposition of embargoes on goods and travelers by other countries. To make matters worse, governments, especially in developing countries, were often ignorant of health conditions in their own countries, making effective reporting impossible. Since the late 1990s, however, there have been immense changes to the way disease surveillance is conducted, and these changes have fundamentally altered the nature of the contemporary global health regime.

In the mid-1990s, dramatic advances in communications technology, especially e-mail and the Internet, reformed the global health surveillance system almost overnight. Surveillance shifted from being a weakly enforced and often flouted system of reporting by state governments to WHO, to an open system of communications involving a variety of sources—including health professionals, nongovernmental organizations (NGO) representatives, and government officials. Because of this, WHO began to receive information on dozens, if not hundreds, of diseases, and for the first time state governments did not have complete control over the flow of health information leaving their countries. The establishment of computerized surveillance programs able to detect disease outbreaks (or events) and alert appropriate responders, immediately and dramatically, altered the global system of disease monitoring. This is evidenced by the fact that in recent years approximately 65 percent of first reports of infectious disease outbreaks have come "not from country notifications, but from informal sources, including press reports and the internet."[12]

The significance of this shift cannot be underestimated as effective disease detection is the cornerstone of any containment program and is essential in limiting global fallout from outbreaks. As two high-level WHO officials have noted, "[I]nadequate surveillance and response capacity in a single country can endanger national populations and the public health security of the entire world. As long as national capacities are weak, international mechanisms for outbreak alert and response will be needed as a global safety net that protects other countries when one nation's surveillance and response systems fail."[13]

Although the most notable changes in the surveillance of disease outbreaks starting in the 1990s concerned nongovernmental actors, there were some important alterations in WHO arrangements for reporting outbreaks. The main vehicle for reporting outbreaks, before the 1990s was the Weekly Epidemiological Record (WER), which was created as early as 1926 by the Office International d'Hygiene Publique (OIHP). Between 1951 and the mid-1990s, under the authority of the WHO, it published suspected and confirmed outbreaks of the diseases that were specifically noted in the IHR.[14] In recent years, reflecting the shift in disease surveillance, the WER has published reports on a much wider spectrum of disease outbreaks. Beginning in 1996, WHO published an online list of officially confirmed disease outbreaks called *Disease Outbreak News*.

The following section highlights and explains the significance of a handful of surveillance bodies that have developed over the past several years. Although this listing does not purport to be comprehensive, it does provide an overview of some of the most important surveillance mechanisms currently available as well as an idea of the effect they have had on the nature of disease surveillance in general. Before examining the newer surveillance groups, however, it is necessary to mention one of the oldest and best-established surveillance bodies in the global health regime, the WHO Global Influenza Surveillance Network. This initiative is important because due to its effectiveness, it paved the way for future initiatives to gain legitimacy and become respected members of the global health regime. The network was established in 1952 and is currently comprised of 117 National Influenza Centers (NICs) located in 88 countries, four Collaborating Centers located in Australia, Japan, the United Kingdom, and the United States, and the WHO. The role of the network is to provide recommendations to states about which vaccine will be effective against circulating influenza viruses. To this end, the NICs collect 175,000 samples of influenza viruses each year. These samples are sent to the WHO Collaborating Centers for analysis, and eventually a vaccine is developed and recommended for widespread use. In fact, "more than 250 million doses of influenza vaccine are produced annually which contain the WHO recommended influenza strains."[15] The network serves an important secondary purpose as well, and that is to monitor the mortality rates of influenza viruses and to alert the medical community if a virus develops with the potential to cause a pandemic.

For most of the latter half of the twentieth century, the WHO Global Influenza Surveillance Network stood alone as virtually the only organized, multilateral initiative to provide accurate information on the nature and spread of a disease. However, as previously noted, technological innovations in the early 1990s revolutionized the entire system of global disease surveillance. In response to these changes, the global health surveillance system began to change starting in 1993. In that year a group of medical experts met to consider the creation of the Program for Monitoring Emerging Diseases (ProMED) and an electronically linked network of health professionals throughout the world, called ProMED-Mail. The deliberations were successful, and in 1994, ProMED and ProMED-Mail were launched. The program is "an Internet-based reporting system dedicated to rapid global dissemination of information on outbreaks of infectious diseases and acute exposures to toxins that affect human health, including those in animals and in plants grown for food or animal feed."[16] Importantly it accepts information from a variety of sources—not just government. The information is then vetted by experts, published on the ProMED-Mail Web site, and distributed to its subscribers.

ProMED was initially administered by the Federation of American Scientists, but, as of 1999, responsibility was transferred to the International Society for Infectious Diseases. Soon after its founding, it had 40 subscribers in 7 countries. Currently, it has more than 30,000 subscribers in 150 countries. It is available in English, French, Spanish, and Portuguese. It is presently funded by the Gates Foundation, the Rockefeller Foundation, and the Oracle Corporation, and its e-mail services are provided by the Harvard School of Public Health. ProMED has become one of the most important sources of disease outbreak news in the world owing to its careful screening of reports and wide distribution base.[17]

Another important contemporary surveillance system is the Global Public Health Intelligence Network (GPHIN), which was created by the Canadian government in 1997 in collaboration with the WHO. GPHIN monitors media sources from around the globe for information on disease outbreaks, bioterrorism threats, contaminated food and water supplies, nuclear material leaks, and natural disasters. A sophisticated computer program filters the information for relevance and accuracy, which is then further screened by officials working for the Public Health Agency of Canada. Information is then released to GPHIN subscribers who can further disseminate the information. The main characteristic of GPHIN that sets it apart from other surveillance systems is that it operates around the clock. News sources are scanned 24 hours a day, and pertinent information is released to appropriate health experts almost as soon as it is discovered. It currently scans reports on numerous Internet sites in Arabic, English, French, Russian, simplified and traditional Chinese, Farsi, and Spanish. GPHIN's importance to current disease containment issues can be clearly demonstrated by the fact that information on 40 percent of the approximately 250 outbreaks that WHO investigates every year comes from GPHIN.[18]

Although ProMED is an example of a network of private individuals and GPHIN is an example of a government-administered surveillance organization, there is another important actor in the disease surveillance realm and that is the military—particularly the U.S. military. Most militaries are, in varying degrees, concerned with infectious disease agents owing to the likelihood that their troops will make the first contact with either a deliberate or naturally occurring outbreak. As a result, the U.S. Department of Defense "is playing an increasingly important role in global disease surveillance, particularly with regard to building the epidemiological capacity of foreign laboratories."[19] As part of this expansion of duties, the U.S. military also runs the Global Emerging Infections Surveillance and Response System (GEIS), which was created by a presidential directive in 1996. GEIS is a network of domestic and overseas military research units with a mandate of supporting surveillance, training, research, and appropriate responses to infectious diseases. Overseas, it is linked with five army and navy laboratories (located in Egypt, Kenya, Indonesia, Peru, and Thailand) that monitor infectious diseases of concern to the military and host countries.[20]

The growing importance of the WHO Global Influenza Surveillance Network and the development of initiatives such as ProMED, GPHIN, and GEIS should highlight the fact that surveillance regarding the international spread of diseases has improved significantly in recent years. However, the earlier discussion is not designed to suggest that disease surveillance has become entirely transparent and effective: there is, in fact, much room for further improvement. In developing countries—precisely where accurate surveillance is most necessary—the medical infrastructure is often so lacking that simple diagnostic tests for common diseases such as TB and HIV/AIDS are impossible to carry out. "Basic health indices, such as death rates or causes of death, are unknown in such contexts. Health ministries may generate health reports, but the data are generally unreliable."[21] Members of medical NGOs such as Medecins sans Frontieres (MSF) and Merlin may have access to information in certain cities or regions of developing countries, and they may be willing to share that information with groups like ProMED and GEIS, but NGOs cannot be expected, and nor are they equipped, to amass epidemiological data on entire countries. Therefore, until state health infrastructures are strengthened and linked into the growing global network of disease surveillance groups, we are still at risk that an outbreak with the potential to threaten the globe could occur.

Effective surveillance mechanisms are crucial to contain disease outbreaks; however, merely knowing that an outbreak is occurring is not sufficient to prevent its spread. Containing a disease once an outbreak has begun requires other social and economic factors as well. Evidence of such threats can be seen in recent occurrences regarding avian influenza outbreaks in Southeast Asia. In many instances, farmers dealing with outbreaks in poor communities were unwilling to have their flocks culled and therefore quickly sold birds without reporting symptoms of the disease to authorities. To make matters worse, the governments of some Asian countries afflicted by avian influenza were unwilling to release information to WHO for fear of causing panic, and losing tourist and export dollars.[22] But as Dr. Juan Lubroth, who runs the emergency prevention system for infectious animal diseases at the Food and Agriculture Organization (FAO) states, "any benefits of hiding data are short-lived" because lack of information sharing makes it virtually impossible to develop appropriate pandemic preparedness plans.[23] Surveillance regarding zoonotic diseases is in an even worse state as "the World Animal Health Organization cannot accept information on wildlife diseases in a country unless that information has been submitted officially by a national agricultural authority—few of which are mandated or organized to monitor wildlife diseases."[24] Essentially, surveillance of animal disease outbreaks has remained where surveillance of human outbreaks was until the 1990s: it has not evolved concomitantly with human outbreak surveillance. This is potentially disastrous as "more than 60 percent of the 1,415 infectious diseases currently known to modern medicine are capable of infecting both animals and humans" making it likely, if not probable, that a pandemic will begin in animals before affecting humans.[25]

Overview of Emergency Multilateral Interventions

This section provides a description of a handful of significant disease outbreaks that have occurred over the past several decades. The discussion provides an analysis of how the outbreaks came to light, what was done to contain them, and what roles different actors played in the containment process. It should be noted that minor outbreaks of infectious diseases occur throughout the world every day; fortunately most are not serious and thus do not attract the world media or the major international health organizations. In recent years WHO has become involved in verifying the medical characteristics of approximately 250 outbreaks annually. In approximately 20 percent of these outbreaks, WHO regional commissions became involved, and in about one percent of all cases—the cases that pose the most severe threat—WHO headquarters assumes an active role in containing the outbreak. Before continuing with the review on the multilateral interventions, however, a description of the different actors commonly involved in outbreak interventions is necessary.

The Actors

Generally, six types of actors are involved in managing a contemporary outbreak intervention: WHO; the WHO regional office of the area experiencing the outbreak; one or more advanced research laboratories such as Centers for Disease Control and Prevention (CDC) or the Pasteur Institute; one or more medical NGO such as MSF or Merlin; the Ministry of Health (MoH) of the state in question; and one or more United Nations (UN) body such as United Nations Children's Fund (UNICEF).

The WHO is often at the center of international efforts to control disease outbreaks, but its main efforts generally concern the mobilization and coordination of other expert individuals and groups. Countries experiencing outbreaks often approach WHO for assistance as the first point of call—this can be likened to a global equivalent of dialing 911 in an emergency. WHO then acts as a facilitator as it has the capacity, knowledge, and legitimacy to mobilize the most appropriate people to assist with the disease outbreak in question. Although the facilitator or coordinator role is undoubtedly the predominant role WHO plays, it does also have infectious disease experts who can be deployed in an emergency to provide on-the-ground medical expertise. Representatives from WHO regional offices are often particularly helpful in this regard as they have more local knowledge regarding language, local customs, endemic diseases, weather patterns, and infrastructure conditions, all of which are important factors in developing an appropriate outbreak response plan. Also, in some recent cases a representative of WHO and/or the WHO regional office has assumed a central role in relaying information to the media. With increasing frequency, WHO issues statements that inform the world about the evolution of a disease outbreak, via media releases and its Web site. Thus, the central roles of

WHO bodies during outbreaks are legitimizing the inclusion of foreign medical experts into the outbreak response, facilitating the involvement of appropriate humanitarian health organizations, providing general advice to the MoH, and providing information to the media and the public. The main roles of WHO in outbreaks can be summarized as follows:

> The work of coordinating large-scale international responses to the unexpected [outbreak] . . . is facilitated by WHO operational protocols which set out standardized procedures for the alert and verification process, communications, coordination of the response, emergency evacuation, research, and relations with the media. WHO has also revised its guidelines for the behavior of foreign nations during and after field operations in the host country.[26]

National research laboratories play crucial roles in an emergency intervention. Understanding the precise nature of the virus, bacteria, or microbe causing an outbreak is of key importance in developing the proper response protocols. As seen in the discussion on Ebola outbreaks, scientific research facilities are even more important when an outbreak of a new disease occurs. In this situation, there is no precedent to follow; experts on the ground need as much technical knowledge about the new disease as possible to determine how to proceed with a containment strategy. One of the best-known research facilities is the CDC based in Atlanta, Georgia. It is known as "a world leader in outbreak investigations."[27] CDC has advanced research facilities as well as a high caliber staff of medical experts. As such they are frequently called upon to supply information, equipment, or expert personnel in outbreak interventions. Other important laboratories involved in outbreak research are the U.S. Army Medical Research Institute of Infectious Diseases (USAMRIID)[28] located at Fort Detrick, MD, the global network of Pasteur Institutes that have their headquarters in Paris, France, the British Porton Down Institute and the National Institute of Virology in South Africa. Most of the national research laboratories that participate in controlling disease outbreaks are affiliated with WHO as Collaborating Centers. WHO creates agreements with these laboratories ensuring that they will provide specialized assistance if called upon during medical crises. There are presently close to 300 research institutions that have the status of WHO Collaborating Centers. This system of linkages gives WHO considerable leverage in coordinating outbreak response efforts. It is significant that the activities of foreign research institutes in outbreak response efforts are politically more acceptable as they operate under a WHO umbrella.

Numerous NGOs have become involved in providing health assistance in recent years; however, only a few have developed a reputation for being sufficiently organized and possessing sufficient medical training to assist in disease outbreak situations. Three prominent examples of members of this select group are MSF, the International Committee of the Red Cross (ICRC) and various national Red Cross groups,[29] and Merlin. MSF, which was founded by a group of French doctors in 1971, maintains and operates medical facilities in third world countries afflicted by poverty, drought, famine, and/or war. It also has teams of emergency responders who are capable of assisting with the medical treatment of victims of natural disasters and disease outbreaks.[30] The ICRC was founded in 1863 in Geneva as a humanitarian organization dedicated to alleviating the suffering of soldiers in wartime. In 1919, the organization expanded its mandate, and a second group, the International Federation of Red Cross and Red Crescent Societies (IFRC), was created. Currently, the 185 national Red Cross and Red Crescent offices are autonomous but are loosely coordinated by the IFRC. Owing to the asset of name recognition, Red Cross and Red Crescent groups are able to mobilize large amounts of funding from individual donors in developed countries as well as large numbers of volunteers in both developed and developing countries. Merlin (which takes its name from the caption "Medical Relief, Lasting Health Care") was established as a humanitarian health organization in 1993. It is based in the United Kingdom, but it has run emergency and long-term health operations in Rwanda, Afghanistan, Kenya, Sudan, and many other countries. Its personnel, made up of health professionals including volunteer doctors, nurses, and health specialists, provide medical treatment in disaster situations such as earthquakes, tsunamis, conflict zones, and disease outbreaks.

The MoH of the country experiencing an outbreak is often the first to know about the disease. If unable to manage the crisis with available resources, the MoH can call upon the international community for assistance. This often takes the form of a call to the WHO. A call or invitation is still considered necessary by custom and convention, and indeed it is a legal requirement of the IHR before WHO can organize a foreign team to assist in the health emergency. After permission has been granted to allow a WHO-coordinated team into the crisis zone, the MoH is involved in relaying information from the expert team to the public. The MoH usually provides trained medical staff to work with the expert team as well as material goods, such as hospital supplies and diagnosis equipment.

The last group of actors that are commonly involved in emergency outbreak situations are UN bodies. Groups such as the UNICEF often have a presence in developing nations, and they can provide valuable assistance when an outbreak occurs. UNICEF is frequently an important source of material assistance during outbreaks. For example, they have been known to provide oral rehydration salts during cholera outbreaks, basic hospital supplies such as soap, and importantly vaccines and medicines to treat common diseases, especially those that predominantly affect children. Halting the spread of a disease can be greatly facilitated if a program of immunization can be administered quickly and effectively, making UNICEF's contributions to outbreak assistance very significant.[31] As seen in the discussion on avian influenza, the FAO also becomes involved in disease containment in which animals are involved. The FAO has expert teams of veterinarians and animal health specialists who can provide valuable advice on how to best control diseases that spread from animals to humans.

Over the years, these six types of outbreak response actors developed a loosely coordinated network that allowed for better communication and more effective response procedures. In April 2000, the network was formalized under the WHO-led Global Outbreak Alert and Response Network (GOARN).[32] GOARN consists of a large group of more than 120 governments, NGOs, and multi-partner health initiatives. It was created in recognition of the fact that "no single institution or country has all the capacities to respond to international public health emergencies caused by epidemics and by new and emerging infectious diseases."[33] The network cooperates to accomplish four tasks: conducting epidemic intelligence, verifying outbreak rumors, alerting appropriate groups in outbreak situations, and organizing rapid response reactions when necessary.[34] Owing to the existence of this network, WHO can mobilize GOARN partners and send medical teams to states experiencing outbreaks within 24 hours of notification. Between 2000 and 2004 it launched operations involving response teams to 17 developing countries in Africa and Asia. GOARN is led by a Steering Committee made up of health experts, and an Operational Support Team that is based within WHO headquarters. It receives funding support from WHO regular and extra-budgetary accounts. It is significant that the WHO Outbreak and Alert Response Team, which meets every morning to assess rumors and reports of outbreaks,[35] is composed of health experts generally associated with the WHO secretariat, and is not accountable to a governmental or intergovernmental body.[36] In many ways GOARN can be seen as the consolidation of collaborative efforts since the mid-1990s—including the revision of the IHR between 1996 and 2005.

The Outbreaks

Cholera has been a scourge of humanity for millennia; however, medical advances in treatment of the disease have greatly reduced the number of cases and the mortality rate since the mid-1900s. In fact, in modern times, the fatality rate is usually as low as 1–2 percent because effective medical treatment is easy to administer, inexpensive, and readily available. Nevertheless, cholera outbreaks—particularly in poor countries—can still be devastating without prompt and proper treatment, and the death rate can skyrocket to levels reminiscent of the nineteenth century. An outstanding example of this occurred in the Democratic Republic of the Congo in 1994. Refugee camps were set up for survivors of the Rwandan genocide; and when cholera broke out, medical assistance and supplies were nonexistent, resulting in a 49 percent fatality rate. Shockingly, 23,800 of the 48,000 infected persons died.[37] This tragedy was an example of what happens when surveillance and response mechanisms fail.

The best-known and the most widespread outbreak of cholera, in recent years, began in Peru in 1991 and spread throughout the Americas. In 1991 and 1992, there were 400,000 cases with 4,000 deaths, and in the period between 1991 and 1995, 1.4 million cases were reported with more than 10,000 deaths in 19 countries. The cause of the outbreak, still not determined, is often cited to have been the discharge of contaminated water from a foreign vessel in a Peruvian port. Foreign reactions to the outbreak were dramatic. Bolivia, Chile, and Ecuador banned imports of perishable foods from Peru; Argentina banned fish imports; the EC banned all fish and all goods from Peru; and the United States required tests of all foods coming in from Peru.[38] A team of medical specialists from the Pan-American Health Organization (PAHO) was active in assisting Peruvian and other Latin American authorities with control measures. The PAHO officials also argued that bans on fish, foods, and goods were not effective measures against cholera. The U.S. CDC also sent doctors to Peru to provide advice on treatment options and control measures.[39]

The crisis led the WHO to create the Global Task Force on Cholera Control that is composed of experts on cholera containment, which can be called on by countries facing serious outbreaks. It was created with the passing of Resolution 44.6 at the 1991 World Health Assembly (WHA) and was officially launched in 1992. The task force has two primary goals: to reduce the morbidity and mortality rates of the disease and to reduce the socioeconomic effect of outbreaks. To this end, "it brings together governmental organizations and nongovernmental organizations, UN agencies, and scientific institutions to coordinate activities against epidemic enteric diseases and to develop technical guidelines . . . for cholera control."[40] Since its inception, the task force has assisted cholera-afflicted countries in several ways, such as giving medical advice, disseminating information on the disease, and training health professionals.

Plague has been one of the most harmful infectious diseases in human history, and major outbreaks often originated in southern Asia. Owing to the disastrous impacts of past outbreaks, it is not surprising that people from both within and outside the region fear any rumor of a plague outbreak in the Indian subcontinent. However, these fears are generally exaggerated today because plague can be completely cured with very inexpensive antibiotics.[41] In September 1994, the media reported a number of cases of plague in Surat, India, and this set off a flight of 500,000 people from the city. As it turned out, the outbreak was not particularly lethal and resulted in less than 6,500 cases with 56 deaths, but over much of September and October people feared a much larger disaster.[42]

Soon after the first reports of the plague outbreak, India called on WHO for assistance. The latter then organized a team of experts from Geneva headquarters, the regional WHO office, the United States, and Russia. The WHO team recommended control measures to the Indian government, and they were largely accepted. These measures included mandatory screening of airline passengers, fumigation of aircraft, inspection of vessels for rats, and the requirement of deratting certificates from ships. Early in the crisis, WHO provided advice to travelers moving to and from the infected area of India, but it stated that there should not be travel restrictions, and there should be no vaccination requirements.[43] During the crisis of September and October the Gulf States, Pakistan, and Sri Lanka banned entry of all travelers and goods from India. The Gulf States even banned the entry of mail. Their policies of imposing an embargo on travelers and goods from India were also adopted by Russia, China, Egypt, Malaysia, and Bangladesh. The European Union and North American States kept trade and travel routes open with India, but air passengers were subject to inspection. The total loss to India's economy was approximately $2 billion. Laurie Garrett accuses WHO of being weak in allowing the imposition of all these restrictions, but there was not a lot that it could have done at the time given popular fears in the Middle East and parts of Asia. The degree of public concern in the world is indicated by the fact the U.S. CDC established a plague hotline for its citizens and also distributed information sheets on the plague to travelers in its airports and hospitals. Medical specialists were certainly not convinced that the threats were serious, but they had to do something to allay public anxieties.[44]

When people think of virulent, epidemic-prone diseases in the late twentieth century, they generally think first of diseases like Ebola hemorrhagic fever. The disease was first discovered through several outbreaks in Sudan and Zaire in the mid-1970s. After a nearly two-decade hiatus in Ebola outbreaks there have been, on an average, annual outbreaks in Africa since the mid-1990s. The incubation period for the disease is generally between 2 and 10 days, and it kills between 50 and 80 percent of the people who contract it. The fact that hemorrhagic fever leads to profuse bleeding heightens fear of the disease.

The most publicized case of Ebola was the outbreak in Zaire (now the Democratic Republic of the Congo) in 1995. There were 316 cases and 245 deaths over a period of several months. Contact was first established between the Zairian government and WHO thorough interpersonal channels, and WHO soon responded by sending several staff members to Zaire. The head of the infectious diseases division at WHO, David Heymann, assumed a role of press secretary for the multiorganizational effort to control the Ebola outbreak. WHO staff also assumed a role of coordinating the increasing number of foreign medical staff arriving at the outbreak zone in Kikwit. The biggest problem facing the medical teams was the lack of adequate medical supplies necessary to deal with the outbreak. The success of the small WHO team in coordinating foreign workers is remarkable as it had such a small staff, poor equipment, and very limited financial resources and because there were so many health workers from different countries and organizations. In fact, most foreign financial assistance (approximately $2 million) was provided by a group of European corporations and foundations but an additional $1 million came from the U.S. CDC and several NGOs provided material assistance. Journalist Laurie Garrett, in fact, has attributed the success of the international effort largely to the efforts of these NGOs (particularly MSF) because they provided the necessary health care materials and skills. Volunteers from the local Red Cross group also provided crucial assistance as they helped care for patients. An interesting comment concerning the international effort in Zaire was that "nearly all Europeans, who took part in Kikwit did so under the aegis of the American CDC, *Medecins sans Frontieres*, or WHO—not under their own country's sponsorship."[45] This indicates a kind of ad hoc adjustment of foreign medical staff to the diversity of backgrounds, resources, and expertise, and the size of different medical assistance groups. Regarding the testing of blood samples to determine the nature and lethality of the virus, CDC, USAMRIID, and the Pasteur Institute worked out their own coordination of research efforts.

An equally virulent outbreak of Ebola occurred in Uganda between 2000 and 2001. There were 425 cases and 224 deaths. The disease was reported to WHO in the fall of 2000. WHO immediately called for assistance from its network of governmental, intergovernmental, and nongovernmental bodies. Within 24 hours, a WHO-led investigative team arrived in Uganda and created an isolation ward for infected patients. CDC also sent a group of medical scientists who confirmed the outbreak of Ebola.[46] Soon 190 foreign experts from 22 different medical institutions were on the scene, many of whom had been mobilized by WHO. The major organizations apart from WHO that participated in the containment effort were the International Committee for the Red Cross, the IFRC, the

International Rescue Committee, MSF, and nine governmental agencies. WHO acted as a coordinator of these organizations, and it also acted as spokesperson of these agencies to the world media.

Rift Valley fever is a viral disease that is transmitted to humans by mosquitoes that carry the disease as a result of biting infected animals. Every year approximately 18,000 cases are reported, and there are approximately 600 deaths in East Africa where the disease is concentrated. Also, deaths of animals cause major economic damage in endemic areas. A serious outbreak of Rift Valley fever occurred in Kenya and Somalia in December 1997 and January 1998 that killed about 500 individuals. WHO was informed of the outbreak, which together with a number of foreign medical laboratories and NGOs sent medical assistance. WHO assumed a role as coordinator among the various agencies, but its policies sometimes elicited criticisms. The laboratory work throughout the crisis was performed by the South African National Institute of Virology and the CDC. WHO sent groups from both Geneva and its regional commissions, and medical assistance was also provided by the IFRC. In addition, international bodies that specialized in livestock, such as the International Livestock Research Institute and the FAO, also sent representatives. The medical experts did warn people in the region about the need for protection from mosquito bites, but they did not recommend that travelers alter plans to visit the area.[47]

In talking to health professionals about their fears of future disease pandemics, they usually mention the likelihood of an influenza outbreak along the lines of the 1918–1919 Spanish Flu, or the smaller but still deadly influenza pandemics of 1957 and 1968. The Spanish Flu pandemic is estimated to have killed approximately 50 million people.[48] A virus with a comparable mortality rate could kill many times that number in today's interconnected world of fast and easy air travel.[49] Fears along these lines have been accentuated by the mutation of a dangerous influenza virus—the H5N1 virus—in Asia since the late 1990s. Avian influenza has been recognized as a common affliction for a variety of species of birds (and occasionally pigs) for centuries; however, recently the virus has changed such that it can now cause illness in humans.

The first known case of the virus jumping the species barrier from birds to humans occurred in Hong Kong in 1997. In total, 18 people contracted the disease, 6 of whom died. Importantly, the disease was (and remains) transmissible predominantly via direct contact between an infected animal and a human. As the virus was not easily communicable between humans, it did not cause a pandemic. Nevertheless, the particularly high mortality rate combined with the frightening similarities between H5N1 and the virus that caused the Spanish Flu pandemic led influenza experts to call for a dramatic response to the 1997 outbreak. The spread of the disease was controlled by the killing of 1.5 million birds in less than a week. The WHO Global Influenza Surveillance Network was activated to prescribe control strategies, and CDC influenza experts played an important role in advising the Hong Kong government.[50] Although contained with relative speed, this outbreak prompted WHO to develop the Influenza Pandemic Preparedness Plan in 1999, which lays out steps to be taken following confirmation of an outbreak.[51]

The disease lay dormant for several years after the 1997 outbreak, but in February 2003 reports of a human infected with H5N1 avian influenza once again emerged from Hong Kong. This second outbreak caused two illnesses and one death, but similar to the first outbreak it was quickly contained by the culling of large numbers of infected and potentially infected poultry flocks. It is now known that the third outbreak of avian influenza began in China in November 2003;[52] unfortunately, however, this outbreak has not yet been contained. In fact, it has now spread throughout Southeast Asia and has affected countries in Central Asia, Europe, and Africa.[53] As of 2007, avian influenza has spread to 12 countries on three continents and it has caused 300 cases of illness with nearly 200 fatalities.

Three hundred cases of illness is certainly a minute number compared to disease goliaths such as TB and AIDS. However, the very legitimate fear that the highly pathogenic H5N1 virus has the capability of becoming easily transmissible between humans makes this disease a predominant concern for global health experts. Hence, under the auspices of the WHO, GOARN has mobilized teams of medical experts to treat patients and explore outbreak sites to learn as much as possible about the source of infection. Due to the importance of understanding the exact nature of the virus, many WHO affiliated laboratories (including the four key Collaborating Centers in Australia, Japan, the United Kingdom, and the United States) that specialize in influenza, have been called upon to conduct research on the samples of virus taken from various victims of the disease. Given that this disease originates in animals that are used primarily as food sources, the FAO and the World Organization for Animal Health (OIE) have also been heavily involved in multilateral efforts to limit the spread of avian influenza. To coordinate the differing activities of these organizations in a better way, the WHO, FAO, and OIE jointly established a regional consultation mechanism for consulting on the prevention and control of the disease. WHO's main role in controlling and containing the current avian influenza outbreak has taken the form of advising state governments on how best to treat patients and prevent new infections. The predominant method for the prevention of new infections has been to cull infected poultry flocks, but this has not been a popular solution in the eyes of many government officials as poultry production is a major source of income in some Southeast Asian countries. In one notable incident in 2003, the Indonesian government initially refused to cull flocks of infected birds but quickly succumbed to international pressure when WHO officials publicly criticized the lack of action. This is an interesting example of WHO successfully employing the tactic of "naming and shaming" to induce compliance with regulations that are not legally binding.[54] Beyond providing treatment and prevention recommendations, WHO has also taken on an active role providing information to the public and it releases avian influenza outbreak updates to its Web site almost daily.

Without question the SARS crisis of 2002 and 2003 was the most notable disease outbreak in recent decades. The significance of the SARS outbreak derives from its rapid global spread and financial impacts as well as the variety, strength, and innovation of the multilateral responses combining governmental and nongovernmental actors. The key health, financial, and political impacts can be broken down into the following categories. First, infected individuals have no overt signs of the disease for about 10 days, meaning that the disease was unknowingly spread from human to human. Second, SARS can progress very quickly into severe pneumonia and respiratory collapse; and death can come within a matter of weeks.[55] Third, although the number of people who were infected (approximately 8,000) and the number of people who died (approximately 700) were relatively small, SARS had a profound global impact as the disease spread from China to 30 other countries in less than 4 months. A handful of countries experienced the brunt of the outbreak, particularly China, which accounted for 83 percent of the cases; Taiwan with 8 percent and Canada and Singapore with 3 percent, but numerous other countries suffered from the outbreak as well.[56] Fourth, according to some reports, SARS cost Asian countries alone between $11 and $18 billion in lost trade and income. Estimate as to the global losses owing to SARS ranges between $40 and $80 billion.[57] In the case of Canada, the drop in passengers between Toronto and Asia went from 27,000 passengers a week to 19,000.[58] Fifth, the scope and impacts of multilateral collaboration, largely through WHO, can be justly called "one of the great success stories in global public health efforts on infectious diseases."[59] The nature of the multilateral activities was of such diversity and importance that one can honestly look at the international collaborative efforts as demarcating a change in the nature of the international health regime. To quote a major study on the development and effects of SARS; "the quality, speed, and effectiveness of the public health response to the SARS brilliantly outshone past responses to international outbreaks of infectious disease, validating a decade's worth of progress in global public health networking." It went on to say that the accomplishments are significantly due to WHO efforts.[60] However, it is important to highlight that WHO's role was significantly enhanced by its cooperation with numerous research institutes from around the world.[61]

We now know that the first cases of SARS originated in Guangdong province of China in November 2002. The earliest information regarding the outbreak was reported by two electronic reporting networks—GPHIN and ProMED—although they could not identify its character. For several months it was labeled as a case of unique pneumonia by Chinese authorities. Central to the spread of the disease from Guangdong was a trip by a Chinese doctor to Hong Kong in mid-February 2003 where he infected 12 people at a hotel. They then carried the disease to Singapore, Vietnam, Canada, Ireland, and the United States. Both WHO and the CDC sent a team to China to investigate the outbreak but were not allowed to enter Guangdong province. On February 28, 2003, a WHO representative in Vietnam identified some of the unique features of the disease, and this was followed on March 12 by a WHO global alert about the outbreak of an atypical pneumonia. The alert included recommendations that humans who contracted the disease should be immediately isolated, be subjected to strict infection control, and also be subject to vigorous contact traces to determine the source of infection.[62]

On March 15, WHO issued the first of its now famous Travel Advisories. It called on travelers and health professionals to adopt certain practices to avoid contraction or spread of the disease, and it called on all states to report suspected outbreaks. However, it did not call for any restrictions in travel practices.[63] On March 27, WHO issued its second travel advisory in which it called on airport authorities to screen passengers coming from infected areas. It also advised airlines on how to evaluate whether passengers had the disease.[64] On April 2, WHO announced its third travel advisory that adopted a notable recommendation to individuals to postpone nonessential travel to areas that were identified as having infected residents. At this point, Guangdong province in China and Hong Kong were the only areas that were identified as being covered by the travel advisory. On April 4, WHO laid out reporting procedures for governments to adopt regarding the reporting of suspected cases of SARS in its Weekly Epidemiological Record.

Several weeks later, on April 23, WHO added Toronto, Beijing and the province of Shanxi to those areas to which travelers should postpone nonessential travel. The Canadian government objected to the application of the travel advisory to Toronto as there was no evidence of the disease being transmitted to the general population. Following political representations at the highest level, the ban was removed on April 29. The dispute between Canada and WHO officials focused on the criteria that should lead to travel advisories for particular areas, whether Toronto met these criteria, and whether the travel advisory should have been applied to Toronto without prior notification by the WHO. WHO's decision had been based on the number of cases, the number of cases exported, and the mode of transmission.[65] Subsequent to the application of the travel advisory to three areas on April 23, it was applied to Taiwan and several other areas in China in May.[66]

Although WHO's involvement in the SARS crisis is best known for the application of travel advisories to individuals throughout the world, there was a host of other WHO activities that were very important from both health and political perspectives. Of great significance was the issuance of more than 20 sets of guidelines and recommendations regarding the control of SARS.[67] They were not legally binding, but they had marked effects on states' and nongovernmental actors' management of the disease outbreak. Many of these sets of recommendations or guidelines emanated from three networks that were created by WHO. First, there was the network of researchers from 13 laboratories in 10 countries that tackled the problem of identifying the etiology of the SARS virus. It was only with such knowledge that it was possible to prescribe many control strategies. One of the 13 laboratories, the British Columbia Cancer Agency in Vancouver, announced that it had succeeded in isolating the SARS pathogen in April 2003. The Agency released data on the previously unknown *coronavirus* on April 12. Two days later, the CDC in Atlanta announced that it had replicated the success of the BC Cancer Agency, and on April 16, the WHO released internationally accepted data on the *coronavirus*. It is significant that during the crisis WHO was very helpful to the CDC and other national laboratories in securing disease samples from China where the disease started.[68] Second, WHO created a network of 50 clinicians in 14 countries who developed definitions of the disease and control guidelines. Its members had regular teleconferencing meetings throughout the crisis.

Finally, WHO formed a network of 32 epidemiologists from 11 countries that were responsible for collecting data on the disease and conducting studies on the characteristics of SARS—including those features influencing its transmission and control. To quote an Institute of Medicine study, "A virtual network of epidemiologists brought together public health institutions, ministries of health, and WHO Country Offices to analyze the spread of SARS and to define appropriate public health measures."[69] In the case of Vietnam, the WHO team of scientists specializing in SARS came from nine different countries.

In addition to the above activities to control the outbreak, GOARN mobilized 115 experts from 26 institutions in 17 countries to help manage the outbreak. Approximately two-thirds of the experts employed by

GOARN came from the CDC. Most of them were sent by the Western Pacific Regional Office of WHO that was one of WHO's six regional offices.[70] According to two WHO officials the most important partner institutions of GOARN were GHPIN and the WHO Global Influenza Surveillance Network of 117 laboratories.[71] Finally, it should be noted that throughout the crisis there was a Global WHO Senior Management Group of between 6 and 8 members who met twice a week (often by teleconferencing) and issued 18 recommendations after March 15. Relevant to the activities of all these networks was WHO's establishment of a SARS Web site that received between 6 and 10 million hits each day during the outbreak from March through July. The data for this Web site came largely from "The Daily Country Summary of Cases of SARS."[72] A number of NGOs with personnel in various countries were also active in efforts to control the disease. This was particularly the case with the IFRC that distributed information on treatment strategies.

WHO's relations with China during the crisis constitute an important landmark in its promotion of state compliance with recommendations and directives. Following the March 15 travel advisory calling on states to report possible outbreaks, WHO specifically called on China to provide information. On April 4, China finally began to send electronic reports—in part because information on cases of SARS was reaching the outside world through NGOs within and outside of China. On April 16, WHO expressed "strong concern over inadequate reporting." Fidler has noted that "WHO's public criticism of the Chinese government presented a radical break with the traditional diplomacy that characterizes relations between the Organization and member states."[73] To mute external criticism, the Chinese Premier, on April 20, fired the health minister and the mayor of Beijing on the grounds of their promoting a cover-up. A WHO publication of May 20, noted,

> Cases during the earlier phase of the SARS outbreak [in China] were not openly reported, thus allowing a severe disease to become silently established in ways that made further international spread almost inevitable. This is the most important lesson for all nations: in a globalized, electronically connected world, attempts to conceal cases of an infectious disease, for fear of social and economic consequences, must be recognized as a short-term stopgap measure that carries a very high price—loss of credibility in the eyes of the international community.[74]

Despite the retreat by China in May 2003, the deputy minister of health argued on May 30, that China had never concealed the truth. In response to this statement, WHO announced that it would remove all staff from China if the deputy minister did not recant. Within a couple of days he reversed his stance, revealing a remarkable amount of effective political pressure by WHO officials.[75]

It is significant that in the last week of May 2003, the WHA passed resolutions that supported WHO's practices during the preceding three months of the SARS crisis. It supported the ability of WHO to create communications networks, to draw on nongovernmental sources of information, to send teams of experts into countries to assure that they were following effective policies, to promote increased national capacities for monitoring and control, and to undertake containment efforts.[76] On July 4, WHO was able to declare that the SARS outbreak had been contained and that the world now looked at WHO as a much stronger and more important organization than had ever been the case in the past.

The above section has provided an overview of outbreaks of half a dozen diseases—cholera, plague, Ebola hemorrhagic fever, Rift Valley fever, avian influenza, and SARS. In analyzing these examples of outbreaks of infectious diseases, one can observe that representatives from all six different types of actors involved in disease containment are usually present in outbreak situations. This fact exposes the important trend that disease containment processes in the twentieth century are almost always multilateral in scope. There are virtually no cases in which outbreaks are managed solely by one state or one actor; rather the different actors have developed a complex, loosely governed arrangement whereby the different actors are responsible for different aspects of the containment procedure. Although there are still gaps in cooperation and incidents of overlapping activities, the regime governing disease containment is moving toward one of greater coordination.

The 2005 IHR: Rule-Making for Contemporary Global Health

The first stage in the negotiations to revise the IHR occurred from 1996 to 1999 following the authorization of the negotiations by the WHA in 1995. The deliberations produced a draft IHR in January 1998. In the foreword to that draft there were several important points. One statement concerning a change in the basic strategy of regulation read:

> It is now clear that international infectious disease control is more effectively undertaken by surveillance and intervention strategies taking advantage of the considerable evolution in communications technology, laboratory science and diagnosis, treatment and control of infections, rather than by the application of quarantine practices or other measures at sites distant from the source of the infection.[77]

This represents a major strategic change from seeking to control the spread of diseases at points of entry (ports, airports, and borders) to reducing the incidence of diseases within bounded territories. At the same time the actual changes in the regulations relating to surveillance and medical interventions concerning disease outbreaks that were integrated into the 1998 draft IHR were very modest.[78]

Of greater significance than the above trend was a major change that was noted in the foreword to the 1998 draft IHR, and that was the change in disease coverage from three epidemic-prone diseases (cholera, plague, and yellow fever) to a host of diseases that fell under six syndromes—acute hemorrhagic fever, acute respiratory, acute diarrheal, acute jaundice, acute neurological, and other notifiable diseases.[79] As it turned out, field trials concerning the diseases that fell within the syndromes in 1998 and 1999 did not prove very successful since many countries did not have the medical resources to evaluate the outbreaks. Consequently the entire focus on syndromes was dropped in 1999. However, at the same time that WHO was dropping the syndromic approach in developing a revised IHR, there was also a culmination of thinking within WHO about a variety of changes in disease controls. These proposed revisions of the IHR appeared in a number of publications between 2000 and 2004, and they culminated in the Interim Draft of the IHR in January 2004. In November 2004 an international conference was convened to consider the January draft during which some changes were recommended. At a subsequent conference in May 2005, the participants approved the 2005 IHR.[80]

The first key publication in the 2000–2004 period was coauthored by nine WHO officials and appeared in the journal *Emerging Infectious Diseases* in early 2000. It focused on outbreak verification and envisaged a proactive role for WHO in sending verification teams to states where disease outbreaks were reported and in assisting states in building their surveillance capabilities.[81] Another important WHO publication issued in 2002 was *Global Crises—Global Solutions* and this was followed in 2003 and 2004 by a number of publications that focused on the lessons of the SARS crisis and which influenced the reform of the IHR. Some of these publications appeared after the Interim Draft of the IHR in January 2004 and after states' comments on the Interim Draft in the early months of 2004. There were a large number of issues and interstate differences in the deliberations to formulate the new IHR, and they were partially rooted in states' experiences in controlling diseases during the 1990s. The proposed revisions also flowed from resolutions of the annual meetings of the WHA in the post-1998 years.[82] The subsequent discussion on the 2005 IHR provides an overview of its major provisions, and explores some of the reasons for changes in the regulations. As will become clear, many of the changes emerged from established state and WHO practices over the decade between 1995 and 2005.

Throughout most of the twentieth century the character of WHO institutions were similar to that of other UN bodies. The WHA and Executive Board could adopt recommendations on a variety of matters by simple majority or two-thirds votes; accepting a new convention required a two-thirds majority.[83] In fact, the IHR was the only binding treaty that the WHA approved between 1948 and 2000. The director general could adopt a mediatory role in interstate conflicts, but with the exception of one interstate conflict in 1970, the director general was not an active mediator.[84] The recent disease outbreak in which the director general took an active role in recommending governmental responses to a disease outbreak was the SARS crisis of 2003 in which Director General Brundtland recommended certain dramatic policy changes for states and travelers. However, her role here was not a mediatory one between states; it was an international executive's recommending remedial policies for both states and individuals to reduce the incidence of infections and deaths.

The most important institutional changes in the 2005 IHR concerned a number of new bodies that operate under the WHA. First is the IHR Expert Roster that is composed of one person from each member state.[85] Second is the Emergency Committee that is appointed by the director general from the IHR Expert Roster and other expert bodes, and it gives its views on the existence of "public health emergencies of international concern" and necessary control measures that are referred to as "temporary recommendations."[86] Third, there is the Review Committee whose membership is also taken from the IHR Expert Roster and other expert groups, and its decisions are taken by simple majority. It is particularly charged with proposing amendments for the IHR as well as "standing recommendations" pertaining to long-term health problems.[87] Fourth, there are a variety of approaches for dispute settlement that are suggested in the 2005 IHR—namely, negotiation, mediation, conciliation, and arbitration (particularly by the WHO director general or the WHA), but there is no legal obligation to accept the judgment of a particular body.[88] Finally, it should be noted that the 2005 IHR, like the previous versions, provides states with an option to reject the agreement or make reservations concerning particular provisions within 18 months of the IHR acceptance by the WHA.[89] The remarkable thing about these provisions in the past is that so few states have rejected the IHR in its entirety or voiced reservations.

As has been noted earlier, the IHR were not important to global health politics and law during most of the twentieth century. States did not comply with the rules in many circumstances, and there was little effort to expand the scope of the IHR beyond the three diseases of cholera, plague, and yellow fever. In fact, David Fidler has pointed to the "obscurity" of the IHR in his work on international heath law.[90] Although there was considerable optimism that the IHR would be revised and their importance would be enhanced during the late 1990s, this was not the case. The negotiations to revise the IHR in the late 1990s attracted little political attention, and in fact there was considerable opposition to the 1998 draft that focused on expanding coverage to six groups of syndromic diseases.[91]

There was a significant transformation in the political importance of the negotiations on the IHR's revision starting in 2000. This change in political thinking was marked by the creation in 2000 of the GOARN that legitimized a broad range of interventionist strategies. The change was due significantly to a variety of disease outbreaks throughout the world. Particularly, the SARS crisis of 2002–2003 had the most dramatic impact on states' perception that the IHR required important changes. Between 2002 and 2005 the member states of the WHO approved some important revisions in the IHR, but it would be an exaggeration to claim that revolutionary changes occurred.

A notable change in the 2005 IHR is an expansion in the values that the IHR promotes. In the case of previous IHRs, the most recent being the 1983 version, they were designed to limit the international spread of infectious diseases and to reduce interference with the flow of international commerce. In the 2005 IHR, states are called upon also to promote human rights, environmental protection, and security as well as the original two goals. David Fidler has labeled this spreading of political goals as "integrated governance."[92] It is quite possible that this augmentation of regime goals will be regarded as the most significant change in global health governance. One should not underestimate the IHR's commitment to "avoid unnecessary interference with international traffic and trade," but at the same time one should not ignore the growing importance of human rights, economic development, environmental protection, and security in the health regime.[93] The first principle in the 2005 IHR states "the implementation of these regulations shall be with full respect for the dignity, human rights and fundamental freedoms of persons."[94] This commitment harkens back to the preamble of the WHO constitution that was approved in 1948. It states that "the health of all peoples is fundamental to the attainment of peace and security and is dependent upon the fullest cooperation of individuals and states." The preamble also posits that "the enjoyment of the highest attainable standard of health is one of the fundamental rights of every human being without distinction of race, religion, and political belief, economic or social conditions."

The major obstacle in developing an effective set of Health Regulations during the twentieth century was the long-standing clause that WHO could only publicize information on disease outbreaks that it received directly from the government of the afflicted state. This inevitably led to many outbreaks going unpublicized as states often chose not to release information on outbreaks for fear of expensive trade embargoes or quarantines being imposed on goods and citizens. As explained earlier in this chapter, this began to change in the 1990s owing to advancements in information technology that prevented states from controlling the flow of information from their countries. WHO began to accept nongovernmental sources of information with the informal establishment of GOARN in 1997; however, the practice was only formally approved in the 2005 IHR. According to the most recent Regulations: "WHO may take into account reports from sources other than notifications [from states] or consultations [with states] and shall assess these reports according to established epidemiological principles and then communicate information on the event to the State Party in whose territory the event is allegedly occurring."[95]

Although it is certainly true that some states chose not to report outbreaks owing to fear of financial losses, it was also understood that states sometimes did not report disease outbreaks as they lacked the technical capacities to monitor the health of their citizenry and thus were simply unaware that an outbreak was occurring. During the negotiations leading up to the 2005 IHR, this point was often stressed as many countries wanted to strengthen state obligations to detect, assess, and share information regarding outbreaks. The main provision in the current IHR on states' obligation to develop surveillance capacities is "Each State Party shall develop, strengthen and maintain . . . the capacity to detect, assess, notify and report events in accordance with these Regulations as specified in Annex 1."[96] The Regulations, and more specifically Annex 1.A, spell out the capacities that states should acquire. To enhance the surveillance capacities of both states and WHO, the Regulations specify that every state should create "a National IHR Focal Point" for communicating with other states and WHO, and WHO commits itself to establish "IHR Contact Points" for communications with states.[97] Also, WHO is obligated to assist states in developing their communications and surveillance capabilities, and the WHO must provide guidelines for developing these capabilities.[98]

A central obligation of State Parties to the IHR is that they must report,

all events which may constitute a public health emergency of international concern within its territory in accordance with the decision instrument, as well as any health measure implemented in response to those events. If the notification received by WHO involves the competency of the International Atomic Energy Agency (IAEA), WHO shall immediately notify the IAEA.[99]

It is also important to highlight that in the 2005 IHR, states are obligated to report public health emergencies of international concern "irrespective of origin or source." This opens the door for WHO to address security threats that do not concern infectious diseases.[100] Some countries, such as the United States, wanted all State Parties to be obligated to report emissions of materials that could be used for weapons. This was fought by some developing countries including Iran and Brazil. In the end an article was accepted that satisfied the outlooks of both developing and developed countries. The negotiated provision states, "If a State Party has evidence of an unexpected or unusual public health event within its territory, irrespective of origin or source, which may constitute a public health emergency of international concern, it shall provide the WHO all relevant public health information. In such a case, the provisions of Article 6 . . . shall apply in full."[101]

The most important issue during deliberations on the 2005 IHR was how State Parties should determine which disease outbreaks constitute public health emergencies of international concern, and therefore which ones must be reported to the WHO and the broader international community. Articles 5 and 6 (and Annex 2) of the 2005 IHR identify three ways to classify disease outbreaks. The first classification applies to diseases that are *always* deemed a public health emergency of international concern and must therefore always be reported. This group of diseases includes smallpox, poliomyelitis (owing to wild-type poliovirus), human influenza caused by a new subtype, and SARS. The second classification includes a group of diseases that *sometimes* pose a public health emergency of international concern, and these are cholera, pneumonic plague, yellow fever, viral hemorrhagic fevers (including Ebola, Lassa, and Marburg), West Nile fever, and other diseases of special national or regional concern. If an outbreak of one of these diseases occurs, it is examined in terms of four criteria for determining its potential global impact, and these are whether it is serious; unusual or unexpected; capable of posing a serious risk of international spread; and/or capable of posing a significant risk to international trade or travel. The third classification for disease outbreaks provides a channel for reporting emerging or reemerging diseases because it includes any disease outbreak that possesses two of the above four criteria.[102]

An interesting provision in the 2005 IHR pertains to the "transport and handling of biological substances, reagents and materials for diagnostic purposes." It provides that "States Parties shall, subject to national law and taking into account relevant international guidelines, facilitate the transport, entry, exit, processing and disposal of biological substances and diagnostic specimens, reagents and other diagnostic materials for verification and public health response purposes under these Regulations."[103] This provision is very important in that it establishes that States Parties and WHO can request that particular biological substances be sent to them, and the recipient of the request is obligated to comply. This is a significant measure for international surveillance of diseases in that it assures that states and medical laboratories have access to specimens for research purposes. It is, however, important to stress that the WHO has found it difficult on occasion to enforce compliance with this rule.

Most of the substantive recommendations related to the promotion of public health in the 2005 IHR are in Parts 5 and 6. They are concerned with public health measures and conditions of ports and ships, travelers, goods, containers, and health documents. They clearly focus on the facilitation of commerce. In Annexes 4 through 8 there are specific guidelines with regard to the character and conduct of the maritime and air transport industries.[104] These articles and annexes deal only marginally with national public health systems, and in so far as they do, it is largely with regard to points of entry and exit.

It is important to note that a large body of recommendations regarding particular international health problems emanate from the WHA and its sub-bodies, and many of these sub-bodies in the past have been groups of medical experts from a number of countries. It is very likely that these groups of experts will continue to be central to WHO practices and decision-making processes. It is, of course, probable that the newly created Review Committee and Emergency Committee will assume crucial political roles and that the WHO director general will have an enhanced role in proposing international health strategies like Dr. Gro Brundtland proposed during the SARS crisis of 2003. Brundtland and her advisory committee of experts from within and outside the WHO had crucial impacts throughout the crisis. In retrospect it is remarkable that WHO member states accepted such a broad and important role for WHO organs in the SARS crisis as they did. For example, the director general's issuance of "travel advisories" symbolized an acceptance of the director general's status and influence that had not existed in the past.

A contentious issue concerning IHR regulations during the twentieth century was labeled the problem of "excessive measures" or "more stringent measures." Some states favored restrictions on countries' ability to adopt regulations that are more stringent than those in the IHR, and other states wanted significant freedom for states to legislate more stringent rules. From the early twentieth century through the late twentieth century the developed countries opposed the right of states to adopt more stringent measures since their application could impede the flow of commerce. This thinking changed recently as more developed country governments judged that they desired greater freedom of action to control outbreaks of emerging diseases. In the negotiations on the 2005 IHR this issue was dealt with under the title "Additional Health Provisions."[105] The convention gave countries significant leeway in adopting more stringent measures. All that was required of states was that they discuss the more stringent measures that they intended to implement with WHO officials. In other words, states' sovereign rights of legislation have won out in the debate over excessive measures.

An issue that arose at a number of points in the negotiations was whether the rules of the IHR should be legally binding as they had been in the past. Of course, states often did not treat them as legally binding—indicating this by their frequent noncompliance with the rules. The prevailing attitude among the developed countries was that even if many states did not treat the IHR as a legally binding treaty, maintaining the IHR's original legal status would enhance the probability of compliance with the rules (which they generally favored). Also, many developed countries moved toward strong support for their own political autonomy into health crises, and ironically this brought them closer to the views of the developing countries. Relevant to this change in policy orientation Fidler has remarked that "the revision process has moved away from binding legal rules on notification—one of the classic regime pillars—to reliance on global information networks."[106]

It is valuable to note that there have been other international organizations apart from WHO that have become involved in preventing the transnational spread of infectious diseases. The key global bodies are the International Maritime Organization (IMO) and the International Civil Aviation Organization (ICAO). However, their roles are relatively minor in comparison to those of WHO. IMO is responsible for three major conventions: the International Convention for the Prevention of Pollution from Ships (knows as MARPOL 1973), the Convention on the Prevention of Marine Pollution by Dumping of Wastes and Other Matter (known as the London Convention, 1972), and the Convention on Facilitation of International Maritime Traffic (1965). Another convention that has recently been accepted at an IMO conference is the International Convention for the Control and Management of Ships' Ballast Water and Sediments (2004). Most of the substances that are banned or controlled by the MARPOL and London convention do not threaten outbreaks of infectious diseases, and the same is largely true of the Ballast Water convention although ballast water can spread some infectious diseases such as cholera. The Facilitation Convention largely concerns practices of port authorities, and this includes support for WHO standards in ports.[107]

The key health regulations prescribed by ICAO are in Annex 9 (the Facilitation Annex) of the Convention on International Civil Aviation. Provisions in annexes are not formally regarded as legally binding, but there is a very high level of compliance. Almost all of the provisions that are directly and indirectly related to the protection of health support WHO standards. They state that ICAO members should comply with the IHR, should use methods of disinfection prescribed by WHO, should utilize the International Certificate of Vaccination and Revaccination prescribed by WHO if vaccinations are needed, and should maintain facilities in ports that are necessary for the promotion of public health.[108] It is clear that IMO and ICAO largely defer to WHO on regulations that concern health matters. However, ICAO does have an Aviation Medicine Section of its Secretariat that recommends a variety of control strategies regarding particular disease problems.

Conclusion

This chapter focused on certain developments relating to disease containment. It first addressed the governance strategy of disease surveillance, which is important as an issue in-and-of-itself and as an issue that influences other strategic approaches. It then addressed controlling emergency outbreaks. Finally, the chapter analyzed reforms of the IHR that are particularly concerned with preventing the transborder spread of diseases.

A major problem of the global disease-control regime throughout the twentieth century was the continuing reluctance of states to provide the outside world with information on disease outbreaks because they feared embargoes of their goods and citizens. A major change regarding this issue occurred in the mid-1990s when transformations in information technology made it very difficult (if not impossible) for states to block the spread of information regarding disease outbreaks within their borders. The particular change that revolutionized what states could do was the development of the Internet. From this point on, the emergence and impacts of diseases were significantly more transparent.

Owing to technological changes, health experts and national officials soon began to establish institutions that would facilitate the sharing of information on disease outbreaks. The first significant institutional development was the creation of a network for sharing information among health professionals who sent information on outbreaks to a Web site in the United States. Its title is ProMED and it was created in 1993. It stands as one of the two most important medical networks for distributing information on outbreaks. The other very important information network (the GPHIN) has quite a different structure. In 1997, the Canadian government in partnership with the WHO created an electronic system that collects information from a large number of Web sites that publish data on disease outbreaks throughout the world. Canadian government employees then organize the data and send it to WHO and a large number of other health organizations who evaluate the reports.

After ProMED and GPHIN the most important surveillance organizations are probably media groups such as CNN and BBC as well as humanitarian NGOs such as MSF and Oxfam that are exposed to a great deal of information on local disease problems in the course of their work. In considering these comments on disease surveillance it is important to realize that by the late 1990s information technology had given most people a de facto right of access to news on disease outbreaks throughout the world. Embedding such a right in a legal text was valuable, but not crucial.

One of the three most important strategies for controlling the spread of diseases is the provision of material and financial assistance to areas with existing and potential disease outbreaks. Sometimes the problems that states face are long-term infrastructure issues that require the improvement of health systems (see chapter 5), but at other times countries face short-term problems of emergency outbreaks. Five of these emergency situations are reviewed in this chapter, and the patterns of external assistance are remarkably similar. WHO encourages and coordinates assistance from a wide variety of sources. Governments provide research assistance and funds although they some times operate under the umbrella of WHO (either its global headquarters or one of its regional commissions). In fact, the research labs operating as WHO Collaborating Centers are national bodies that sign assistance agreements with WHO. There are also usually NGOs that provide assistance to states in need, but again the funding often comes from states. In reviewing programs to control emergency outbreaks it is important not to exclude the local MoH since it often coordinates various groups participating in control efforts. The government of the afflicted state also plays a crucial role in that it must request assistance from various actors, but particularly WHO. Without this formal invitation, WHO is not legally permitted to send emergency response teams to the outbreak site. WHO staff are often active in advising state officials, particularly from local ministries of health, regarding treatment protocols. Owing to WHO's strong network of health experts, they are often able to persuade states to comply with medical practices even without a legal structure to force compliance. Much of WHO's legitimacy derives from the widely accepted view that it has a genuine interest in improving global health outcomes. In fact, UN bodies are generally perceived as having a bias for improving the welfare of developing countries, and this is why bodies such as UNICEF, FAO, and even the World Bank are often participants in international efforts to assist developing nations. The final group of actors that are important participants in health assistance networks are NGOs such as MSF, Merlin, Oxfam, and CARE. A number of these bodies are often active partners, and their strong presence demarcates contemporary international assistance efforts from those in the past.

A variety of changes in international health practices occurred during the early 1990s, but starting in the mid-1990s WHO turned its attention to the revision of the IHR that are the most important legal arrangements concerning health governance. The negotiations on IHR reform began in 1996 and ended in 2005, but the key deliberations took place between 2003 and 2005. Although a wide variety of changes were accepted, the number of major, substantive alterations in the Regulations was relatively small.

First, the key change in reforming the IHR concerned broadening its coverage of diseases from just 3 to more than 15, with the door open to include more. Second, the 2005 IHR for the first time formally permitted WHO to accept information on outbreaks from nongovernmental sources. WHO's inability to receive and disseminate such information was a major object of criticism during most of IHR's history. Third, states committed themselves to acquire capabilities to gather and distribute information on diseases. Fourth, states were given greater latitude to adopt more stringent measures than in the past. This provision indicated that the developed countries were moving in the direction of the developing countries on the issue of legislating "more stringent" measures. Finally, WHO was given new decision-making bodies to create more specific rules or guidelines with respect to emergency outbreaks and long-term health problems— referred to as "emergency recommendations" and "standing recommendations." In addition to these provisions concerning the powers of the WHO membership it is important to point out that the WHO secretariat was recognized as having the power to "name and shame" states if they refused to comply with directives of major WHO bodies. This particularly developed in the context of the SARS and avian flu crisis.

It is clear that states still fear the multiple negative ramifications of outbreaks of new and old diseases. Paradoxically, increased medical knowledge in the twentieth and twenty-first centuries regarding infectious diseases has made us more aware of the fragility of human health and the dangers of global interdependencies in terms of the spread of disease. This understanding has driven states into the acceptance of a decidedly stronger surveillance and containment regime than they were willing to accept in the past. One of the most powerful forces driving the evolution of a stronger regime is the increasing awareness that the health of peoples in the industrial world is profoundly influenced by the health conditions in the developing world. Health-oriented nongovernmental groups have always had a strong humanitarian foundation for their grassroots political pressure. Nowadays, the deeper understanding of the self-interested benefits of disease containment has made it easier to argue that a strong global surveillance and containment system is not just desirable for humanitarian reasons but necessary for survival reasons.

CHAPTER 4

DISEASE CONTROL: TRANSFORMATION
OF HEALTH ASSISTANCE PROGRAMS

The most extensive, complicated, and controversial of issues in international health collaboration concerns the provision of health assistance or financial and material aid programs aimed at improving health standards in developing countries. The importance of aid programs has been highlighted by a significant expansion in health assistance initiatives since the early 1990s. Marked changes in the perceived impacts of deficient health systems have dramatically expanded the scope of this strategy and the ways in which actors collaborate with one another in providing health assistance. To explore these changes and understand how collaboration to provide aid has evolved, this chapter is divided into four sections. The first section provides an overview of recent trends in the health assistance arena and suggests some possible explanations for these trends. The second section provides an overview of the actors that are currently involved in the provision of health assistance, with a focus on the roles they play. The third section analyzes and explains the four methods used to distribute aid, which are bilaterally between state governments; bilaterally from nongovernmental organizations (NGOs) to recipients; multilaterally through international organizations; and multilaterally through global health partnerships (GHPs). This section also examines the motivations for employing each of the delivery methods, but prominent focus is given to the last category as it is a new phenomenon in global health politics and because explaining this kind of aid helps us to understand multilateral governance programs. The final section provides an analysis of the nature and effectiveness of contemporary health assistance.

Trends in Health Assistance

This section examines *three* broad trends that have been shaping health assistance for the past 15 years, and it identifies *four* factors that are driving or influencing the general trends. The three trends are an increase in the amount of funding for assistance programs, an increase in the number of actors involved in these programs, and a growing focus on aid effectiveness.

During the 1990s, Official Development Assistance (ODA)[1] steadily decreased; in fact, it declined nearly 25 percent over the course of the decade reaching a low point of $58 billion in 1997. In 1998, however, ODA began to rise, and reached $70 billion in 2003 and $105 billion in 2004.[2] The increases in ODA in the early years of the new millennium raised ODA from an all-time low of 0.22 percent of gross national income of donor states in 1997 to approximately 0.25 percent by 2003. Although this is certainly an improvement, it should be noted that this figure still falls well short of the goal of 0.7 percent set by the Organization for Economic Cooperation and Development's (OECD) member states in 1970.[3]

Increases in ODA in recent years have largely been allocated to debt relief, emergency and disaster relief, technical cooperation, and administrative overhead.[4] In terms of geographical allocation, it is not surprising that Africa has traditionally been the largest recipient of aid money receiving approximately 35 percent of the total; Latin America and the Caribbean receive around 14 percent; East Asia and South Asia receive 11 percent; and the Middle East receives the remaining 7 percent.[5]

Development assistance for health (DAH) is the portion of development assistance that is specially earmarked for health programs. Not surprisingly, the trend in DAH mirrors the trend in ODA and as such has begun to rise in recent years. In the early to mid-1990s, DAH measured approximately $2 billion per year.[6] It increased to $10 billion in 2003, $14 billion in 2004, and by all accounts is still rising.[7] Journalist Laurie Garrett neatly summarizes the trend as follows: "Today, thanks to a recent extraordinary and unprecedented rise in public and private giving, more money is being directed toward pressing health challenges than ever before."[8] The recent upsurge in health aid has numerous experts being optimistic regarding the capacity for future endeavors to succeed. For example,

> Donors and developing countries are testing and implementing innovative approaches to the use of DAH, while simultaneously seeking ways to raise the effectiveness of existing streams of aid and more traditional financing mechanisms. In short, DAH has entered a dynamic phase that holds considerable promise.[9]

An important dimension of this study on the nature of health aid collaboration is an explanation of how much aid is given through bilateral channels and through multilateral channels. Therefore, it is interesting to note that bilateral assistance for health rose from an annual average of $2.2 billion (3.8 percent of the total) during 1997–1999 to $2.9 billion (6.8 percent of the total) in 2002. The United States is by far the largest bilateral provider of health assistance money. In fact, although the United States is often criticized for giving less than the global average of 0.25 percent of gross national income, this country alone supplied approximately 40 percent of all bilateral aid during this time frame.[10]

Health assistance dispersed through multilateral channels is also on the rise. UN system health assistance has risen from an average of $1.6 billion per year during 1997–1999 to $2 billion in 2002. Furthermore, the budget for the World Health Organization (WHO) increased significantly to $3.3 billion (almost $1 billion in regular budget monies and another $2.3 billion in extra-budgetary or voluntary monies) in the 2006–2007 fiscal year. Financing via development banks has remained consistent during the early years of the twenty-first century with an average annual commitment of $1.4 billion. However, it is important to note that World Bank funding for health issues was almost nonexistent in the early 1990s, but spending on communicable diseases tripled from $157 million to $507 million in the decade between 1993 and 2003. In 2003, World Bank general health spending reached a high-water mark of $3.4 billion, but has gradually decreased since then.[11]

The second major trend in global health assistance has been the expansion of the number and type of actors involved in this sphere. Since the early 1990s, the assistance realm has changed very dramatically, from being dominated by state-to-state politics to a variety of different types of actors. Although a handful of nongovernmental actors (such as the Red Cross and the Rockefeller Foundation) have been active participants in the health sphere for many decades, over the past 15 years hundreds of nonstate entities have entered this arena, and the scope of their influence and impact has increased to an unprecedented degree. The contemporary health regime is comprised of a mix of actors including governments, intergovernmental organizations (IGOs), humanitarian organizations, medical NGOs, private businesses, and philanthropic groups. In the words of a recent World Bank report, "proliferation of aid channels is particularly pronounced in the health sector. In fact, more than 100 major organizations are involved in the health sector, a much higher degree of proliferation than in any other sector."[12]

It is particularly interesting to learn that the number of donor states that are funding development and health projects is higher than ever before. Numerous countries outside the traditional assistance framework[13] are now providing financial and material assistance to poor countries, and other sources of financial and material assistance, such as private companies, are beginning to have significant impacts. Viewed from the perspective of a developing country, it is noteworthy that,

> The average number of donors per country nearly tripled over the last half century, rising from about 12 in the 1960s to about 33 in the 2001–2005 period. The combination of more bilateral donors and of an increasing number of multilateral channels has led to an increasingly crowded aid scene. Aid channel proliferation . . . has been substantial, particularly after the end of the Cold War when the number of countries with over 40 active donors and international organizations grew from zero to thirty-one. The number of international organizations, funds and programs is now higher than the number of developing countries they were created to assist.[14]

An increasing focus on aid effectiveness is the *third* major trend in the health assistance realm.[15] Over the past decade, dozens if not hundreds of reports have been released annually from governmental and nongovernmental sources all arguing as to how aid money should be spent, and perhaps more importantly, how it should not be spent. The Paris Declaration on Aid Effectiveness, issued in 2005, was in many ways the culmination of these efforts. The Paris Declaration was signed by more than 100 governmental ministers and well-known officials. It describes steps that must be taken to ensure that aid money is used in the most effective manner, and it lays out quantifiable progress indicators designed to measure improvements in aid spending.[16] Aid effectiveness is crucial because despite the fact that aid money flowing toward health problems is increasing, it is still not enough to pay for all the programs that are deemed necessary to create functioning health care systems in poor countries. Furthermore, developed donor countries have often experienced negative feedback from their constituents when it has been demonstrated that aid money has been mismanaged or misspent, making it in the best interests of both rich and poor countries to develop effective results-based aid policies. Interestingly, NGOs who have spontaneously taken on the role of global watchdog have often spurred development agencies to develop new and arguably better policies. For example, ActionAid, a U.K. based NGO and lobby group, has criticized ODA for being wasted on overpriced and unnecessary products and services, tided aid, and excessive administration costs. Public criticism in this vein has prompted many reputation-sensitive states and international organizations to examine and in some cases alter the way they give aid.[17]

As the earlier section has explained, health assistance programs are currently mobilizing more money than ever before, and that money is coming from a wider variety and larger number of actors than ever before. The next section identifies and explains some of the reasons why health assistance programs have expanded in such a dramatic way. The five reasons are linkages between the promotion of health and other values; the Millennium Development Goals (MDGs); the AIDS pandemic; the increasing impact of civil society groups in health programs, and the establishment of GHPs.

First, although the global health agenda has always had a strong moral and humanitarian draw it is only within the past few decades that convincing linkages have been made between health and economic development and between health and security. The clear links between improved health conditions and improved global economic development and stability have resulted in health being granted more prominence in government and governance agendas, as it can now be persuasively argued that poor health of those living in developing countries can have a negative effect on the developed countries. In particular, DALYs,[18] as a measurement of lost productivity, has provided some insights for economists and development experts into the vital links between health and economic growth. Regarding security, there have been numerous studies in recent years explaining how various diseases, but particularly the AIDS pandemic, has the capacity to destabilize entire regions of the world by decimating a country's political and military leadership, and destroying the productive age group. In the words of a former U.S. ambassador to the UN,

> AIDS is as destabilizing as any war . . . in the post-Cold War world, international security is about more than guns and bombs and the balance of power between sovereign states. Vice President Gore, who chaired that Security Council session, put it eloquently when he said AIDS is "a security crisis because it threatens not just individual citizens but the very institutions that define and defend the character of a society."[19]

Second, the MDGs, which were adopted by all 189 member states of the United Nations in September 2000, have done much to highlight the inequities and flaws of the existing global health system.[20] There are 8 MDGs, which are subdivided into 15 targets and all must be realized by 2015 to meet the stipulations of the UN Resolution.[21] Goals 4, 5, and 6 are directly related to health and they are, respectively, to reduce child mortality, improve maternal health, combat HIV/AIDS, malaria, and other major diseases.[22]

Since the passing of the MDG Resolution, the goals have had a powerful influence on the global development agenda. The MDGs differ significantly from previous development programs in two key areas. First, as the earlier list demonstrates they are far-reaching and broad-based. Second, the targets behind the goals are quantifiable; there are numerical, measurable targets to be reached by 2015, making it easier to track progress than previous more nebulous development objectives. Furthermore, because the Goals were negotiated and agreed upon by all UN member states, many developed country governments have changed their own foreign aid programs and goals to correspond with the MDGs, making them the focus of state governments as well as the broader UN system. As such, Hecht and Shah identify "donors' increasing attention to the challenges presented by the MDGs" as a key reason for increased financial support for health projects.[23] It should be noted here that although the MDGs are undoubtedly responsible for increased mobilization of aid money, many low-income countries are not on track to reach the goals. In fact, most estimates indicate that aid financing needs to be at least tripled or the MDGs for health will not be met.[24]

Third, few events in history have galvanized more public concern for a health issue than the HIV/AIDS pandemic. According to the WHO, nearly 40 million people around the globe (but disproportionately located in Africa) have the disease; it kills about 3 million people each year and about 4 million new infections occur every year.[25] AIDS has had a truly devastating impact on human health since it was discovered just 25 years ago. As Kofi Annan stated in 2006,

> [Since 1981], AIDS has fundamentally changed our world—killing more than 25 million men and women, orphaning millions of children, exacerbating poverty and hunger, and, in some countries, even reversing human development altogether. . . . What was first reported as a few cases of a mystery illness is now a pandemic that poses among the greatest threats to global progress in the twenty-first century.[26]

Widespread knowledge of the destruction and devastation caused by HIV/AIDS has resulted in a "strong global mobilization to confront the AIDS pandemic in developing countries."[27] Further impetus for combating the pandemic has come about owing to the recognition of grossly unequal and unfair access to drugs that can dramatically improve victims' lives. Human rights groups have made access to antiretroviral drugs a major global political issue, and as a result there are now numerous assistance programs devoted specifically to providing drugs to HIV/AIDS patients. For these reasons, "HIV/AIDS is clearly the top priority in international health assistance."[28] In fact, an argument can be made that this disease has actually gained too much prominence in health and development circles because it is largely responsible for the increase in health assistance funding. Development assistance is finite, and donor countries often choose to support health projects that resonate with domestic populations. This means that HIV/AIDS projects receive more funding than lesser-known but still devastating diseases such as dracunculiasis and leishmaniasis. As one report states,

> The increased share of ODA from OECD donors devoted to health in recent years has essentially been a response to the HIV/AIDS crisis; resource allocations towards combating HIV/AIDS and to a lesser degree improving reproductive health are much higher than those that would have been expected had the "burden of disease criterion" been used to set priorities, as measured by disability-adjusted life years lost due to any given disease.[29]

The *fourth* reason for increased health assistance is the establishment and dramatic growth of multilateral collaborative initiatives. A central feature of the evolving world of international health assistance is the collaboration between the public sector (governments and IGOs), the private sector (commercial firms), and civil society (humanitarian NGOs and philanthropic foundations). In the category of philanthropic foundations, the Bill and Melinda Gates Foundation has had profound impact on the development of partnerships because of the sheer size of their financial contributions and because of the perceived legitimacy their involvement brings to a cause. This has manifested in the development of broad-based partnerships, bringing together a variety of groupings of these different actors. These multifaceted groupings are referred to as public-private partnerships (PPPs) or more specifically for our purposes as GHPs. According to Gordon Conway, former president of the Rockefeller Foundation, "creating public-private-community partnerships is the new twenty-first century role of philanthropy." He remarked that the collaboration among the aforementioned three sectors of society is based on the strengths and weaknesses of each,

> Each of these has its drawbacks—governments are sometimes slow and inefficient, markets can deepen inequities, rather than ease them, and community organizations, while they have the needs of poor people at the forefront of their goals, tend to lack scale and resources. But done right, partnerships between these actors can be extraordinarily successful, harnessing the scale and political clout of the public sector, with the innovativeness and enterprise of private industry, and the self-help and commitment of community organizations.[30]

In the early 1990s there was a mere handful of GHPs; today there are close to 70 active partnerships.[31] These partnerships have done much to increase awareness of health issues, mobilize funds, and raise political support at a global level. In the words of an admittedly pro-GHP report sponsored by the Gates Foundation, "GHPs have become the dominant organizational model for addressing today's complex global health issues. They produce benefits beyond what individual partners could achieve, including attracting attention and funding to diseases, spurring countries to craft smarter policies . . . for the future, encouraging countries to strengthen program monitoring and accountability, and boosting wider stakeholder participation. Early evidence suggests that GHPs work."[32] Inevitably, there are serious concerns regarding accountability, representation, and effectiveness of these partnerships. However, they have become an entrenched feature of the contemporary global health governance system and they are changing the nature of collaboration in this sphere in significant and interesting ways that are discussed in more detail in the third section of this chapter.

Overview of Actors

As the preceding discussion on the proliferation of actors involved in the provision of global health assistance indicates, there are now numerous—sometimes cooperating, sometimes competing—actors in this sphere. This section provides a description of the six key groups of actors—states, IGOs, development banks, NGOs, foundations, and private businesses—and attempts to explain the nature of their role within the complex sphere of health assistance.

States

The largest providers of financial assistance for health are members of the Development Assistance Committee (DAC) of the OECD. The governments of more than 20 rich countries[33] are members of the DAC and they use this forum to track and disperse aid monies.[34] Out of the approximately two dozen rich donor countries, the two biggest by a wide margin are the United Kingdom and the United States, which donated more than $10 billion and $27 billion in total aid respectively in 2005.[35] The DAC has not developed specific policies for health aid, but it has produced a number of guidelines that have contributed to the coordination of international health assistance. They include the importance of a defined plan by recipient countries, regular meetings between donors and recipients, and the utilization of donor consortia. There is also cooperation among states to work with a single ministry in recipient states, so as to avoid administrative confusion. The DAC was and continues to be integrally involved in developing and implementing the provisions of the Paris Declaration on Aid Effectiveness and, in fact, it hosts the Working Party on Aid Effectiveness.[36]

Since the 1970s, bilateral ODA has accounted for approximately 70 percent of all aid flows. Multilateral aid flows make up the remaining third of total ODA. Multilateral contributions vary from state to state with some donors channeling as little as 9 percent of aid through multilateral channels and others as much as 64 percent.[37] An interesting aspect of contemporary bilateral development assistance is the aforementioned increase in new donors. Outside of the DAC country donors, there have been some surprising new state actors joining the development arena. Many of these new donor states, particularly China, donate exclusively through bilateral channels, and often it is difficult to track the level and nature of aid they are providing, making accurate assessments regarding the impact of their aid flows virtually impossible.[38]

One of the most important contemporary state-driven, bilateral aid initiatives in the health field is the President's Emergency Plan for AIDS Relief, or PEPFAR. Announced in 2003 in President George W. Bush's State of the Union Address, it consists of a $15 billion fund to be distributed over five years to combat the spread of HIV/AIDS and provide antiretroviral drugs to those already infected. This makes PEPFAR "the largest commitment ever by any nation for an international health initiative dedicated to a single disease." The goals of the program are (1) to treat 2 million HIV-infected people with antiretroviral therapy; (2) to care for 10 million people already infected with HIV/AIDS, including children and orphans; and (3) to prevent 7 million new HIV infections. PEPFAR focuses on 15 countries—12 in Africa, 2 in the Caribbean, and 1 in Asia.[39] Although bilateral in structure, $1 billion of the total fund is dedicated to the multilateral Global Fund to Fight AIDS, Tuberculosis, and Malaria.

International Organizations

The most important UN affiliated bodies in the international health sphere are the WHO, the United Nations Development Program (UNDP), the United Nations Children's Fund (UNICEF), and the United Nations Population Fund (UNFPA).[40] WHO, which was created as a UN specialized agency in 1948, plays a vital role in designing and implementing polices to improve health at a global level. Its central objective, as stated in its constitution, is the attainment by all peoples of the highest possible level of health. In fact, health is portrayed as a basic human right in the WHO constitution. WHO headquarters are in Geneva, but it has six regional offices in Africa, Southeast Asia, the Americas, the Eastern Mediterranean, Europe, and the Western Pacific. It is governed by its 192 member states through the World Health Assembly (WHA), which meets once a year.

Most of its decisions are taken by simple majority, but international agreements and treaties require a two-thirds majority vote.

WHO's regular budget in 2004/2005 was $908,468,000 and approximately half of this went to technical assistance, which is controlled by the regional offices. The distribution of funds to the regional offices is made by the WHA. The regular (voluntary) budget has remained very stable over the past two decades, whereas extra-budgetary contributions have increased dramatically over recent years. In fact, the amount of funding for extra-budgetary purposes has almost doubled between the 2001/2002 fiscal year and the 2004/2005 fiscal year. In 2004/2005, WHO received $1,898,000,000 from its developed member states in the form of extra-budgetary contributions.[41] Extra-budgetary contributions are given to WHO for particular health assistance projects, and they are controlled by committees of donors. There are separate committees that make decisions for each assistance program. This indicates that WHO now has built into it a strong correlation between contributions and voting power over financial grants.

The UNDP was established in 1994. Its headquarters are in New York, but it has country offices in 130 states and a presence in an additional 36 states. For funding, it is completely dependent on voluntary contributions from states, other IGOs, and NGOs. Its total budget in 2004/2005 was $5.6 billion.[42] It gives money in five general categories: democratic governance, poverty reduction, crisis prevention and recovery, energy, and the environment. Funding for health-related projects comes from both the Poverty Reduction and HIV/AIDS programs. The UNDP is ruled by an executive board, which is made up of representatives from 36 countries. Of course, as all funds are voluntary and most donations come from developed countries, they have significant leverage over funding decisions.[43]

The UNICEF was created in 1946 and is headquartered in New York at the UN. It is governed by an Executive Board, which is made up of representatives from 36 states. Board members are elected by the UN Economic and Social Council. UNICEF provides assistance in five areas: immunization projects, HIV/AIDS, education for girls, child protection, and early childhood education. According to its 2001 financial report, 24 percent of its regular budget was allocated for immunization and seven percent for HIV/AIDS. Its total budget in 2001 was $1,218,000,000: 64 percent of this total sum was provided by governments and IGOs; 33 percent from NGOs and private companies; and 3 percent from other sources;[44] 45 percent of its budget is distributed by decisions of the executive board, and 55 percent is earmarked to particular purposes by the donor states, IGOs, and NGOs. Again, the donor states have a very strong role in allocation of funding.[45]

Development Banks

Among the most important sources of funding and strategic thinking in the field of development assistance are the development banks, particularly the World Bank Group. The World Bank was established at Bretton Woods in 1944. It is headquartered in Washington, DC and has 109 country offices. Currently, the bank has approximately 10,000 permanent and temporary staff in Washington and around the world. The World Bank's highest decision-making body is its board of governors, which meets once in every year at the bank's annual meeting to determine the bank's overarching strategies and policies and to vote on key budgetary issues. The number of votes controlled by member states is correlated to the size of its economy and its financial contributions to the bank. Thus the bank employs a weighted voting system that effectively gives rich states a veto over financial decisions. Governors are usually the minister of finance or development of their country. Day-to-day decision making is done by the board of directors, which is made of up 24 executive directors. One member comes from each of the five largest share-holders—France, Germany, Japan, the United Kingdom, and the United States—and 19 are selected by the remaining member states. The board is responsible for the day-to-day running of the bank, and it approves loans and grants and authorizes assistance strategies for developing nations.[46]

The World Bank Group consists of five bodies: the International Bank for Reconstruction and Development (IBRD); the International Development Association (IDA); the International Finance Corporation (IFC); the Multilateral Investment Guarantee Agency (MIGA); and the International Centre for Settlement of Investment Disputes (ICSID). The IBRD and the IDA, which provide low-interest loans, interest-free credit, and grants to poor countries, are the relevant component bodies concerned with health assistance.

The IDA receives its funding from approximately 40 developed countries, with contributions being made every 4 years. At the 2002 contribution round, the IDA received $9 billion in donations and obtained another $6.6 billion from World Bank Group resources. In 2002, the IDA provided $8.1 billion in financing for 133 projects in 62 low-income countries. The IBRD, on the other hand, provides low-interest loans to higher-income developing countries, with the money it raises from the world's financial markets. It raised $23 billion in 2002. During that year, the IBRD provided $11.5 billion in loans to 96 projects in 40 countries. These loans funded a wide variety of development programs from poverty reduction programs to improved environmental standards.[47] Total IBRD/IDA lending for 2002 was 19.5 billion; 12 percent of which went to "Health and Other

Social Services," and a further 3 percent went to "Water, Sanitation and Flood Protection," which has a spillover effect into the health sphere.[48]

Interestingly, the World Bank did not offer any funds for health projects until the early 1970s. However, since the 1990s "the Bank's activities in [the health] sector have grown rapidly to the point where it is now the single largest external source of Health Nutrition and Population (HNP) financing in low- and middle-income countries."[49] As of 2002 there were 154 active and 94 completed bank HNP projects, totaling $13.5 billion (1996 prices). An important document in the bank's evolving role in the health sphere was the 1993 World Development Report titled *Investing in Health*, which analyzed the economic rationale for providing health sector grants. This document has had a major impact not only on the lending polices of the bank but also on the policies of major funding states and other IGOs.

Starting in the 1990s, the World Bank Group has been a major contributor to programs combating HIV/AIDS. Since 1999 "the Bank has provided $1.5 billion in grants, loans and credits to fight HIV/AIDS, most of which has come through the Multi-Country HIV/AIDS Programs (MAPS)."[50] To complement these more microlevel initiatives, the bank established a Global HIV/AIDS Program in 2002 to combat the pandemic from a cross-sectoral perspective. Further to these efforts, the bank supports research on an AIDS vaccine through its membership in the International AIDS Vaccine Initiative (IAVI), and it was one of the original cosponsors of UNAIDS, which seeks to promote funding to combat the disease and to coordinate international responses to it.

However, HIV/AIDS is not the only health focus of the World Bank. It has financed tuberculosis control programs in more than 30 countries, spending more than $560 million. The major emphasis has been on large-scale programs in India and China, where this disease is a particularly serious problem. Beyond its bilateral aid programs, the bank is also the fiscal agent for the Stop TB Trust Fund, which is the financing mechanism for the multilateral Stop TB Partnership. The bank has also become involved with combating malaria in poor countries; it supports more than 40 malaria control projects in 35 countries. It is a founding partner of the multilateral initiative Roll Back Malaria, and it supports vaccine research through donations to the Medicines for Malaria Venture and the Multilateral Initiative on Malaria. Other health issues of concern to the bank are SARS, polio, measles, malnutrition, poverty, and lack of access to clean water.[51]

Regional development banks have also been prominent in the development assistance field, although they have not been major sources of assistance to health sectors. The Inter-American Development Group was created in 1959 and stands as the oldest, largest, and most active of the regional development organizations. The group is comprised of three bodies: the Inter-American Development Bank (IDB), the Inter-American Investment Corporation, and the Multilateral Investment Fund, all of which are headquartered in Washington, DC. Together, the group is the "main source of multilateral financing for economic, social and institutional development in Latin America and the Caribbean."[52]

The bank is the body that deals with the social sector, and it is thus the only member of the IDB group that funds and supports health assistance projects. The bank lends mainly to public institutions, although private projects occasionally receive support. The bank has 46 member countries, of which 26 are borrower countries and 20 are donor countries. The bank is governed by a board of governors, and its decision-making processes are on the basis of a weighted voting system, which is, in turn, based on states' subscriptions to the IDB. The 26 Latin American countries have 50.02 percent of votes; the United States has 30.01 percent; and the remaining votes are distributed among the other donor states.[53] An interesting fact about the IDB is that it is stipulated in the Articles of Agreement that the borrower member countries cannot fall below holding 50.005 percent of the total votes. This has prevented the donor countries from gaining a formal veto over bank decisions and, thus, has fostered a strong sense of entitlement and commitment on the part of the borrower members to the IDB. Over the past four decades, the bank has provided $128.9 billion in loans and guarantees with total investments totaling $291 billion. Health assistance falls under the category of Social Sector Reform. It has received $2.7 billion in funding or 2.1 percent of total bank expenditures.[54]

The two other important regional development banks are the African Development Bank Group (AfDB) and the Asian Development Bank (AsDB). The African Development Bank (ADB) was created in 1964 and is headquartered in Abidjan, Cote d'Ivoire. This regional development bank has had a turbulent history, and has been much criticized for its policies in the past, although the consensus is that the AfDB is an essential component of Africa's development agenda.[55] Its three component bodies are the ADB, the African Development Fund, and the Nigerian Trust Fund. The AfDB has 77 members, about two-thirds of which are from Africa. Similar to the World Bank, the ADB uses a weighted voting system, which gives the donor states a veto over most issues. Both the ADB and the African Development Fund provide public sector funding; together they have allocated loans and grants totaling $19.8 billion since the AfDB began financial operations in 1967. These two bodies did not start contributing to the health sphere until the publication of a bank health sector policy paper in 1987. Since that time, health has been categorized under the social sector heading, which also includes education and poverty reduction. Slightly more than 5 percent of all loans and grants from the ADB have been allocated to the social sector.

The Asian Development Bank (AsDB) was established in 1966. It is headquartered in Manila, Philippines and has 24 subsidiary offices around the world. It currently has 63 members, 45 of which are from the Asia-Pacific region. The AsDB follows the same weighted voting method as the other regional development banks; Japan and the United States are the two contributors to the bank and as of late 2003 they both held 12.942 percent of total ADB votes. In 2003, the bank approved $6.1 billion in loans and actually dispersed $3.8 billion. Traditionally, agriculture and rural development have received most of the bank's lending. In recent years, however, the Social Infrastructure Sector—including health, education, and water supply—has increased in importance, reflecting ADB's poverty reduction drive. Social infrastructure lending has accounted for about 7 percent of total bank loans.[56]

NGOs

One of the most striking features of the development of international health assistance has been the growing prominence of NGOs. To a large degree, NGOs have put global public health on the agendas of world leaders. They have lobbied governments, raised countless millions of dollars, and mobilized supporters and volunteers from around the world.[57] Although there are hundreds, if not thousands, of NGOs of varying wealth and size active in international health, only a few prominent ones are discussed here. The representative sample of six health-oriented NGOs— the Red Cross, Medecins Sans Frontieres (MSF), the People's Health Movement (PHM), Christian Children's Fund (CCF), the Aga Khan Foundation, and the Carter Center—are discussed to provide insights into the similarities and differences between important types of nonstate actors active in global health.

The Red Cross is the oldest, largest, and among the best-known international NGOs. The concept behind the Red Cross originated in 1859, when a young Swiss man, Henry Dunant, stumbled across the aftermath of a battle in Solferino, Italy. Witnessing the suffering of the tens of thousands of soldiers left on the battlefield, Dunant decided to create a society that would care for wounded soldiers in times of conflict. Four years later, in 1863, the Red Cross Movement was officially launched. Today, the Red Cross has more than 180 national societies, giving it a truly global scope. It has 97 million members; 300,000 employees; and 233 million beneficiaries worldwide each year. The Red Cross classifies itself as an independent, impartial humanitarian organization. It is involved in disaster response, disaster planning, health care, and the strengthening humanitarian law, especially rules surrounding warfare and the Geneva Conventions.[58]

This organization has three main component bodies at the international level: the International Red Cross and Red Crescent Movement, the International Committee of the Red Cross (ICRC), and the International Federation of Red Cross and Red Crescent Societies (IFRCS). It produces a quarterly magazine detailing the activities of the organization, and it periodically organizes conferences. The ICRC was also founded in Switzerland in 1863, and it is still located in Geneva. It is involved in fund-raising activities and focuses mainly on the promotion and strengthening of international humanitarian law.

The IFRCS is the most recent addition to the Red Cross group, being founded in Paris in 1919. After World War I, it was deemed necessary to form a body that could foster increased cooperation among the autonomous national societies. To this day, the IFRCS, which has a Secretariat in Geneva, is the overarching, coordinating body for the societies. Further-more, a segment of the Red Cross movement believed that the Red Cross should expand its mandate to a more generalized program of providing assistance to those in need, rather than maintaining the focus on assisting soldiers and victims of war.[59] Funds for the Red Cross are raised through the National Societies and the ICRC, which accept donations from governments, corporations, and private citizens. The National Societies also mobilize public support in the form of money and volunteers. The group of Red Cross bodies has clearly benefited from a growing humanitarian sentiment in the world.

Another internationally recognized NGO that is active in the health sphere is MSF, commonly referred to by its English title, Doctors without Borders. It was created in 1971 by a small group of French doctors and now has an international office in Belgium, national offices in 18 countries, missions in more than 80 countries, and a volunteer roster of more than 2,500 people. MSF's national offices, which are located in industrialized countries, are responsible for fund-raising, recruiting volunteers, organizing field missions in crisis situations, and lobbying governments on behalf of developing countries. In the field, MSF supports doctors and other medical personnel in providing emergency medical treatment for people in times of crisis. In countries with insufficient medical infrastructures, it often takes on a capacity-building role as well, working with the Ministry of Health and providing medical training for locals. MSF is also a strong advocate of assistance to the poor and sick people in developing countries. In 1999, it established one of the most successful recent campaigns to assist the poor in developing countries—the Access to Essential Medicines Campaign. It also spearheads a program called the Drugs for Neglected Diseases Initiative (DNDi), which is designed to foster increased research for medicines and vaccines for diseases that predominantly affect people in poor countries. MSF's prominent status among the plethora of humanitarian NGOs was recognized in 1999 when the organization received the Nobel Prize for Peace.[60]

The PHM provides an important approach to public health by creating community partnerships that are designed to empower the poor. PHM is an advocacy group that leads numerous campaigns in important health issue areas. It is a civil society–based initiative that evolved out of the People's Health Assembly in 2000 that was a gathering of almost 1,500 individuals representing 75 countries to affirm the WHO's 1978 Alma-Ata Declaration that promised "health for all by 2000" and was signed by 134 nations. The assembly gave birth to the People's PHM, which is a grassroots organization that focuses on people-centered health initiatives.[61] The PHM consists of a global secretariat and a steering group of representatives of regional focal points, as well as the eight organizations that cosponsored the assembly.[62] The PHM's goal is to allow for the organized articulation of local demands for health services on the basis of what the poor in an affected area want, and not on what global institutions and NGOs define as priorities. This approach has begun to influence organizations such as the World Bank, which in 2001 published a report indicating that empowerment of poor people was a key pillar in poverty reduction.[63]

Many humanitarian aid organizations are "faith based" and one of the more prominent of these is the CCF, which was created in 1938. Although it is based in Richmond, Virginia it has an active presence in 31 developing countries. This means that personnel representing CCF are active on the ground in these countries. CCF is active in the education and economic aspects of development, as well as the health sphere. Its budget for 2002 was $133 million, and approximately 25 percent of its resources are devoted to health and sanitation projects, with a further 12 percent allocated to nutrition projects. CCF's funding is entirely voluntary and is comprised of contributions from government and private sources.[64]

Although nondenominational, the Aga Khan Foundation is another extremely important NGO that was founded on a religious ideal.[65] Founded in 1967 by the leader of the Ismaili Muslim people, His Highness the Aga Khan, the institution is currently active in more than 15 countries, and has an approximate annual operating budget of $150 million. The Aga Khan Foundation is particularly focused on development projects in Asia and Eastern Africa. Its assistance programs have won several awards over the years, including the Most Innovative Development Project for 2005, awarded by the Global Development Network.[66]

An interesting NGO that was created in 1982 is the Carter Center, founded by former U.S. president and former first lady Jimmy and

Rosalynn Carter. Its activities are concentrated in the peace and health
fields, with more than three quarters—77.5 percent—of its funding going
to health programs. In the 2002–2003 fiscal year the Carter Center
received $117 million in donations from governments, foundations, indi-
viduals, corporations, and international organizations. Interestingly, nearly
half—46.7 percent—came from corporations. It has been particularly
active in combating tropical third world infectious diseases such as guinea
worm, onchocerciasis, trachoma, lymphatic filariasis, and schistosomiasis.
The Carter Center is well known for its collaboration with both IGOs and
NGOs.[67]

Foundations

Foundations have played a prominent role within the health assistance
sphere since the early twentieth century, beginning with the establishment
of the Rockefeller Foundation in 1913. In its first several decades,
Rockefeller's International Health Commission focused on the control of
hookworm, malaria, yellow fever, and schistosomiasis. These programs had
a profound impact on health programs in the southern United States and
parts of Latin America. One indication of how significant the Rockefeller
Foundation's impact has been on the health sphere is that its New York
Laboratory developed the vaccine for yellow fever in 1935. It has continued its involvement in controlling third world diseases since World War II,
and in 1977, it commenced a project studying neglected diseases of the
third world: African trypanosomiasis, leprosy, malaria, schistosomiasis,
hookworm, onchocerciasis, and childhood diarrhoeas. By the end of the
decade-long program, 360 scientists had been trained in 26 countries. In
fact, one of Rockefeller's major contributions has been the training of
scientists from developing countries. Currently, the major focus of the
Rockefeller Foundation within the health sphere is increasing health equity
for the poor regions of the world. It is also still involved in research and
drug development for tropical diseases and vaccine development through
the Global Alliance for Vaccines and Immunizations.[68]

Today by far the most prominent foundation concerned with international health is the Bill & Melinda Gates Foundation, which is headquartered in Seattle and has an endowment of more than $30 billion. The three
main areas in which it works are global health, education, and libraries. It
has provided large amounts of funding for projects such as vaccine development and the Global Fund to fight AIDS, TB, and Malaria. Although a
comparatively young organization, being founded in 2000, the Gates
Foundation has made commitments to donate more than $13 billion to
global health development causes over the past seven years making it one

of the biggest players in the global health arena—governments and international organizations included. The foundation has had a particularly influential role in shaping the health research agenda since 2005 when it announced the Gates Grand Challenges in Global Health Initiative. The Grand Challenges project provides grants, totaling more than $400 million, to a large number of scientists to encourage them to conduct research on diseases that affect the inhabitants of poor countries. This foundation is both creating a new research agenda and carving out a new and deeper role for itself in the health governance regime.[69]

Examples of other notable foundations active in the health sphere include the Nippon Foundation, which is based in Japan and is predominantly concerned with the elimination of leprosy. It has contributed more than $200 million to this cause.[70] Another example is the United Nations Foundation, which was founded by a $1 billion donation from Ted Turner in 1997. It is involved in grant making and supporting PPPs that work in a variety of UN areas, including international health.[71] A final example of a foundation involved in global health projects is the William J. Clinton Presidential Foundation, which was established by former U.S. president Bill Clinton and, in the health sphere, is particularly involved in the HIV/AIDS crisis and increasing access to essential drugs.[72] Foundations have long played an important role in public health and in the contemporary period that role is becoming more diverse, more collaborative, and, arguably, more significant.

Private Businesses

A notable development in health multilateralism over recent decades has been the emergence of private businesses, particularly pharmaceutical companies, as important contributors to and participants within health partnerships. In 2002 alone, pharmaceutical companies spent $564 million on assistance programs—particularly on the provision of vaccines and remedial drugs.[73] Since 1998, 10 major drug companies, through their membership in the Partnership for Quality Medical Donations, have donated products worth $2.7 billion.[74] Some of the more notable grants from private drug companies to the public health sector include a drug donation of Albendazole worth $1 billion by GlaxoSmithKline to eradicate lymphatic filariasis by 2020, and a $122 million donation by Novartis to establish a tropical disease research center in Singapore.[75] Increasingly, pharmaceutical companies are expanding the scope of their participation in the public health sphere. In the words of one expert, "the contributions from the companies concerned have gone beyond the provision of products and have included involvement in supporting activities to ensure efficient distribution and effective use."[76] In 2003, the African Malaria Partnership (which is led by GlaxoSmithKline) launched a 3 year, $1.5 million initiative to combat malaria in rural African communities.[77] Examples such as this demonstrate how, over recent years, private pharmaceutical firms have become significant players in charitable health programs. Although the role of private companies in GHPs is often deemed controversial owing to potential conflict of interest issues, they have become entrenched, and in many cases valuable contributors.[78]

As this section has made clear, there is presently a wide variety of actors involved in the provision of health assistance. Governments of rich states, which until recently, were responsible for all aspects of health assistance are now predominantly the suppliers of financial resources. They no longer provide medical personal or treatment facilities, but rather contract out medical services to civil society or nongovernmental groups. IGOs, including UN bodies and development banks, provide technical expertise and often act as information hubs and/or convening bodies, bringing together a wide array of experts. Foundations, NGOs, and private businesses are all civil society actors that are currently carving out roles for themselves in the global health governance field. These actors, which have only recently been deemed as legitimate assistance health donors have proven to be skilled at carving out niche roles that fill gaps in governance. As such, the governance system in which these competing actors operate can seem chaotic and messy, and although that is no doubt true to a degree, there are certain cases in which cooperative initiatives have exploited the skills of the varying actors and developed highly effective aid programs.

Methods for Providing Assistance

The provision of financial, material, and technical assistance to improve global health is more complex than at any time in history. Dozens of participants are funding scores of health assistance programs, and it is the goal of this section to provide insights into the different forms donor initiatives take and what spurs their creation. To this end, we have categorized the methods used to disburse assistance in four ways: bilaterally between states; bilaterally from NGOs to recipients; multilaterally among international organizations; and multilaterally among groups of actors participating in GHPs.

As the preceding section on trends in assistance flows indicated, *bilateral donations* (from state to state) continue to make up the lion's share of international health assistance. Approximately two-thirds or 70 percent of official development aid is given directly from one state to another, and by some accounts certain donors are making bilateral aid an even larger portion of the total.[79] This trend has been augmented by an increase in the number of states providing assistance. In fact, the number of bilateral donors has grown exponentially in the past 50 years, from just 5 donor states in the mid-1940s to 56 donor states as of 2007.[80] In the words of a recent International Development Association (IDA) report, "non-DAC and emerging donors are becoming increasingly important as ODA providers."[81] The report goes on to identify four groups of donor countries that are not part of the DAC. These are OECD countries that are not members of DAC such as Korea, Mexico, Turkey, and several European countries; new EU countries that are not members of the OECD; Middle East and OPEC countries (particularly Saudi Arabia); and non-OECD donors that do not belong to any of the previous groups including Brazil, China, India, and Russia. Although increased financial support to poor countries is welcomed by many governmental and nongovernmental advocates, the increase in sources of aid makes it difficult to track aid flows and thus avoid duplication of aid assistance programs.[82]

There are two key reasons that states continue to give bilaterally. First, bilateral aid programs give the donor states more control over how their aid money is allocated. Given that most donor states are democratic, their governments must answer to their electorates regarding how tax dollars are spent; thus it is often necessary to keep a tight reign on aid spending. Aid that is given bilaterally has often been criticized for being motivated by geopolitical and strategic reasons rather than humanitarian reasons and this is often justified.[83] Furthermore, it is easier for donor states to ensure that domestic priorities are satisfied when aid is given bilaterally. Probably the prime example of this is the aforementioned U.S. PEPFAR program, which has been criticized internationally but lauded domestically for its bias toward funding sexual abstinence programs (as opposed to condom or safe-sex awareness programs).

Second, bilateral aid is often easier to disburse and arguably more effective. For example, a high proportion of the $1.3 billion spent in 2005 by the U.S. government was given in bilateral aid, the majority to specific countries in sub-Saharan Africa chosen by the Bush administration. In contrast, the Global Fund has consistently struggled to obtain funds from donor countries and in 2005 only disbursed $292 billion.[84] "In terms of outcome, PEPFAR is providing urgent care more quickly. In two years, PEPFAR has placed 800,000 adults and children on ART, provided HIV testing for 19 million and provided treatment to more than half a million HIV positive pregnant women to prevent transmission to their children."[85]

Assistance provided to developing countries from *nongovernmental and civil society actors*[86] has increased to an unprecedented level in the twenty-first century. More NGOs exist now than at any time in history and they are able to command more funds, mobilize more volunteers, and garner more media attention than ever before. Small volunteer-based groups are active all over the developing world in a wide variety of programs. From building hospitals, to digging wells, to fostering children, NGOs are having a large cumulative impact owing to the expansion of numerous small, local-level aid initiatives. Although large NGOs, including MSF, Oxfam, and CARE, often work multilaterally in health partnerships, they also focus a considerable amount of funding and effort on bilateral projects. Nongovernmental development activity forms a complex mixture of low-level and high-profile, bilateral and multilateral efforts.

The Bill and Melinda Gates Foundation is probably the prime example of a nongovernmental organization that sometimes chooses to work bilaterally. This foundation has committed more than $13 billion since its creation in 2000; and much of it has gone directly to on-the-ground aid projects. Specifically, the Gates Grand Challenges is a funding initiative designed to foster research into medical and scientific solutions for global health problems. This bilateral, NGO-to-individual-researcher program has arguably done more to influence the research agenda than any event in the twentieth century. NGOs can choose to work autonomously rather than as part of a broader coalition when they are either very big or very small. The very big NGOs sometimes have the power to work alone because of their financial resources and perceived legitimacy. The very small NGOs usually work at a localized level on disease specific projects and they often do not want to divert scare resources to forming large, potentially cumbersome partnerships with government and intergovernmental actors.

Recent analyses of *institutional collaboration* often focus on cooperation among NGOs, but these analyses often underplay the continued salience of IGOs. The most prominent health-oriented intergovernmental body is the WHO, but international development banks (especially the World Bank) and other UN groups play active and important roles in improving global health conditions. WHO financial and material assistance programs are undoubtedly vital for the recipients, but what global intergovernmental bodies such as WHO contribute most to health assistance is their ability to facilitate dialogues and promote cooperation among governmental and nongovernmental actors. International cooperation of various forms (especially remedial and preventative guidelines) requires communication, and global bodies such as WHO play an important facilitation role.

GHPs, which have already been mentioned several times in this chapter, are a fascinating new feature of global health governance because they bring together large number of diverse institutions. There were just a handful of GHPs in the early 1990s, but now there are more than 70 active health partnerships.[87] GHPs are often categorized by their main area of activity, and the most widely accepted mode of classification was developed by the British Department for International Development (DFID) several years ago. The DFID typology classifies GHPs by their major functions in four ways: research and development (which includes product discovery and development of new diagnostics, drugs, and vaccines); technical assistance and support services (which includes improving access to services, discounted or donated drugs, and medical assistance); advocacy (which includes raising the profile of diseases and advocate for international and national response, and resource mobilization); and financing (which includes funding for specific disease programs).[88]

The following pages describe five of the most notable and successful GHPs. The DNDi is included here as an example of a prominent GHP in the research and development category. The Onchocerciasis Control Program and the Guinea Worm Eradication Program are examples of GHPs that provide technical assistance/service support. It is interesting to note that the majority of health partnerships fall into this category. UNAIDS is an example of the third category of advocacy, and the Global Fund is an example of a GHP that focuses on financing mechanisms. These examples are included here to provide insight into how GHPs operate and what they bring to global health governance.

An important, recently established initiative, which has attracted significant attention is the DNDi. Its origins lie in an MSF-initiated study on neglected diseases in 1999. "Neglected diseases" are those diseases that occur only in poor countries and garner little or no drug research and development (R&D) by private pharmaceutical firms because there is no possibility for profit. As one prominent expert on health assistance explains,

> Historically, drugs and vaccines have become available through an informal division of responsibilities between public entities and private companies . . . This division of labour constitutes a poorly defined partnership in which the outcomes desired by different parties have never been explicitly negotiated. In the more economically advanced countries it is generally regarded as reasonably successful, having led to the availability of a broad range of effective drugs and vaccines. However, this kind of system is not particularly responsive to the specific health needs of the world's poorest populations.[89]

Recognizing this fact, and combining it with the knowledge that MSF's medical personnel in poor countries were treating patients with outdated, toxic, or useless drugs, MSF banded together with six like-minded organizations to create DNDi in 2003. It is based in Geneva at the Medecins Sans Frontieres headquarters.

The purpose of DNDi is to stimulate, fund, and conduct drug research for four diseases: malaria, trypanosomiasis, leishmaniasis, and Chagas. DNDi's goal is to have at least 6 drugs registered and a further 8 R&D projects established within 12 years at an estimated cost of $250 million. On its first anniversary in 2004, DNDi announced that it was launching clinical trials for two malaria treatments, and it has seven R&D projects for the other three target diseases. MSF has provided sufficient money to fund DNDi for its first five years, after which time money will be raised from rich governments, foundations, and individuals. DNDi's founding partners are MSF, the Brazilian Oswaldo Cruz Foundation, the Indian Council for Medical Research, Institut Pasteur of France, the government of Malaysia, and the Kenya Medical Research Institute. The UNICEF/UNDP/World Bank/WHO Special Programme for Research and Training in Tropical Diseases (TDR) is also associated with the initiative. These partners contribute to the initiative either through direct financial support, or through "donations" of scientific knowledge and expertise.[90]

One of the more notable initiatives directed at a tropical disease is the Onchocerciasis Control Program (OCP), which was founded in 1974 and continued operations for almost 30 years. Onchocerciasis, commonly referred to as "River Blindness," is predominantly an African disease, which has 90 percent of cases presently occurring in Africa; the remaining 10 percent occur in Latin America and Yemen. The disease is caused by a parasitic worm that is transmitted by a black fly that inhabits areas around fast flowing water. The major catalyst for the 1974 initiative was the development of an effective aerial spraying process that killed the black fly vector. This technique was aimed at reducing case numbers by preventing new infections. In the mid-1980s, however, the initiative expanded its scope to provide treatment to those already infected. This was possible because the pharmaceutical company Merck & Co, which had developed the effective drug Mectizan (ivermectin) several years previously, decided to donate the drug to all in need for as long as necessary.[91]

The program membership included a large number of organizations—the World Bank, WHO, UNDP, UNFAO, research organizations, donor states, 30 NGOs, and the corporate sector. The various participating organizations had particular roles. The World Bank was the fiscal agent for the OCP, and it was responsible for the mobilization and administration of funds. WHO was the executing agency, concerned with overseeing the overall implementation of the program. The UNICEF, UNDP, World Bank, and WHO Special Programme for Research and Training in Tropical Diseases (TDR) were responsible for promoting scientific research and the distribution of research findings. The UNDP provided modest funding. Industrialized countries likewise were responsible for providing funding.

NGOs were particularly involved with administering treatment and training locals.

When the program closed in 2002, it had covered 11 African countries, with a total population of 30 million people. It cost approximately $550 million and lasted 28 years. Operations ended in 2002, at which time OCP handed over the remaining tasks of disease monitoring and drug distribution to the governments of the 11 states within the scope of the program. It is estimated that the program cured 1.5 million people, prevented 300,000 people from going blind, and paved the way for 25 million hectares of arable land to be reclaimed for habitation and agricultural usage. Thus the OCP became "a pioneer and successful model of public-private partnership for health."[92]

Guinea Worm Disease, or dracunculiasis, is an ancient affliction of humankind, which is caused by a parasite found in water fleas that inhabit bodies of stagnant water. When water from these sources is drunk, parasitical larvae are ingested. The larvae hatch and grow into a worm within the host's body, and about one year later the fully grown, meter long, worm emerges from the host, usually through the foot. Dracunculiasis has been deemed a feasible candidate for eradication for decades because it is easily and inexpensively preventable and it has no animal reservoir. For this reason, the Guinea Worm Eradication Program was established by the U.S. Centers for Disease Control and Prevention (CDC) in 1980. Since 1986 the program has been directed by the Carter Center.

The eradication program currently involves more than 100 partners including governments, foundations, corporations, individuals, UN organizations, Ministries of Health of afflicted nations, and NGOs. The four major partners spearheading the eradication effort are the Carter Center, CDC, UNICEF, and WHO. The Carter Center coordinates the activities of the program partners, advocates on behalf of the afflicted, raises funds, and provides technical assistance and medical supplies. The CDC has a Guinea Worm Task Force, and it is mainly involved in monitoring and scientific research concerning Guinea worms. UNICEF is most directly involved with the prevention aspect of the program through the provision of water filters, the digging of wells, and the use of larvicide. WHO, through its Collaborating Center for Research, Training and Eradication of Dracunculiasis and its country offices in endemic areas, assists with detection of cases, dissemination of information, and training of local persons and health officials in how to prevent contraction of the disease. Teaching and remedial care for indigenous peoples is usually undertaken by on-the-ground NGOS, such as the Red Cross, MSF, and CARE.

Funds for the eradication program come largely from governments of developed countries and foundations. Of particular note was the $28.5 billion donation made by the Bill and Melinda Gates Foundation in 2000. According to the terms of the grant, the Carter Center is the lead agency for countries with case loads more than 100 per year, although WHO is the lead agency for those with less than 100 cases per year. Also, WHO is responsible for the technical aspects of precertification and certification. UNICEF remains involved in the provision of clean, sanitary drinking water.[93] The 25 private companies involved in the program provide support in the form of medical supplies such as drugs, and prevention tools such as nylon filter cloths for filtering fleas out of the infected water, and larvicides for killing the dracunculiasis larvae. Growth in assistance efforts from pharmaceutical companies highlights the growing sensitivity of these types of actors regarding their role and reputation in health governance.

The eradication program has been remarkably successful. In fact, it has reduced disease incidence by 99 percent since its inception. In the mid-1980s, more than 3.5 million cases of Guinea Worm disease occurred every year; by the early twentieth century, that number had dropped to approximately 50,000 cases annually. In 2005, there were fewer than 11,000 cases, and the disease has now been geographically limited to just nine African countries, with most cases occurring in Sudan, Ghana, and Nigeria.[94] Eradication in Sudan poses the biggest obstacle in the global eradication effort because of the internal conflict that makes it virtually impossible to allow medical workers and scientists to treat infected persons. Nevertheless, experts believe that Guinea Worm Disease can be eradicated from Sudan within five years of effective access being granted to the Eradication Program.[95]

The Joint United Nations Programme on HIV/AIDS (UNAIDS) was created in 1996 by a group of six cosponsors. They were the UNICEF, the UNDP, the UNFPA, the UN Educational, Scientific and Cultural Organization (UNESCO), the WHO and the World Bank. The UN Office on Drugs and Crime (UNODC) joined the initiative in 1999; the International Labour Organization (ILO) joined in 2001; the World Food Programme (WFP) joined in 2003; and the UN High Commissioner for Refugees (UNHCR) joined in 2004. Together, these 10 UN bodies form the Committee of Co-sponsoring Organizations, which meets once per year to deliberate on key issues and develop policies and strategies for UNAIDS. The ultimate goal of this initiative is to foster an expanded, global response to HIV/AIDS that focuses on "preventing transmission of HIV, providing care and support, reducing the vulnerability of individuals and communities to HIV/AIDS, and alleviating the impact of the epidemic."[96] Overall, UNAIDS' main function is coordination and information sharing, but it plays a very limited role in field activities.

To achieve these goals, UNAIDS provides leadership and coordination among key UN bodies and acts as an information hub. Its members and secretariat collect and disseminate information on the nature and scope of the epidemic, which helps to mobilize support for programs that combat HIV/AIDS. It also plays a large role in engaging civil society and afflicted communities to improve assistance programs. UNAIDS is governed by a Programme Coordinating Board (PCB), which is made up of 22 governments from all geographic regions, the UNAIDS Cosponsors, and five representatives from NGOS. The PCB holds a regular session once a year in Geneva, and in alternate years it also holds thematic sessions outside Geneva, as requested by the members. This initiative is funded through voluntary contributions from governments, foundations, corporations, private groups, and individuals. In 2003, more than $118.5 million was received from 30 governments, philanthropic organizations, and individuals from around the world.[97]

Perhaps one of the most important new health initiatives is the Global Fund to Fight AIDS, Tuberculosis and Malaria. In recognition of the fact that AIDS, TB, and malaria (combined) kill more than 6 million people per year, and in light of the growing understanding of connections between development, poverty, and health, the Global Fund was launched in 2002. It was created owing to the belief that these three diseases are contemporary scourges of mankind, and that appropriate funding to combat them was lacking from the world community. Thus, the Global Fund was designed to act as a unique and powerful financing mechanism and to raise and distribute monies for projects combating any one or all of the diseases in question. As such, the fund does not design, implement, or control projects. Rather, it provides funding for country or local projects. Financial commitments to the Global Fund, from rich governments, foundations, corporations, and private individuals, through 2004 totaled approximately $2 billion, with $0.5 billion actually dispersed. Despite the significant increase in health assistance funding that this represents, it is estimated that at least $2 billion more is needed to close the funding gap.[98]

The fund's secretariat, which is based in Geneva, approves grants for health projects under its system of Country Coordinating Mechanisms (CCMs), and it monitors them through an independent Technical Review Panel. Approximately 40 percent of applicants have received grants to date. After a project is granted funding, the money is allocated to a principal recipient, which is an on-the-ground representative that becomes legally responsible for utilizing funding along the lines of the grant application approved by the Global Fund. Fifty-one percent of principal recipients are governments of poor countries; twenty-four percent are NGOs, and the remainder are divided relatively evenly between academic institutions, faith-based organizations, and private companies. Since its inception, the majority of Global Fund disbursements—56 percent—have been allocated toward HIV/AIDS prevention and treatment programs; 31 percent has gone to tuberculosis programs; and the remaining 13 percent has targeted malaria. Geographically speaking, sub-Saharan Africa has received most Global Fund money, with 61 percent of total disbursements; East Asia, Southeast Asia, and Oceania together have received 18 percent; Latin America, 9 percent; Eastern Europe and Central Asia, 7 percent; and South Asia, the Middle East, and North Africa, 5 percent.[99]

The Global Fund's membership is diverse, including governments of rich and poor countries, diverse civil society, private sector representatives, and members of affected communities. The fund is governed by a 23 person International Board, which includes representatives of both donor and recipient governments, NGOs, corporations, foundations, and affected communities. UN bodies (especially WHO and UNAIDS) as well as the World Bank, which is the fiscal agent, are key partners of the Global Fund. As the Global Fund does not implement projects, the roles of the various partners within the initiative are essentially similar: to advocate on behalf of the fund, to raise money, and to assist in determining overall policy and fund-disbursement guidelines.

As the above five examples of GHPs make clear, these initiatives have much potential to positively impact the health situation of people in poor countries. In the words of one report, "despite some concerns, individual GHPs are seen overall as having a positive impact in terms both of achieving their own objectives and of being welcomed by countries studied."[100] Although GHPs should not be viewed as a "panacea"[101] for the world's ills, they are playing an important role in the contemporary governance system. A particularly interesting aspect of these partnerships is that they have arisen spontaneously; they have not been deliberately created but have rather emerged as a response to health crises or gaps in governance. As such, one commentator remarks that these partnerships "should generally be viewed as social experiments that are attempting to learn how to tackle intractable health problems in better ways. There is no formula for constructing them and it is unlikely that a universally applicable one will be found."[102]

Despite the fact that there is no formula or coherent organizing principle driving the creation of GHPs, certain patterns can be discerned regarding the nature of these groupings and the roles played by different actors within them. In general states, foundations, and private individuals fund GHPS. International organizations often act as coordinators or communication hubs that bring the appropriate people together. Development banks often provide funding, accountancy advice or recommendations, and economic guidelines. Private businesses provide financial resources, material goods (pharmaceutical companies especially provide discounted or donated drugs), and personnel. Nongovernmental groups provide manpower, often both in terms of untrained volunteers and trained medical professionals. The fact that the roles within GHPs can be relatively clearly delineated speaks to one of the key characteristics that contribute to the success of these partnerships, and that is the exploitation of each actor's comparative advantage. Effective health partnerships are more than the sum of their parts because they take the skills, expertise, and resources from diverse actors and combine them to combat a particular problem.

Although their marked success with regard to certain projects indicates that GHPS are a valuable addition to global governance, many important questions still surround these groups including questions of accountably, representation, legitimacy, and lack of coordination. As previously mentioned, GHPs tend to coalesce in response to a specific issue, which necessitates a narrow focus; however, health issues are intrinsically interconnected. Thus a negative ramification of GHPs is the proliferation of vertical, autonomous institutions that operate in isolation from one another, as opposed to a coordinated, harmonized approach to improving a health system in general. Another key problem is that, owing to their diverse composition, GHPs are not directly accountable to any body, organization, or institution and without effective accountability mechanisms partnerships can potentially waste resources, develop inappropriate programs, and negatively impact health systems.[103]

Conclusion

Health assistance, as a strategy of global health governance, has developed in significant ways in recent years, and it is now a deeper, more complex area of governance than ever before. Increased recognition of global interdependencies has led to more funding for health programs, more participants in the health field, and more attention being paid to health issues. Studies that focus on multilateralism often assumes a growing predominance of multilateral institutions and regimes. Although this assumption is true to a degree in health governance, this chapter has attempted to highlight the continued salience of bilateral health assistance in that it accounts for 70 percent of total aid flows. States have often wanted to maintain control over aid disbursements for political and economic reasons because aid can buy political influence for a state, and can promote economic benefits for national exporters. Countries may have humanitarian motivations for aid transfers, but these motivations are generally accompanied by other self-interested considerations. While recognizing the importance of bilateral transfers, it is also necessary to recognize that it is sometimes difficult to make clear distinctions between bilateral and multilateral assistance. This is especially the case today when there are so many complex collaborative arrangements between different international donors.

Despite the continuing prominence of bilateral assistance, developments in multilateral health efforts are significant and important. The emergence of new infectious diseases has made many health experts believe that global cooperation to combat these diseases is a medical necessity. Advances in medical knowledge regarding treatment of diseases have convinced many humanitarian and development professionals that cooperation between rich and poor countries to improve health is a moral necessity. The increased involvement of several actors in the health arena, particularly rich foundations and private pharmaceutical companies, along with the increased activity of powerful NGOs, has encouraged the growth of PPPs for distributing material and financial assistance. The participants in GHPs have strengthened each other's commitment to international health collaboration through their frequent interactions and their varied forms of cooperation, and this trend is likely to continue into the foreseeable future.

CHAPTER 5

DISEASE CURES: INTERNATIONAL PATENT LAW AND ACCESS TO ESSENTIAL MEDICINES

Access to essential medicines has long been a concern for health professionals, development experts, and governments globally; however, since the formal establishment of the World Trade Organization (WTO) in 1995, this issue has become a serious concern for trade specialists as well. The concept of essential medicines was popularized in 1977 with the publication of the first World Health Organization (WHO) Model List of Essential Medicines. According to WHO "[e]ssential medicines are those that satisfy the priority health care needs of the population."[1] Today, the term is strongly associated with medicines for infectious diseases that kill millions— particularly diseases such as HIV/AIDS, malaria, and tuberculosis, although it covers numerous drugs designed to meet basic health needs.

Lack of access to essential medicines is a critical issue within global health governance, as demonstrated by the fact that an estimated 10 million deaths annually could be prevented if access was improved.[2] In poor parts of Asia and north and central Africa a third of the population lacks access to the most essential drugs; in the poorest parts of sub-Saharan Africa half the population does not receive essential medicines. This is in large part owing to the prohibitively high cost of the medicines; however, issues such as government corruption,[3] undeveloped health infrastructure, and lack of capacity to deliver medicines to people in rural areas are also important factors that impede access.[4] The price of pharmaceutical products is of key concern to developing countries due to the significant proportion of health spending that they devote to acquiring medicines: "Pharmaceutical expenditures in developing countries represent between 10 to 40 percent of public health budgets; and between 20 and 50 percent of total health care expenditures, compared to an average of 12 percent in OECD countries."[5] The problem of the high cost of drugs has been particularly highlighted in recent years as the need for antiretroviral therapy (ART) treatment for HIV/AIDS patients has come to the forefront. For example, in the Ivory Coast in 2000, the daily cost of using the antiretroviral drug *didanosine* was $3.48 per head, but the government-run health service was only able to afford spending of $0.03 per person, per day.[6]

Another salient feature of the access issue is that very few new drugs are being created to treat diseases of poverty, such as malaria, chagas, and cholera. This is because the major developers of new drugs are private, profit-oriented pharmaceutical firms. These firms predominantly focus their research dollars on creating drugs for diseases and afflictions of the comparatively wealthy, such as obesity, cancer, and smoking related illnesses. From the perspective of these companies, there is no viable market for medicines in developing areas because their inhabitants cannot afford to pay prices that would make the high research and development (R&D) costs worthwhile in the long run.[7] In fact, although developing countries account for approximately 80 percent of the world's population, they only account for 20 percent of global pharmaceutical sales, and profit-oriented drug companies that must answer to their shareholders must consider this reality when they are determining how to spend their research budgets.[8] As a result, the nongeneric pharmaceutical industry rarely produces drugs for diseases prevalent in the developing world. A remarkable figure that bears this out is that of the 1,223 new medicines that were developed between 1975 and 1997, only 13 (1 percent) of them were useful for treating tropical diseases.[9] More up-to-date figures indicate that there is still a serious disconnect between health needs and drug R&D priorities; between 2000 and 2004, 163 new drugs were developed and only 4 were targeted for neglected diseases.[10] This gap exists despite the fact that the overall amount of money being spent on drug development has increased significantly in recent years from $30 billion in 1990 to nearly $106 billion in 2001.[11] This issue of lack of R&D into diseases of the poor is commonly referred to as the "10/90 gap" as approximately 10 percent of global drug R&D is focused on the medical problems that cause 90 percent of the global disease burden, a problem that was first noted by the Commission on Health Research for Development in 1990.[12]

Both the affordability of existing drugs and the lack of research into new and better drugs to treat diseases of the poor are major components of the broad issue of lack of access to essential medicines. In recent years, health and development activists have argued that the affordability issue has become more serious owing to the development of an intellectual property (IP) rights regime that promotes increased protection for IP and that one of the consequences of this regime has been an increase in drug prices. The second issue, lack of research, is being dealt with in interesting ways, as a handful of nonprofit-based organizations have recently become involved in drug development. It is feasible that new projects involving universities and nonprofit research groups could have great success in treating diseases of the poor because "[a] high proportion of deaths in the developing world are due to illnesses which are in principle curable with medicines which currently exist . . . [M]any other deaths result from diseases for which medicinal treatments could, with little effort, be developed using knowledge already available."[13] As James Orbinski and Barry Burciul have argued in a recent publication, the lack of drugs for treating "neglected diseases" is not due to lack of knowledge or the capability of scientists, but rather due to "market failure" as the current system is arranged such that the major developers of new drugs have no vested interest in researching medicines for those who are arguably most in need of them.[14]

The issue of IP rights and access to essential medicines is particularly complex, and as it has attracted significant attention in recent years, there is a wealth of information surrounding the topic. To develop a reasonably succinct chapter while still maintaining a high level of discourse and analysis, we have made certain value judgments regarding the topics on which to focus, and which matters to avoid. Three issues are most germane to the purposes of this book and are the key themes that recur throughout the subsequent pages. First, the crux of the access issue is the contention that patents on pharmaceutical products are a necessary and justifiable facet of IP law. The second key theme that runs throughout the chapter is the idea that loopholes, such as compulsory licenses, to protect public health are a necessary dimension of the regime.[15] The third major theme of the chapter is the reframing of IP rights away from the trade arena and toward the human rights arena.

In exploring these themes, the chapter is organized in the following manner. It begins with a chronological breakdown of the major economic treaties that are relevant to the pharmaceutical industry. It then provides a description of major political and legal events that have occurred over the past decade and have influenced the debate over access to essential medicines. The third section provides an analysis of the role played by nongovernmental organizations (NGOs) in this field. The final section consists of concluding comments and an assessment of the different governance strategies that have been used in this issue area.

WTO Agreements and the Access Issue

As is the case with most international trade issues, one must begin the discussion with the creation of the General Agreement on Tariffs and Trade (GATT) in 1947. It was created as a provisional body, but was the central global, multilateral trade body for nearly 50 years. A core provision of the GATT international trade regime was nondiscrimination, commonly known as the Most Favoured Nation principle, which entails obligations to apply identical trade barriers and benefits to all member states, and to treat all foreign firms equally. After nearly a decade of negotiations that took place between 1986 and 1994, the GATT was succeeded by the WTO, which officially began operations in 1995. It absorbed the many trade agreements developed under this early trade regime, as well as legitimizing several new and important trade liberalization agreements. The WTO currently has 151 member states.[16]

Establishing the appropriate balance between a desire for unrestricted trade (and thus increased economic development and profit) and the duty of governments to protect the health of their citizenry has always been an issue of major contention within international trade agreements. In an attempt to achieve this balance, the GATT included an important health safeguard. Article XX specified that states could override the nondiscriminatory principle and impose higher barriers on products that protected people's health. Thus, if it were necessary to protect their public's health, a member state could ban imports of meat, for example, from Country A although allowing the same type of meat to be imported from Country B and C, as long as the member state imposing the ban could medically and/or scientifically prove that meat from Country A posed a threat to human health. However, the limiting stipulation within this GATT clause was that any import ban must not unnecessarily stymie international trade. This was, at least in part, to prevent states from spuriously applying the health exception as an unfair barrier to trade. On this matter, Article XX (b) stated,

> Subject to the requirement that such measures are not applied in a manner which would constitute a means of arbitrary or unjustifiable discrimination between countries where the same conditions prevail, or a disguised restriction on international trade, nothing in this Agreement shall be construed to prevent the adoption or enforcement by any contracting party of measures . . . necessary to protect human, animal or plant life or health.[17]

During the Uruguay Round, which led to the creation of the WTO in 1995, four major agreements were negotiated that had relevance to public health. They were the Agreement on Sanitary and Phytosanitary Measures (SPS), the General Agreement on Trade in Services (GATS), the revised Agreement on Technical Barriers to Trade (TBT), and the Agreement on Trade Related Aspects of Intellectual Property (TRIPS). All four agreements entered into force on January 1, 1995. Following the precedent set by Article XX of the GATT, the four health-related WTO agreements included provisions that allow states to impose standards in excess of those prescribed, on the basis of a need to protect public health. To quote David Fidler,

> The main dynamic that operates in international trade law with respect to infectious diseases contains two elements. First, international trade law recognizes the sovereign right of States to adopt measures to protect public health from threats posed by products flowing in international commerce. Second, international trade law imposes on this sovereign right disciplines that constrain the ability of the State to misuse its power to protect public health.[18]

In all cases the agreements have loopholes or "safeguards" that allow for the protection of public health, and in all cases disagreements have arisen between WTO members as to what constitutes reasonable and legitimate trade barriers in this context. However, only the TRIPS agreement is discussed in detail here for two reasons. First, although the SPS, TBT, and GATS agreements are relevant to the broader health sphere, they do not influence the access-to-medicines debate, which is, of course, the focus of this chapter. Second, unlike disputes regarding the SPS, TBT, and GATS agreements, clashes that have occurred under TRIPS have mirrored a larger axis of international conflict regarding terms of economic competition and well-being between industrialized countries and developing states.

The TRIPS agreement was negotiated between 1986 and 1994, but it followed in the wake of some very important changes in the global trade regime that took place from the late 1970s through the late 1980s. In the late 1970s, IP rights-based businesses and industries were facing serious threats to the violability of their property rights because "[t]echnological change had made the appropriation of intellectual property-based goods and processes easy, inexpensive and lucrative."[19] Initially, the IP lobby, which was and still is predominantly housed in the United States,[20] approached the U.S. government with its goals for trade liberalization. It gained significant victories in getting domestic laws passed in 1979, 1984, and 1988 that enhanced the rights of IP holders. As seen in later discussions, probably the most notable achievement was persuading the U.S. government to include the Special 301 provision in the Trade Act in 1988, which enabled the United States Trade Representative (USTR) to act unilaterally against countries that failed to protect U.S.-held IP.[21] Thus the 1980s witnessed a strong and growing trend in U.S. economic policy toward favoring the IP industry. This trend carried over into the TRIPS negotiations in many important ways. First, the IP industry lobby directed their negotiations away from the World Intellectual Property Organization (WIPO) and toward the WTO because the consensus within the IP lobby was that the WIPO was too weak to enforce compliance, too concerned with North-South politics, and too sympathetic to developing nations' opposition to the protection of IP rights.[22] Second, the IP lobby approached counterparts in the European Union and Japan to gain support for their proposals for the structure and principles of the TRIPS agreement.[23] They succeeded in getting this support, and so the United States, European Union, and Japan formed a very strong bloc during the negotiations. This trilateral bloc was further supported by numerous IP rights experts largely employed within the pharmaceutical industry.[24]

At the start of TRIPS negotiations, the developing country representatives were unwilling to support increased protection for IP as "[p]rior to TRIPS, many governments in developing countries had adopted an explicit policy preference not to honour intellectual property protection for pharmaceuticals in an effort to promote self-sufficiency in the production of basic medicines and as in the case of India, develop a competitive local industry."[25] However, the developing nations did not have a coordinated or organized opposition to the United States, European Union, and Japan since they were represented at the negotiating table by general trade specialists, rather than IP law experts. "In the absence of the necessary legal expertise, [negotiation] fatigue resulted because developing countries simply did not have the knowledge necessary to negotiate effectively on the content of the TRIPS agreement."[26] In the end, the developing countries compromised their preference for a more lax regime, in exchange for developed country concessions in certain other trade sectors, particularly textiles and agriculture.[27] And so, on January 1, 1995, the TRIPS entered into force along with the other WTO agreements, and the IP architects of TRIPS got 95 percent of what they wanted.[28]

The key elements of the TRIPS agreement are increased protection of patents, copyrights, trademarks, and industrial design. TRIPS extends patent rights for a minimum of 20 years, it requires that all countries offer patent protection to IP goods, including pharmaceutical products and requires that patent rights are enforced with a strong system of penalties and consequences for states that do not comply. Thus, TRIPS "created global standards for intellectual property law with real power."[29] The rationale for increased IP protection includes the encouragement of technological innovation and the dissemination of technological advances.[30] Thus, central to the TRIPS agreement is a requirement that WTO members "establish minimum standards for protecting and enforcing intellectual property rights" that translates into increased protection for patents.[31]

Patents are in essence temporary, legal monopolies. They give an individual or firm that developed a product, procedure, or technology the right to sell it with no competition for a certain period—thereby creating artificial scarcity and sustaining a higher price than the market would bear under normal, competitive circumstances.[32] Patent laws are justified and encouraged because they provide the incentive for firms to invest the large sums of money that are often required to develop new products. This is especially true for medicines as the estimated cost to develop a new drug is in the hundreds of millions of dollars.[33]

The price differential between patented and generic versions of drugs is extremely significant. For example, the patented version of an important drug in treating a type of meningitis that often affects HIV/AIDS patients costs between $14 and $25 per dose; the same drug drops to $0.75 in countries where competition comes from generic producers.[34] In India, where the HIV drug *fluconazole* is generically produced, it costs $55/150 mg; the same amount costs $697 in Malaysia, $703 in Indonesia, and $817 in the Philippines where it is under patent protection.[35] Another example is the generic drug manufacturer Cipla, based in India. Cipla can produce a drug regimen for treating AIDS victims for $350–$600 per patient per year whereas the same regimen costs between $10,000 and $15,000 when purchased from the patent holder in the United States.[36] Not surprisingly the majority of patents are held by developed countries; in fact, developed countries hold 97 percent of all drug patents, and 80 percent of the patents granted in developing countries are owned by residents of developed states.[37]

The period for patent protection under TRIPS is 20 years, but certain industrialized countries, particularly the United States, have emphasized the fact that TRIPS establishes minimum standards. Therefore, they argue that TRIPS permits longer patent protection periods, which are known as "TRIPS-Plus." Although it is generally accepted that patent protection provides incentives for R&D into new products by preventing competition for a limited period, there is a debate as to whether this logic applies to products in the developing world, as these countries are too poor to pay the higher prices that a patent would guarantee,

> Patent protection for pharmaceutical products is an area where the problem of finding a proper balance is particularly acute—namely, between the goal of providing incentives for future inventions of new drugs and the goal of affordable access to existing drugs. It is especially important from a social and public health point of view that new drugs and vaccines to treat and prevent disease are generated, and that the incentives provided by the patent system effectively promote this. Precisely because of the social value of the drugs so generated, they need to be widely accessible as quickly as possible.[38]

Although TRIPS was "a stunning triumph for commercial interests and intellectual property (IP) industry lobbyists who worked tirelessly to achieve the global agreement," it also included several important loopholes regarding the health interests of developing countries.[39] Given that the disease burden is much more significant in developing countries, and given that developing countries are generally too poor to afford effective health care, these loopholes had particular resonance for poor countries in Asia, Africa, and parts of Latin America.

The first key health-oriented provision in TRIPS is Article 8(1) that states "members may, in formulating or amending their laws and regulations, adopt measures necessary to protect public health" The next crucial provision is Article 27.2 that allows a government to deny patent protection for specific inventions if they are necessary to protect human, animal, or plant life or health . . . in order to protect "*ordre public.*" However, there is no universally accepted definition of what this term means and so governments have shied away from using this provision.[40] Article 30 states "[M]embers may provide limited exceptions to the exclusive rights conferred by a patent, provided that such exceptions do not unreasonably conflict with normal exploitations of the patent and do not unreasonably prejudice the legitimate interests of the patent owner, taking account of the legitimate interests of third parties."[41] Taken together, the meaning of Articles 8(1) and 30 is very significant to the access to medicines issue as these two clauses provide an "override" or "loophole" to the patent laws implemented by the TRIPS agreement, albeit under extreme circumstances that are elaborated in the following section.

Article 31 of the agreement is of particular importance to the issue of access to essential medicines. It is entitled "Other Use without Authorization of the Right Holder," and it sets out the conditions under which a product that is still under patent can be produced by an entity other than the patent-holder. The subsections of the Article go on to state that a member state can request or order a third party to produce the product in question if public health is at risk. However, the member state must first approach the right-holder with the option to negotiate a mutually beneficial solution. (In the case of a national emergency, the step of approaching the right-holder may be bypassed). Furthermore, cases in which a non–patent-holder produces the product, the patent-holder must be reasonably compensated. The commonly used term for this process is "compulsory licensing," that is, the member state would issue a compulsory license to a third party, ordering the production of "x" amount of the patented product. However, the term compulsory license was not officially used in WTO nomenclature until the release of the Doha Declaration on TRIPS and Public Health in November, 2001.[42]

Although the provision for compulsory licenses provided governments with an important tool for the treatment and prevention of disease, a severe restriction was placed on the issuing of such licenses. According to Article 31(f) "any such use shall be authorized predominantly for the supply of the domestic market of the member authorizing such use." This limitation was a major cause of concern for many developing countries, because any state without a functioning and relatively advanced domestic pharmaceutical industry would not be able to take advantage of this clause. In other words, the "domestic market" limitation of Article 31(f) rendered impotent the power of the compulsory license for the least developed states that would be most in need of exploiting this acceptable patent-violation clause. It was not until 2003 that a solution regarding this issue was agreed upon. The solution is discussed in the following text.

Major Political and Legal Events

In the decade after the WTO and the TRIPS agreement entered into force in 1995, several important events occurred relevant to the issue of access to essential medicines for developing countries. A brief chronology of those events is provided here, and they are discussed in more detail in the following text. In 1996, Brazil began to provide free ART to all HIV/AIDS patients. The methods that the Brazilian government used to attain sufficient quantities of ART drugs at a low price were later challenged by some of the developed countries on the basis of a violation of patent rights. In 1997, South Africa passed the Medicines and Related Substances Amendment Act, which allowed for the importation of comparatively inexpensive generic drugs from other developing countries. Immediately following the passing of the Act, the South African government was put under great pressure to repeal it from both the U.S. government and the national pharmaceutical lobby. Then, in 1999, some important developments occurred that supported the Brazilian and South African positions. Medecins Sans Frontieres (MSF), one of the most influential health NGOs in the world, began a highly effective Access to Essential Medicines Campaign. In the same year, President Clinton of the United States announced a dramatic about-face in U.S. policy by stating that the United States would support Africa's program to provide HIV/AIDS treatment to its citizens. By 2001, the South Africans had won their struggle regarding the Medicines Act and the challenge case against Brazil by developed countries had been dropped. In late 2001, the WTO approved the most important international legal accords regarding access to medicines—the Doha Declaration on TRIPS and Public Health. The most recent major development related to this issue was the August 2003 decision regarding the domestic industry provision of the compulsory license clause.

The Brazil Case

In 1996, the government of Brazil launched a broad-based AIDS prevention and treatment program. The prevention aspect of the program was effective in providing critical education to at-risk groups, and the number of people who were HIV positive in the country dropped significantly through the late 1990s. Under the treatment program, the government of Brazil provided free and universal access to ART to all HIV/AIDS patients. The program resulted in a steady increase in those receiving ART, and between 1996 and 1999 it reduced AIDS-related mortality by more than 50 percent, saving Brazil more than $450 million in hospital and treatment costs.[43]

To provide the necessary drugs to run this program, Brazil, which has a well-developed pharmaceutical industry, produced generic versions of many of the more expensive drugs that are still under patent in other countries. This action was justified under TRIPS Article 31. Not all drugs can be produced domestically, however, and Brazil has had to import *nelfinavir* made by the pharmaceutical company Roche and *efavirenz* made by Merck. Citing the prohibitively high cost charged by Roche and Merck, the Brazilian government has threatened to use compulsory licensing to break the patent for these two drugs and produce them domestically. This means that it threatened to order Brazilian firms to produce the drugs and hence violate the foreign patent laws. The threat alone has been an effective negotiating tool, and the foreign companies in question have reduced their prices sufficiently for Brazil to afford importation. Thus far, Brazil has not carried out its threat of violating the patents.[44]

In February 2001, the United States requested that the WTO create a panel to review the activities of the Brazilian government, based on the contention that Brazilian trade law that permits for the above-described activities contravenes TRIPS. In April 2001, the UN Human Rights Commission approved a resolution proposed by the Brazilian delegation that established access to medicines during pandemics as a basic human right. At least in part owing to the publicity caused by the resolution, and the sentiment that fostered it, the United States withdrew the WTO challenge case against Brazil on June 25, 2001.[45] In exchange for dropping the case, the Brazilian government agreed to notify the U.S. government in advance if it developed plans to issue a compulsory license.[46] Brazil's success in dealing with both its AIDS pandemic and the politics and economics of access to essential medicines has made it a model and a "trailblazer" for other AIDS-afflicted nations.[47]

The South Africa Case

The first practical application of compulsory licenses regarding essential medicines began in South Africa in 1997 when the government passed of the Medicines and Related Substances Amendment Act. The provisions of the Act introduced a legal framework that facilitated access to affordable medicines—by allowing the South African Minister of Health to revoke patents on drugs necessary to treat AIDS, to issue compulsory licenses for the generic production of antiretroviral drugs, and to conduct parallel importing of generic versions of patented drugs from countries such as India and Brazil.[48] It is important to note that these provisions within the Medicines Act were compliant with the TRIPS agreement according to the previously discussed Articles 30 and 31.[49] Nevertheless, in early 1998, a case against the South African government was launched by a coalition of 39 pharmaceutical companies, because the Medicines Act violated the South African constitution and in fact, would not increase access to medicine.[50]

The position of the pharmaceutical manufacturers was strongly supported by both the United States and the European Union. In an attempt to persuade the South African government to repeal the Medicines Act the U.S. government applied heavy bilateral economic pressure, including placing South Africa on the U.S. Trade Special 301 Watch List, and denying coverage of the Generalized System of Preferences for certain South African exports.[51] However, the South African government received strong backing from a coalition of NGOs led by MSF. MSF's Campaign for Essential Medicines, which was launched in 1999, was extremely effective and caused considerable embarrassment to the pharmaceutical manufacturers and their developed country allies. This led the United States to withdraw its opposition to the Medicines Act, a decision that was officially announced by President Clinton during the 1999 WTO Seattle Ministerial Meeting.[52] The decision was reaffirmed a year later, when the Clinton administration issued an executive order stating that "the US shall not seek, through negotiation or otherwise, the revocation or revision of any intellectual property law or policy of a beneficiary sub-Saharan African country, as determined by the resident, that regulates HIV/AIDS pharmaceuticals or medical technologies."[53]

By the time the case launched by the South African pharmaceutical lobby against the government came to trial in March 2001, it had become a highly politicized event. The trial was attended not only by the lawyers and parties involved, but also by numerous protestors from human rights and AIDS-activist groups, bearing signs with pictures of dying children and anti-Pharma slogans.[54] On the basis of this type of pressure from NGO groups, the change in the U.S. position, and the desire to avoid further negative publicity, the South African pharmaceutical firms unconditionally dropped the case against the government in April 2001 and announced that it would cover the legal costs incurred by the South African government.[55]

Although the significance of this case should not be overlooked, it is important to note that in other less publicized cases developing countries were less successful in opposing developed countries' pressure. For example, in the late 1990s the government of Thailand was determined to produce a generic version of an antiretroviral drug, but this was met with threats of trade sanctions by the USTR. This type of pressure was effective in convincing the Thai government not to follow through with its plans to produce generic drugs.[56]

The Doha Declaration on TRIPS and Public Health

The fourth WTO Ministerial Conference took place in November 2001 in Doha, Qatar. It was an important conference for many aspects of the international trade regime, and particularly so for IP rights and public health. In the lead-up to the conference, negotiations on the TRIPS agreement were requested by a bloc of African member states. The request for these talks was not based on a desire to change TRIPS articles relating to public health; the developing nations, in general, felt that clauses 30 and 31 (apart from the domestic-production section outlined in Article 31(f)) provided sufficient leeway to provide for the health of their citizenry. What concerned the developing countries were the obstacles that the developed countries imposed when the developing states tried to employ the prerogatives in the accord.[57] In the words of a commentator, the compulsory licensing clause in the TRIPS agreement "was intended as a lifeline. But in practice, any country reaching for it has been handcuffed by US trade negotiators."[58]

Thus, leading up to the 2001 Doha WTO meeting the developing nations desired a clear, unambiguous restatement of what they were legally allowed to do under TRIPS to protect public health. The key policy document that emerged from the meeting on this issue was the Declaration on the TRIPS agreement and Public Health (commonly referred to as the Doha Declaration). The seven-article Declaration largely satisfied the goals of the developing countries and their NGO allies. The key provisions included the following points:

- The WTO should recognize "the gravity of the public health problems afflicting many developing and least-developed countries, especially those resulting from HIV/AIDS, tuberculosis, malaria and other epidemics." (Article 1)
- WTO and TRIPS should "be part of the wider national and international action to address these problems." (Article 2)
- Protection of IP is important for the development of new medicines, but it should be recognized that such protection can raise

prices such that residents of developing countries cannot afford them. (Article 3)

- "The Agreement can and should be interpreted and implemented in a manner supportive of WTO members' right to protect public health and, in particular, to promote access to medicines for all." (Article 4)
- "Each member has the right to grant compulsory licenses and the freedom to determine the grounds upon which such licenses are granted." (Article 5b)
- "Each member has the right to determine what constitutes a national emergency . . ." (Article 5c)
- Doha also extended the time frame for the implementation of TRIPS patent rules on pharmaceutical products for least developed countries from 2006 to 2016. (Article 7)

As the earlier noted articles demonstrate, the Doha Declaration was a significant victory for the developing nations. In fact, it "marked a watershed in international trade demonstrated that a rules-based trading system should be compatible with public health interests."[59] As a result "[p]ublic health advocates welcome[d] the Doha Declaration as an important achievement because it gave primacy to public health over private intellectual property and clarified WTO members' rights to use TRIPS safeguards."[60]

Interestingly, the anthrax attacks that occurred in the wake of September 11, 2001 proved to be a crucial event that the developing country bloc was able to use to strengthen its negotiating position at Doha. As the scale of the attacks was unknown, the U.S. government became concerned that vast amounts of antibiotics could be necessary to treat victims of anthrax poisoning. The most effective drug in treating anthrax is *ciprofloxacin* or Cipro and is produced and patented by Bayer. As the cost of buying numerous doses of Cipro at the patented price would have been astronomical, the U.S. government openly threatened to use compulsory licensing to ensure that they could produce and purchase sufficient quantities of the drug. Although the U.S. government did not actually issue the license, they were able to use this threat to negotiate a significant reduction in the price of the drug. At the Doha Meeting, which took place just a few weeks after the anthrax attacks, the developing countries made the most of the fact that U.S. government officials had hypocritically threatened to use compulsory licensing, when they had actively harassed Brazil and South Africa for precisely the same action. This greatly enhanced the credibility of the developing bloc and, in turn, it helped to ensure that the Doha Declaration largely reflected the desires of the developing countries and their NGO allies.[61]

However, a major limitation of the Doha Declaration was that it did not clarify the previously mentioned domestic market issue regarding compulsory licensing. Article 6 of the Declaration was drafted in specific response to TRIPS Article 31(f), which states that compulsory licenses must be issued for the state's domestic audience (i.e., its own residents). As previously noted, this clause nullifies the power to issue compulsory licenses for all states that have no functioning pharmaceutical industry. Although Article 6 did not provide a solution to this issue, it officially recognized the problem and called on the TRIPS Council to "find an expeditious solution to this problem." (The council was requested to find a solution by 2002; however, the decision on paragraph 6 on Doha was not released until August 2003.)[62]

WTO Decision on Paragraph 6 of Doha

The solution to the domestic market requirement outlined in TRIPS Article 31(f) took nearly a decade to achieve. Debates on 31(f) began shortly after the TRIPS agreement entered into force in 1995. Many expected that the compulsory licensing issue would be resolved entirely by the Doha Declaration; however, that did not happen. Two years and many failed negotiation attempts followed the Doha Declaration's call for an "expeditious" solution to the issue. On August 30, 2003 the TRIPS council finally announced the accepted resolution, under the title WTO Decision on Paragraph 6, in reference to the section of the Doha Declaration on TRIPS and Public Health that discussed the domestic audience provision.

Article 2 of the decision was extremely significant. According to the article, "The obligations of an exporting member under Article 31(f) of the TRIPS agreement shall be waived with respect to the grant by it of a compulsory licence to the extent necessary for the purposes of production of a pharmaceutical product(s) and its export to an eligible importing member(s)."[63] This means that WTO member states no longer have to produce medicines under a compulsory license predominantly for their domestic audience; rather a member state is allowed to produce a patented medicine, under a compulsory license, and then export it to a least developed country that does not have domestic capacity to produce the drugs itself. There are, of course, limits on issuing and usage of a compulsory license that were outlined by the WTO decision. When a member state feels the need to issue a compulsory license, it must notify the WTO TRIPS council. This notification must include all details of the compulsory license, including the name of the drug and the amount needed. The council must then determine that the importing member state (i.e., the one issuing the license) is not capable of producing the product itself.[64] Another clause was included in the decision on paragraph 6 to address the concern of the pharmaceutical industry that drugs produced under a compulsory license would be smuggled into developed countries and sold on the black market for less than the patent price. Thus, Article 2(b) (ii) of the decision states that all drugs produced in this fashion must be uniquely labeled to differentiate them from the same drug produced under patent.[65]

The decision by the TRIPS council to waive the "domestic-requirement provision" and to facilitate "compulsory licensing" was undoubtedly a significant victory for the developing countries and their NGO allies. "As during the original negotiations on the TRIPS Agreement the US and the EC took the initiative during the paragraph 6 talks. However, unlike the original TRIPS negotiations, the paragraph 6 process was also marked by a far greater degree of involvement on the part of NGOs acting in support of the developing country cause."[66] In fact, as *The Economist* pointed out shortly after the 2003 WTO decision was approved, "The long tussle over generic drugs shows that a united front of developing countries can hold its own against Big Pharma."[67] Nevertheless, many NGOs were not completely satisfied with the results. This is because several prominent NGOs, including MSF, the Consumer Project on Technology (CPTech), Health Action International (HAI), and Oxfam, lobbied hard to have the TRIPS council adopt the European Parliament Amendment 196 to the European Medicines Directive as the solution to this issue:

> This amendment provided the precise solution that the TRIPS Council should have adopted. "Manufacturing shall be allowed if the medicinal product is intended for export to a third country that has issued a compulsory licence for the product, or where a patent is not in force and if there is a request to that effect of the competent public health authorities of that third country." The European Parliament Amendment 196 is only 52 words, but it provides exactly the correct policy framework to balance the objectives of Paragraph 4 of the Doha Declaration, while protecting the legitimate interests of patent owners.[68]

The August 30, 2003 decision, argued the NGOs, was a "gift bound in red tape." Technically it provided what the developing nations needed; however, according to several NGOs active in this issue area, the decision increased the level of bureaucracy and the likelihood that states could be pressured, bi-laterally or otherwise, into not producing compulsory licenses, even if their public health needs warranted it.[69]

However, the developing countries and their NGO allies did attain several concessions within the paragraph 6 negotiations that the developed countries and their pharmaceutical lobbies had been keen to avoid. The decision marks a step back from the more restrictive paragraph 6 solution desired by the United States and the European Union in that it does not limit the diseases for which compulsory licenses can be issued, and it does not require a declaration of national emergency. Thus the paragraph 6 statement essentially supported the developing country position and further entrenched the shift toward limiting the scope of IP rights when global public health is at stake. The shift has taken place at the multilateral level within the WTO and can be counted at least a partial victory for the developing nations and their NGO allies. However, the reaction to this shift in the regime at the multilateral level has been yet another shift in forum by the United States. "[T]he US reaction to developing country success on access-to-medicines issues at the WTO has been to shift negotiations on this subject to bilateral and regional fora. It has succeeded in negotiating significant restrictions on the ability of generic producers to introduce medicines in bilateral and regional deals."[70] Since 2003, the United States, with the support of its IP business allies, has been "pursuing an aggressive course of bilateral and regional intellectual property and investment agreements that threaten to undermine any broader gains for developing countries seeking access to drugs, seeds, and educational materials."[71] Recent Free Trade Agreements, negotiated bilaterally with developing nations have consistently included provisions that restrict the use of the TRIPS safeguards.[72]

NGOs and Essential Medicines: Changing the Nature of the Debate

There can be no doubt of the significant impact that NGOs have had on the politicization of the access to essential medicines issue. Particularly, NGOs that focus on human rights have shifted the debate over property rights versus access to medicines from the boardroom to the public forum. Over the past several decades, the notion of access to essential medicines has become a subissue within the broader agenda to promote, enhance, and entrench the concept of universal human rights. David Fidler argues that this trend began after World War II with the establishment of the post–Westphalian governance system. The Westphalian system, which was founded on principles of nonintervention and impermeable sovereignty, operated from the mid-nineteenth century through the post–World War II era. "In this framework, infectious diseases were conceptualized as exogenous threats to a country's public health and economic interests, with threats to economic interests playing the more powerful role in international cooperation on infectious diseases."[73] Throughout this period, states were unequivocally the dominant political actor within international relations; state-based relations and issues of nationality were paramount. Neither issues regarding individual human rights, nor issues that cut across broad socioeconomic lines were on the radar screen of the world powers at that time.

Since the mid-1940s, however, there has been a gradual yet fundamental restructuring of the global political governance system. Multilateral institutions with global membership, most significantly UN bodies, have carved out important—albeit contested—roles within international relations and nonstate actors have been playing an increasingly important role in world politics in the decades since the war, with an exponential increase in their influence since the emergence of the Internet in the 1990s. Such changes have been a reflection of a shift in perceptions regarding individuals and their inalienable rights. Regarding public health in general and infectious diseases specifically, the post–Westphalian era has been characterized by the belief that "infectious diseases [are] threats to human rights, rather than exogenous threats to a state's interests and power."[74] The notion of health as a human rights issue emerged for the first time in the constitution of the WHO, which entered into force in 1948. According to the constitution "the enjoyment of the highest attainable standard of health is a fundamental human right" and "the health of all peoples is fundamental to attaining peace and security."[75] These statements marked an important change in views regarding health and illness, and opened the door for actors other than states to become involved in health issues. The entrance of nonstate actors into the health sphere has dramatically altered the playing field. Obviously state power and state economic interests are not the concern of many NGOs, and they have broadened the scope of the public health debate to include values such as morality, justice, and fundamental human rights.

Although these terms are now widely used regarding many public health issues, they are used nowhere more frequently than within the debate on access to essential medicines. By employing powerful and evocative slogans such as "lives versus profit," NGOs have attained the moral high-ground in this debate, and have been successful in negotiating with pharmaceutical companies because they have great clout with the international media, and can do significant damage to a firm's reputation if they so choose. The legal battle in South Africa is a prime example of the NGO's use of the threat of negative publicity as a negotiating tool. The most active NGOs involved in this access to essential medicines issue are MSF, CPTech, HAI, ActUP, and Oxfam, all of which have a well-established reputation on the global health scene, and all of which have virtually uncontested legitimacy in challenging the IP rights regime.

Since the early to mid-1990s, the nongovernmental role in the global health sphere has predominantly been one of advocacy. Since the turn of the millennium, however, several NGOs have carved a new niche for themselves in the health sphere. There is nothing NGOs are better at than filling a void and activists new to the health scene were quick to identify the gaping void in drug research and development regarding diseases prevalent in poor countries that was mentioned earlier in this chapter. As a result, in recent years many new initiatives have been launched that are conducting research into new drugs, vaccines, and treatment options. Some of the most prominent among these partnerships are the Drugs for Neglected Diseases Initiative (DNDi), the GAVI Alliance, and the International AIDS Vaccine Initiative (IAVI).[76] These groups are able to coordinate scientific expertise from the private sector, with financial contributions from governments and philanthropic sector.[77] "Significant new hope is placed in the relatively new model of PPPs which bring together R&D for neglected diseases by matching existing capacity, expertise, and resources in both the pubic and private sectors on specific projects or disease."[78] By the end of 2004, these research groups had identified 60 potentially viable drug treatment research projects for 7 different neglected diseases, which indicates that this hope is not misplaced.[79]

All this emphasizes how NGOS have expanded and entrenched their role in global health. They have moved from a contained role of agents of advocacy into the realm of hard science, where they are formulating groups of medical experts and actually creating new drugs. Importantly for the access to medicines issue, drugs created by nonprofit groups such as the MSF supported DNDi will not be put under patent and so will be affordable for those living in poor countries.[80]

Conclusion: The Evolution of Access

As with the previous two chapters, our concluding comments in this chapter fall into two sections. The first section concerns the status of the regime, and the second section concerns the factors that have influenced the evolution of the regime. The most fundamental change in this regime has been a marked increase in international governance activities. Virtually all aspects of this issue have attracted more attention and collaboration in recent years. In the first chapter of this book, we identified four general strategies that states and nonstate actors use to achieve governance. Two of them—rule-making and the promotion of compliance—have increasingly been used to great effect in this particular facet of the global health regime. At the outset, rule-making was the strategy selected by the IP rights lobby because they wanted to achieve their goals of an expanded and codified set of laws that would guarantee increased profits for the IP industry. Rule-making in a multilateral forum through a legally binding international treaty was deemed to be the most effective way to ensure that IP firms could garner profits at a global level and to ensure that state governments would have a mechanism for enforcing compliance with the new rules.

In most aspects of the public health issue-area, soft law is the modus operandi of key actors. One reason for this is that global institutions, such as the WHO, have limited power or legal authorization to enforce their recommendations and regulations.[81] Perhaps even more importantly, these institutions have no power to punish states or other actors for noncompliance with the rules. This lack of legal authorization to compel or punish almost always means that soft law agreements based on guidelines or recommendations are favored by global institutions. However, soft law has not only been chosen because it is the only option; in many instances, soft law has been preferable to hard law because it allows for more flexibility in dealing with fast-paced and evolving areas of law: "Soft law can fill the gaps of a hard law instrument without the need for entering into the laborious procedure of treaty amendment."[82]

Nevertheless, regarding IP rights, states and industry, particularly in developed countries, were adamant that the lengthy procedure of negotiating treaties was worthwhile. For pharmaceutical firms, the internationally binding hard law regulations, outlined in TRIPS provide legal guarantees that their patent rights would be respected for at least two decades. This is extremely significant when a company has to decide whether to invest hundreds of millions of dollars into developing a new drug. If there were no assurances of a reasonable return on investment in the long run, there would be no financial incentives to proceed with research and development into new medicines. As this chapter has demonstrated, the complication with this perspective arises when legitimate industry requirements for strict patent laws lead to unnecessary illness, death, and suffering for citizens of poor countries.

The TRIPS agreement provided legally binding loopholes or safeguards that ostensibly allow developed and developing countries to balance the right of pharmaceutical companies to make profits and the need for inhabitants of developing countries to access drugs they need to survive, that is, through patent denial, compulsory licensing, and parallel importation. In the decade since TRIPS entered into force, many developing countries have attempted to exploit these loopholes, but have been met with bilateral pressure from certain industrialized countries, including the United States and some European Union countries, designed to force them away from using the exception clauses within the TRIPS agreement.[83] Thus, developing countries (and their NGO allies) have a vested interest in pursuing the hard law option regarding access to essential medicines. Initially, the developed nations wanted profit guarantees (in the form of augmented patent rights) to be codified into international trade law. Now, the developing nations and NGOs active within the access issue are trying to use those clauses negotiated within the original TRIPS agreement legally to enforce their rights not to purchase patented drugs. Thus the access issue provides interesting insights into how both sides of this debate have successfully employed the strategy of rule-making at different times through the development of hard law.

The second category of concluding comments describes the factors that have influenced the evolution of governance in this area. The three main factors are recognition of interdependencies, increased knowledge, and evolving institutions. Interdependencies are an important aspect of any regime, as they are usually the catalyst and driving force for collaboration. Given that the original treaty was international in scope, cooperation between states to develop and implement TRIPS was a necessary precursor. The nature of cooperation remained global, but altered in scope with the increasing activity of NGO in the early years of the twenty-first century. Recognition of the consequences of increased patent protection on global human health, and specifically the health of citizens of poor countries, was an extremely important factor in developing the governance strategies and institutions that have been used in this issue area.

Second, both sides of this debate have successfully used new knowledge to shift the IP negotiations in their favor. IP industries were threatened by advances in technology that made it easy for new inventions to be copied. Therefore the IP lobby pushed the debate for increased IP protection into the WTO forum, as the members were susceptible to the argument that IP must be protected if the industry is to advance and grow. The developing countries and relevant NGOs shifted the debate away from the trade arena and reframed it as a human rights issue. They made calculated and strategic choices to attract global media representatives to their cause as well. In this aspect, NGOs also used the increased knowledge and understanding of the issue area to help frame their debate. They used information about the HIV/AIDS epidemic and on how millions would not be able to afford patented anti-retroviral drugs to reshape the nature of the debate.

Third, changes in the character and role of different international institutions have also had an important impact on shaping this regime. Most notable has been the increased role of nongovernmental actors since 1990. These entities, which were barely on the radar screen of states in the late twentieth century, have developed to a point where they not only have a legitimate voice in the debate, but they are actually helping to define the terms and nature of the debate itself. NGOs in the access issue have carved out an important role for themselves and are now deemed to be legitimate members of the international community. Along the same lines, public-private partnerships that are conducting research on drug development are a new but increasingly important member in the access community. These partnerships, which are often instigated by NGOs, were designed to fill a void in the drug research environment, and although they have only been in existence for a short period, they have already been accepted as having a valuable role to play in this field.

International organizations, especially the WHO and the WTO have played active, albeit contested, roles in the access to medicines deliberations over the past decade. In particular, the TRIPS treaty has in some ways strengthened the WTO and in some ways weakened it. Initially, the WTO was deemed a powerful governance institution as it could influence the rules and the leverage of key actors. However, as the WTO has moved away from full support of the developed country, pro-IP stance, there has been a shift by these actors toward bilateral trade agreements and the WIPO. Nevertheless, the support of the trade loopholes in TRIPS has meant that developing countries are more comfortable working in a mul-tilateral forum such as WTO, and so issues within the health arena may lead to more cooperation and collaboration in other areas as confidence is instilled in most member states.

As discussed earlier, the subfield of global health governance that deals with IP rights and access to essential medicines has become particularly complex in recent years. Similar to the other two subfields of health gov-ernance discussed in the previous two chapters, governance has increased and intensified in this area since the mid-1980s. As this regime evolves we have witnessed increased activity and increased attention on the issue area and as the debate over patent rights versus access rights continues, the regime will hopefully move beyond the current zero-sum game and toward a scenario in which both sides can emerge as victors.

CHAPTER 6

HEALTH AND GLOBAL GOVERNANCE: CONCLUDING PERSPECTIVES

In the first chapter of this study, literature on the nature of global governance is reviewed. The salient features concerning the existence of formal and informal institutions and rules that are created to manage the interdependencies among governmental and nongovernmental actors. Of particular relevance to this study is Oran Young's statement that "the demand for governance in world affairs has never been greater" and that it has become "difficult for states or other autonomous actors to isolate themselves from events occurring in other parts of the world, however much they might wish to do so."[1] As James Rosenau indicated in his seminal book on the topic, *Governance without Government*, both the concept and practical manifestation of governance transcends the scope of governmental activities. Although state governments are an integral part of governance procedures, they also include other groups that are becoming increasingly important and active within the public realm, including civil society groups, private transnational corporations, and wealthy foundations. Nowhere is this multi-actor feature of governance more prominent than within the regime to combat infectious diseases.

The health governance regime (regarding infectious diseases) originated in the early twentieth century as a weak system of often flouted rules governing the behavior of ships and national health authorities. Over the course of subsequent decades, the regime gradually increased in strength and level of activity; however, it was not until the 1990s that global health governance increased to a significant degree. The past 20 years have been characterized by more activity, more complexity, and a much greater degree of politicization of health politics. The field became highly politicized when major disease threats started to emerge, and when economic interests, especially involving conflicts between developing and developed countries, became highly embedded in the development of global health governance. Another causal factor behind the high level of politicization in this field is the existence of multiple actors and goals. The primary and most obvious goal of health governance is to reduce the negative impact of disease on humankind by treating illnesses and preventing small outbreaks from becoming global pandemics. However, from its early years, actors within this governance regime pursued other goals such as facilitating trade and improving overall economic development, global security, and the realization of human rights.

This chapter is divided into three sections. The first section is descriptive and focuses on the first major thematic question of the book as set forth in chapter 1: How has global governance to control the emergence and spread of infectious diseases evolved; and how has the evolving governance system impacted global health conditions? To this end, the section provides an overview of the development of the three strategies of surveillance, assistance, and rule-making discussed in detail in chapters 3, 4, and 5. The next section is explanatory in nature and thus attempts to answer the second thematic question: What developments and conditions have particularly shaped international health governance? The section reflects on the most important features of global health governance and the key factors that continue to shape it. Thus, section 1 is a description of what the infectious disease governance regime looks like, and section 2 is an explanation as to why it looks the way it does. The final section provides a commentary on the contributions of health governance to health conditions in the world, and reflects on what this study contributes to the analysis of global regimes and governance.

Major Characteristics of Contemporary Global Health Governance

Governance is carried out by global actors in a variety of ways, and these actors favor different strategies depending on their interests, goals, and power. Furthermore, preferred strategies can change with time and with fluctuations in the regime, and actors often use a combination of strategies to achieve their desired goals. There are a number of features of international collaboration that are important to explore in describing the contours of global governance. Specifically, these are the three key control strategies on which political actors have focused within the health governance system—surveillance, the provision of financial and material assistance, and rule-making. Arguably, the most important feature defining a governance regime is the nature of its control strategies and actors' ability to employ them successfully.

The importance of the *surveillance* strategy was recognized from the early years of the International Sanitary Regulations (ISR), as knowledge regarding the source, nature, and severity of an outbreak is essential in curtailing its spread. However, surveillance systems remained extremely weak for many decades because numerous states were cautious in releasing information regarding disease outbreaks owing to fears of embargoes of their goods and nationals. This tendency toward restricting the flow of information between states lasted until the latter part of the twentieth century when advances in information technology and the proliferation of nonstate actors made it increasingly difficult for states to block the release of information regarding outbreaks. The development of more transparent surveillance systems is predominantly supported by industrialized countries as they fear the health and economic ramifications of disease outbreaks originating in poor regions of the world (such as Ebola, SARS, and influenza) traveling to their territories. Nonindustrialized countries also fear ramifications of outbreaks. However, they are generally opposed to being responsible for the high cost of developing surveillance mechanisms and also (legitimately) fear trade and travel restrictions that may be imposed on them if news of outbreaks is disseminated. Despite objections from some nonindustrialized states, by the mid-1990s strong programs for gathering and disseminating information, such as ProMED, GPHIN, and WHO-led surveillance initiatives, had become firmly established.

At its core, this study is about the nature of multilateralism within health politics, and surveillance is a critical aspect of the regime. Global disease surveillance, by its very nature, requires a multilateral approach. In today's increasingly interconnected world—where borders are crossed by more than 2 million people each day and international travel occurs within the incubation period of practically all known infectious diseases—unilateral and domestic initiatives to monitor diseases are insufficient to eliminate the risk of a global pandemic. As the SARS epidemic of 2003 clearly demonstrated, it is essential that outbreak information is shared promptly and internationally to reduce panic and the likelihood of excessive reactions. Probably the most significant event in the evolution of the multilateral approach to disease control was the formal creation of the Global Outbreak Alert and Response Network (GOARN) in 2000. Comprising 120 governmental and nongovernmental actors, it is the largest and most important outbreak control organization. The creation of GOARN underscores the fact that "no single institution or country has all of the capacities to respond to international public health emergencies caused by epidemics and by new and emerging infectious diseases."[2] Effective surveillance requires transnational information sharing and high levels of cooperation among state governments and, increasingly, among nonstate actors. Although there are still serious gaps within the system, it can be argued that multilateral efforts regarding surveillance are the strongest and best developed of the three strategies in the infectious disease regime.

The second strategic approach that has become central to disease management is the provision of *financial and material assistance*. The rationale behind this approach is that diseases cannot spread internationally if they are first controlled or contained domestically. Interestingly, this approach emerged in its earliest form in the first decades of the twentieth century through the efforts of nonstate actors such as church-sponsored missionary programs and the activities of the U.S.-based Rockefeller Foundation. It grew in prominence through the assistance activities of the League of Nations Health Organization in the 1920s, and it was also present in the early WHO policies immediately following World War II.[3] An important feature of health assistance is that a high percentage (approximately two-thirds) has consistently been provided via bilateral channels. Nevertheless, the number and scope of multilateral aid initiatives has grown dramatically since the 1990s. Of particular relevance to this point is the recent establishment and growth of multi-actor global health partnerships (GHPs), which bring together the resources of private and public actors. GHPs have quickly become an entrenched feature of contemporary global health governance. Concerns regarding transparency, accountability, and representation within GHPs are legitimate and serious; nevertheless there are numerous specific examples of these types of institutions having a significant and positive impact on disease rates in developing countries.[4] In fact, many health professionals view GHPs as a potentially effective mechanism for filling some of the most serious gaps in health governance such as neglected diseases and drug development issues.[5]

The establishment of GHPs reflects the general trend of the increasing importance of nonstate actors within global health governance. Respected and well-known NGOs, such as MSF, Oxfam, and the Red Cross, have had a strong influence on the humanitarian debate within health governance as well as access to essential medicines. Rich private foundations, particularly the Bill & Melinda Gates Foundation, the Rockefeller Foundation, the Carter Center, and many others, have emerged as significant sources of funding and political influence and, as such, they are able to alter perceptions regarding priorities within health governance. Private companies, particularly pharmaceutical companies, are also playing an active role in providing assistance in the form of charitable donations of drugs to developing countries and promoting the construction of internationally binding trade agreements regarding pharmaceutical products. Thus, although bilateral assistance programs, such as PEPFAR,[6] still account for the bulk of financial and material aid, multilateral activities within this sector are increasing significantly. This trend has been promoted by the need for coordination of diverse funding and material resources and the need to exploit the comparative advantage of various types of actors within the health arena.

International organizations (IOs) have been major sources of multilateral development assistance for decades. Rich member states generally support this strategy because the voting structures within IOs gives them leverage over the distribution of funds. The strongest intergovernmental bodies have always been the development banks, especially the World Bank; and their weighted voting systems give their wealthy members an effective veto power. In the case of the World Health Organization (WHO) most of its funding now comes from extra-budgetary accounts that are controlled by the donors. Similarly, GHPs commonly possess decision-making mechanisms that provide the major donors (be they states, foundations, or private companies) with veto power over their financial contributions. In fact, most international institutions operate by a de facto consensus voting system. On this point Oran Young has commented that "[i]nstitutional bargaining in international society normally operates under a consensus rule that gives the participants an incentive to put together packages of provisions that will prove attractive to as many interests as possible."[7] This pattern of consensus decision making is, in fact, the informal procedure used in the WHO despite the fact that the formal procedure is one of majoritarian voting.[8]

In the early years of global health governance a great deal of attention was paid to *rule-making* regarding sanitary standards in ships and ports. The developed countries were not only concerned with preventing the spread of diseases into their countries, but they were also opposed to states' adoption of stringent measures that could curtail the flow of commerce. In fact, the major focus of the conferences that took place in the early twentieth century was to prevent states from adopting measures that exceeded those in the ISR. However, the developed countries failed in that the early versions of the ISR included a variety of loopholes that allowed countries to adopt more stringent measures in specific circumstances.

States and NGOs significantly increased their influence in developing guidelines (or soft law recommendations) regarding remedial and prescriptive measures to treat diseases in the late 1900s. Within the WHO, the World Health Assembly took some small steps in this direction, but certain constituent bodies, including WHO Collaborating Centers,[9] were particularly active in developing and publicizing medical recommendations for treatment protocols. Owing to the widely recognized medical expertise of WHO-affiliated groups, these recommendations have often become standard treatment protocols. Interestingly, many GHPs that are focused on combating a specific disease have begun to issue recommendations regarding prevention and treatment as well. Even the World Bank has assumed some important roles in the area of treatment standards and protocols, especially regarding the construction of a functioning health system and infrastructure development. Thus, although rule-making with regard to the actual treatment of diseases cannot be enforced by any one body or group at a global level, certain actors within global health governance have garnered sufficient legitimacy and perceived expertise that they can, in fact, develop de facto rules and regulations for disease treatment that are voluntarily adopted by medical practitioners around the world.

As the earlier section indicates, although the record of global health institutions' promotion of compliance with rules and guidelines is often ineffective, there are some areas where their influence has been relatively strong. Most international health rules relate to how states and medical authorities should act in managing disease outbreaks, and these rules take the form of guidelines or recommendations. If governmental authorities and medical experts follow organizational directives, it is generally in their own best interest. In most cases, states are not subject to formal sanctions if they do not comply; however, there are some circumstances in which actors other than states of origin suffer because of the spread of diseases from other countries. In such cases, the parties that could potentially suffer from outbreaks often apply diplomatic pressure on countries where infectious diseases are endemic. In recent years there have been some cases where WHO criticized or threatened to criticize delinquent states if they did not comply with certain rules (especially those related to reporting). For example, during the SARS and Avian flu crises between 2002 and 2006, WHO officials threatened to criticize states in the public media if they did not provide information on the outbreaks. The states that were being criticized eventually complied in response to the WHO threat of "naming and shaming."[10] It is, however, important to point out that a good number of countries complied with the recommendations of WHO bodies voluntarily because of a recognition that compliance was in their own interests. If any parties suffered from the failure to comply with rules, it was the countries where the disease outbreaks occurred.

Within global health governance, a major conflict that has become increasingly prominent over the past decade is the development of a trade regime that will clarify and codify rules regarding intellectual property rights but that will also permit fair access to medicines for the world's poor. As discussed in chapter 5, since 1995 developing-country members of the World Trade Organization (WTO) have been lobbying to secure pharmaceutical companies' and developed states' compliance with an interpretation of the Agreement on Trade-Related Aspects of Intellectual Property Rights (TRIPS) that allows for the easy exploitation of the health protection loopholes integrated into the agreement. The compulsory licensing clause within TRIPS, which allows patent rules on pharmaceutical products to be bypassed in a public health emergency, was designed to protect public health, but the use of the clause by developing countries was severely restricted owing to threats of trade and diplomatic penalties by some developed countries (but particularly the United States, which had the support of some prominent transnational pharmaceutical firms). A combination of pressure from the developing country members of the WTO and an effective public relations campaign by some powerful NGOs (including CPTech, MSF, and Oxfam) forced the developed countries and their pharmaceutical firm supporters to relinquish certain claims in some significant legal battles of the late twentieth century. The access to essential medicines campaign also directly influenced the terms of the Doha Declaration on TRIPS and Public Health that was released in 2001 and which highlighted the health-loopholes in the agreement. The Doha Declaration solidified the public health protection elements of TRIPS, but the agreement itself has since been undermined by the recent U.S. pursuit of bilateral trade agreements between it and developing nations that can supersede TRIPS and often include more stringent patent regulations. The essential medicines debate is an interesting example of how rule-making operates within global health governance, but it is clear that an appropriate balance between patent protection and access to medicines has not yet been achieved, and, hence this will continue to be an area of conflict for health governance actors for the foreseeable future.

The above synopsis of the three strategies that are used by various actors within health governance should provide some insight into the complex and contested nature of this regime. Contemporary global health governance is complicated and messy; it is comprised of numerous and varied actors with competing values, interests, and motivations. Even the goals of establishing a strong health governance regime are varied and contested. For some, the predominant goal of a strong health governance regime is to reduce the incidences of death by infectious diseases; for others it is to bring about improved economic development; for others it is to increase security against the threat of infectious diseases; and for yet others it is to develop a health policy that does not impede the flow of global trade and commerce. Depending on which goals or values the actors prefer, they will employ different control strategies.

Factors That Shape Global Health Governance

There are a variety of factors that are currently shaping the global health governance regime to combat infectious diseases. These include the incidence and pattern of diseases, medical knowledge of the causes of and appropriate responses to different diseases, changes in information technology, varied patterns of interest among actors, and the institutional setting in which health governance actors operate. Each of these factors is discussed in the following text.[11]

A very important factor in shaping health governance has always been the *global incidence and pattern of diseases*. The early deliberations on global health collaboration in the nineteenth century occurred when much of the world was experiencing or had experienced devastating pandemics of cholera and other serious diseases. Memories of the devastating Spanish Flu pandemic prompted the development of the first global disease surveillance system, the WHO Global Influenza Surveillance Network in 1952. The high death rate and horrific effects of smallpox led to the first and only disease eradication effort in human history in the 1970s. In addition, the current global AIDS pandemic has acted as the catalyst for literally dozens of health assistance initiatives, treatment plans, and drug and vaccine programs. These are just a handful of examples that demonstrate that health governance is reactive and spurred by crises. Governance activities regarding infectious diseases are a reaction to and reflection of the global spread and distribution of diseases, particularly diseases that have a high mortality rate.

Since health experts and officials react to disease outbreaks, knowledge of disease patterns directly alters the nature and shape of the governance regime. This fact helps us to understand why health governance activities to control infectious diseases have expanded in number and strength in recent years. We are currently experiencing a resurgence of infectious diseases both in terms of new diseases like HIV/AIDS and Ebola, which have been emerging at a rate of one per year since the 1980s, and old diseases such as malaria and tuberculosis that are developing resistance to known treatment methods and are thus once again posing a grave threat to global human health. In recognition of this fact, programs to combat infectious diseases are garnering more attention and support.

The exponential growth in scientific and *medical knowledge* over the past hundred years means that we now know more about illness and health than at any point in human history. Medical professionals now have the knowledge and capacity to treat and cure diseases that used to decimate entire civilizations, and this has not only made medical interventions technically feasible but also morally necessary. The technical capability to alleviate human suffering has greatly facilitated WHO's efforts to promote its most basic principle—that health is a fundamental human right.

When the health governance regime first began, it was merely a collection of weakly enforced rules regarding the entry of ships into ports in an attempt to prevent the spread of disease. Now that we have the knowledge and capability to cure and control diseases, governance activities have expanded to include remedial health programs, vaccine research and delivery programs, education initiatives, and the development of recommendations regarding the prevention and control of diseases. The three strategies of surveillance, assistance, and rule-making all rely, to varying degrees, on knowledge of how to prevent, treat, and cure diseases, and expansion of the regime could not occur without a sufficient scientific basis.

It should be noted here that although medical knowledge is an important support for health governance programs, it can also inhibit collaborative multilateral disease control efforts, as increased medical knowledge can lead government officials to believe that they can care for the health of their populace single-handedly. In the twentieth century, government health officials and medical experts became increasingly pessimistic about their ability to seal borders from the spread of diseases, but at the same time they became gradually more optimistic about their ability to control disease outbreaks among their own citizens with the aid of modern medicines and public health systems. This belief has, at times, hampered the development of multilateral efforts.

In previous discussions of surveillance it was noted how the inability of states to obtain information on disease outbreaks in other countries meant that the international community could do little to control medical emergencies throughout the world. It was only when developments in *information technology* prompted a new level of transparency in the world of infectious diseases that major steps in global health collaboration regarding surveillance and outbreak containment were possible. As seen during the 2003 SARS crisis, governments can still hinder the spread of information about diseases for a short period, but it is becoming increasingly difficult for them to entirely prevent the dissemination of information on outbreaks.

Contrary to what many international observers may think, international health collaboration began in a very conflictual political environment. The international sanitary conferences of the last half of the nineteenth century pitted groups of developed and developing countries against each other on several key issues. The Western European countries supported controlling the international spread of diseases, but they were more interested in assuring that controls over shipping and port authorities not interfere with the flow of commerce. The developing countries of Asia and the Middle East, on the other hand, wanted the freedom to impose strong regulations on Western ships and travelers as well as on their own societies. This type of conflict regarding *interests and values* in health governance has been a constant characteristic of the regime.

In the contemporary era, global health governance is characterized by a high level of politicization. This is fundamentally because health governance— particularly with respect to infectious diseases—does not operate in isolation from other issue areas. Changes in global health policy can have a great impact on other governance spheres including human rights, commerce, economic development, and security. The opposite is also true in that changes in any of these other spheres frequently impact how health is governed. This means that actors operating within the health regime must be sensitive to issues in related spheres of governance and vice versa. Extrapolating from this, it is important to recognize that decisions regarding the shape and nature of global health governance do not merely rely on what will make humans healthier, but also what impact those decisions will have on other spheres of global politics. To understand the contested nature of global health politics, it is necessary to understand the multiplicity of interests that motivate actors in this and related fields.

A final, but extraordinarily important, factor that has contributed to the shaping of global health governance is the *global institutional setting*. For much of this century the dominant institutions in international decision making were states and intergovernmental organizations or what has often been referred to as the "Westphalian international order."[12] Such bodies, of course, still exist, but they have been joined by a plethora of nongovernmental (or civil society) organizations as well as hybrid partnerships that bring together states, intergovernmental organizations, nongovernmental organizations (NGOs), and private actors.

The explosion of nongovernmental bodies has brought about a fundamental reshaping of the global institutional order. As two scholars, who have analyzed nongovernmental bodies, commented, "States remain the master builders, but the new global management structure—sometimes effective, often not—is increasingly a device built by many hands pulling many levers."[13] This comment is very accurate and indicates the extent to which NGOs have brought about a new political structure. One need only to contemplate the fact that the number of NGOs increased from 6,000 to 26,000 between 1900 and 2000 to grasp the size of this new institutional structure.[14] The numerical increase opened the door to a much larger influence of NGOs and hybrid GHPs. It has also opened the door to states' increasingly using NGOs as channels for their assistance to the developing world. In fact, governments now channel more assistance to the third world through NGOs than they channel directly from themselves.[15]

The increase in power, resources, and influence of NGOs has fundamentally altered the diplomatic processes within governance structures. Nonstate actors are now deemed legitimate actors within decision-making processes, and forums that allow for their inclusion are a necessary feature of the contemporary governance landscape. Relevant to this point, Harold Jacobson has written that IOs "provide readily available frameworks for such collaboration. They also have fixed procedures for how decisions should be taken, and governments seeking to utilize these organizations to achieve certain goals must take these procedures into account." He noted that global politics is increasingly influenced by "the enmeshment of states in webs of international organization networks" and "the necessity of bargaining and the consent of others" that they engender.[16] This comment is similar to Robert Keohane's arguments that IOs reduce uncertainty, costs of specifying and enforcing contracts, and the transaction costs of collaboration.[17] These general observations are clearly relevant to the impacts of the huge increase of international health institutions over recent decades.

Reflections on the Study of Global Governance

Although this study is centrally concerned with health governance, it is also relevant to general global governance issues. It has adopted a host of approaches and conclusions that are germane to the broad study of collaboration in international politics. The two most important of these are that descriptions of it should center on multiple control strategies and that explanations of it should recognize the importance of multiple interests of state and nonstate actors. In describing and explaining health governance, this study identifies and addresses the strategies of surveillance, the provision of assistance, and the process of rule-making. Studies of other issue areas would address different strategies particular to those regimes; however, in many cases similar strategies can be used in numerous regimes.

The discussion of surveillance in the health arena indicates how important it is not just for health, but for other issue areas as well. If political actors do not have an in-depth knowledge of the relevant international interdependencies, they are seriously circumscribed in what they can accomplish. In our present era, technological changes are doing a great deal to promote greater transparency regarding many global issues. Future studies of global governance should pay considerable attention to the transformation in surveillance capabilities that is currently occurring. General lessons regarding international assistance programs can also be drawn from recent experiences within the global health regime. In particular, innovative political developments in this policy sphere indicate the benefits of combining the efforts of different governmental and nongovernmental actors. It is almost certainly the case that governmental and nongovernmental officials will be looking increasingly to experiences in public-private partnerships as the variety of collaborative institutions and programs is so rich.

The study also highlights some of the important issues relating to rule-making that influence global governance activities. Of central importance is that a great deal of rule-making concerns the development of recommendations or guidelines—or what is often referred to as "soft law." These recommendations sometimes involve controlling the spread of harmful substances or behaviors, but they often promote mutually beneficial practices. The promotion of such beneficial practices has been greatly facilitated by the expansion of NGOs that, in cooperation with governmental actors, bring groups of experts together to craft international regimes of prescriptions and proscriptions. Although soft law has come to dominate rulemaking in many international issue areas, hard law, in the form of legally binding rules with concomitant negative sanctions, also remains an important feature of the governance landscape. There are issue areas, such as intellectual property rights, where changes require refashioning international treaties, and there are issue areas where naming and shaming are, in fact, quite effective in influencing the behaviors of actors to comply with the prescriptions of international institutions. It is interesting that very diverse organizations are involved in the promotion of compliance with both hard and soft law. They include intergovernmental bodies that have utilized the strategy of naming and shaming. Nongovernmental bodies exist in many areas of governance, but particularly in health and the environment they are performing a watchdog role of monitoring and publicly critiquing the behavior of states, development banks, and private commercial actors. The watchdog role of such institutions is often overlooked by observers, but it is very important in many policy spheres in which social welfare issues are at stake.

The earlier section explains how governance strategies used in the health sphere could also be useful in analyzing other international issue areas. Another way in which this study is broadly applicable to the study of global governance is in its analysis of the nature of contemporary multilateralism. Central to this study is the issue of why international institutions have opted for multilateral as opposed to unilateral or bilateral approaches to international issues. There are clearly a host of reasons why diverse political actors have taken the multilateral route; and it is valuable to summarize and highlight some of the trends apparent throughout the previous chapters. Multilateralism is often used when actors realize that particular problems can only be managed if numerous state and nonstate participants adopt compatible policies. For example, efforts are currently being made to assure that compatible disease surveillance programs are adopted by all or most countries to ensure that procedures and technologies effectively facilitate the exchange of information. Also, many international problems require diverse contributions from a large number of countries and organizations. That is to say, effective management requires the pooling of resources. This was certainly the case regarding the control of both emergency outbreaks and large projects to reform health infrastructures. Another important support for multilateralism is that international rules and international aid programs are only likely to be viewed as legitimate if they are sponsored by a large and representative body of actors. Donors often want the legitimacy of being part of large international efforts both because they want the support of aid recipients and their own national populations who contribute funds and material resources to aid programs. Both public and private actors are concerned with attaining a reputation of being strong humanitarians in the eyes of many actors.

It is easy to see the failures and gaps in health governance. More than 15 million people die each year from diseases such as measles and malaria that medical professionals have had the knowledge and ability to cure for decades. Millions of people suffer unnecessarily from debilitating diseases that are easily preventable or curable because private pharmaceutical companies have no financial incentive to develop drugs for diseases that afflict people too poor to afford medicines. Global health surveys indicate that up to 2 billion people on the planet are not able to access medicines because of deficient medical infrastructures, government corruption, and high drug prices. These issues are serious and they highlight the critical failures in health governance that need to be addressed. However, this study has also highlighted some of the areas where health governance has improved the quality of life for humans around the globe. Drug research programs such as Drugs for Neglected Diseases Initiative (DNDi) have emerged to counter the market failure with respect to vaccine and drug development. The Dracunculiasis Eradication Program is an example of a success story in that it has brought about a 99 percent reduction in case rates of a debilitating disease that has been a scourge of humankind for millennia. The establishment of GOARN means that outbreak control teams can be at the site of a disease outbreak, treating patients and containing the disease, within 24 hours of the news reaching WHO. Better child-oriented health programs, including measles vaccination drives and the distribution of mosquito nets to combat malaria, meant that in 2006 the number of child deaths dropped to less than 10 million for the first time.[18] Health governance is far from perfect, but more is being done now than at any time in history to combat infectious diseases. We are living in an era characterized by far-reaching independencies, meaning that no country or region, no matter how strong or rich, can single-handedly protect itself from infectious diseases. We must continue to unite *against* contagion or we are doomed to be united *by* contagion.

APPENDIX A

Table 1   Diseases ranked by average number of infections per year.

Very Large (More than 1 billion)	
Helicobacter Pylori	4 billion (120 million symptomatic)
Hepatitis B	2 billion (350 million symptomatic)
Tuberculosis (TB)	2 billion (8 million symptomatic)
Ascariasis	1.25 billion
Hookworm	1 billion
Influenza	1 billion (3 to 5 million severe)

Large (100 million–1 billion)	
Malaria	300 million
Escherichia Coli (E-Coli)	210 million
Schistosomiasis	200 million
Hepatitis C	170 million
Shigella	165 million
Rotavirus	125 million
Lymphatic Filariasis	120 million

Medium (1 million–100 million)	
Dengue	50 million
HIV/AIDS	39.5 million
Pertussis (Whooping Cough)	32 million
Typhoid Fever	22 million
Human Papillomavirus	20 million
Measles	20 million
Onchocerciasis (River Blindness)	18 million
Chagas	17 million
Leishmaniasis	12 million
Syphilis	12 million
Rabies	10 million★
Streptococcus pneumoniae (Pneumococcus)	7 million
Campylobacteriosis	2.4 million
Hepatitis A	1.5 million

Continued

Table 1   Continued

Small (50,000–1 million)	
Meningococcal Meningitis	500,000
Noma (Cancrum Oris)	500,000
African Trypanosomiasis (Sleeping Sickness)	450,000
Lassa Fever	450,000
Leprosy	410,000
Yellow Fever	200,000
Cholera	155,000
Japanese Encephalitis	50,000

Very Small (Less than 50,000)	
Dracunculiasis	32,000
Buruli Ulcer	25,000★★
Typhus Fever	12,000
Legionnaire's Disease	10,000★★★
Diphtheria (Respiratory)	8,500
Mumps	3,500
Plague	2,000
SARS	Less than 1,000 cases per year (Outbreak Disease)
Rift Valley Fever	Less than 1,000 cases per year
Rocky Mountain Spotted Fever	Less than 1,000 cases per year
Ebola Haemorrhagic Fever	Less than 1,000 cases per year (Outbreak Disease)
Poliomyelitis	Less than 1,000 cases per year
Nipah Fever	Less than 1,000 cases per year
Hantavirus	Less than 1,000 cases per year
Marburg Haemorrhagic Fever	Less than 1,000 cases per year (Outbreak Disease)
West Nile Encephalitis	Less than 1,000 cases per year (Outbreak Disease)
Anthrax	Less than 1,000 cases per year (Outbreak Disease)
Avian Influenza	Less than 1,000 cases per year (Outbreak Disease)
Relapsing Fever	Less than 1,000 cases per year

Notes: ★ Number of rabies vaccinations given annually.
★★ See section on Buruli ulcer for an explanation on this figure.
★★★ See section on Legionnaire's Disease for an explanation of this figure.

Table 2 Diseases ranked by average number of deaths per year.

Very Large (1–3 million)

HIV/AIDS	2.9 million
Tuberculosis (TB)	1.7 million
Shigella	1.1 million
Malaria	1 million
Streptococcus pneumoniae (Pneumococcus)	1 million

Large (100,000–1 million)

Rotavirus	740,000
Hepatitis C	600,000
Hepatitis B	500,000
Noma (Cancrum Oris)	450,000
Escherichia Coli (E-Coli)	380,000
Influenza	375,000
Measles	345,000
Human Papillomavirus	300,000
Pertussis (Whooping Cough)	250,000
Typhoid Fever	200,000
Syphilis	125,000

Medium (20,000–100,000)

Ascariasis	60,000
Leishmaniasis	57,000
African Trypanosomiasis (Sleeping Sickness)	50,000
Meningococcal Meningitis	50,000
Rabies	45,000
Yellow Fever	30,000
Dengue	22,000

Small (100–20,000)

Schistosomiasis	15,000
Japanese Encephalitis	15,000
Chagas	13,000
Cholera	5,000
Lassa Fever	5,000
Typhus Fever	550
Diphtheria (Respiratory)	350
Plague	200

Very Small (Less than 100 deaths per year)

Hantavirus
Rocky Mountain Spotted Fever
Anthrax
Avian Influenza

Continued

Table 2 Continued

Ebola Hemorrhagic Fever
Hepatitis A
Legionnaire's Disease
Marburg Hemorrhagic Fever
Mumps
Nipah Fever
Poliomyelitis
Relapsing Fever
Rift Valley Fever
SARS
West Nile Encephalitis

Nonfatal Diseases★

Buruli Ulcer
Campylobacteriosis
Dracunculiasis
Helicobacter Pylori
Hookworm
Leprosy
Lymphatic Filariasis
Onchocerciasis (River Blindness)

Note: ★ Disease is not fatal on its own, but can contribute to death if victim is already weak or ill.

Table 3 Concentration of diseases in developed and developing regions.

Developed and Developing Regions

Anthrax
Campylobacteriosis
Escherichia Coli (E-Coli)
Hantavirus
Helicobacter Pylori
Hepatitis A
Hepatitis B
Hepatitis C

HIV/AIDS
Human Papillomavirus
Influenza
Japanese Encephalitis
Meningococcal Meningitis
Mumps
Pertussis (Whooping Cough)
Rabies
Rocky Mountain Spotted Fever
Rotavirus
SARS
Streptococcus pneumoniae (Pneumococcus)

Continued

Table 3 Continued

Syphilis
Tuberculosis (TB)
West Nile Encephalitis

Developed Regions Only

Legionnaire's Disease (Legionelliosis)

Developing Regions Only

African Trypanosomiasis
Ascariasis
Avian Influenza
Buruli Ulcer
Chagas
Cholera
Dengue
Diphtheria (Respiratory)
Dracunculiasis
Ebola Hemorrhagic Fever
Hookworm
Lassa Fever
Leishmaniasis
Leprosy
Lymphatic Filariasis
Malaria
Marburg Hemorrhagic Fever
Measles
Nipah Fever
Noma (Cancrum Oris)
Onchocerciasis (River Blindness)
Plague
Poliomyelitis
Relapsing Fever
Rift Valley Fever
Schistosomiasis
Shigella
Typhoid Fever
Typhus Fever (Louse Borne)
Yellow Fever

Note: Diseases included in the "Developed and Developing Regions" section of the chart, refer to diseases with at least two percent prevalence in both regions. Nevertheless, most of the diseases listed in this section burden the developing countries disproportionately. In fact, the only diseases where the percentage of cases found in the developed world is more than 10 percent are influenza and hepatitis C. Legionnaire's disease is the only disease, out of 50, to disproportionately affect the developed world. Even HIV/AIDS, which is commonly thought of as a global problem, has 95 percent prevalence in developing countries; only 5 percent of all HIV/AIDS cases occur in developed countries. Diseases are identified as having a concentration in either the developed or the developing countries one region houses more than 98 percent of the total worldwide case load.

Table 4 Availability of vaccines and drugs.

Diseases with Effective Vaccines and Drugs/Treatment

Anthrax
Diphtheria (Respiratory)
Hepatitis A
Human Papillomavirus
Japanese Encephalitis
Measles
Meningococcal Meningitis
Pertussis (Whooping Cough)
Rabies
Streptococcus pneumoniae (Pneumococcus)

Diseases with Effective Vaccines but No Drugs/Treatment

Hepatitis B
Mumps
Poliomyelitis
Yellow Fever

Diseases with Effective Drugs/Treatment but No Vaccine

African Trypanosomiasis (Sleeping Sickness)
Ascariasis
Buruli Ulcer
Campylobacteriosis
Chagas
Cholera
Dengue
Escherichia Coli (E-Coli)
Helicobacter Pylori
Hookworm
Legionnaire's Disease (Legionelliosis)
Leishmaniasis
Leprosy
Lymphatic Filariasis
Malaria
Noma (Cancrum Oris)
Onchocerciasis (River Blindness)
Plague
Relapsing Fever
Rocky Mountain Spotted Fever
Rotavirus
Schistosomiasis
Shigella
Syphilis
Tuberculosis (TB)
Typhoid Fever
Typhus Fever

Continued

Table 4 Continued

Note: By the term "effective," we mean a vaccine or drug that completely prevents or cures the disease, thus excluding diseases like influenza where drugs only exist that mitigate symptoms without affecting a cure and HIV/AIDS where drugs merely slow the progress of the illness.

Table 5 Mortality rates.

Disease	Number of Cases (annual)	Number of Deaths (annual)	Mortality Rate (overall)
HIV/AIDS	40 million	3 million	100%
Noma (Cancrum Oris)	500,000	450,000	90%
Avian Influenza	Less than 1,000 cases per year (Outbreak Disease)	<100	72%
Ebola	Less than 1,000 cases per year (Outbreak Disease)	<100	50–90%
Plague	2,000	200	50–60%
Nipah Fever	Less than 1,000 cases per year	<100	50%
Hantavirus	Less than 1,000 cases per year	<100	35%
Japanese Encephalitis	50,000	15,000	30%
Marburg Hemorrhagic Fever	Less than 1,000 cases per year (Outbreak Disease)	<100	25%
Yellow Fever	200,000	30,000	15%
SARS	Less than 1,000 cases per year (Outbreak Disease)	<100	11%

Continued

Table 5 Continued

Disease	Number of Cases (annual)	Number of Deaths (annual)	Mortality Rate (overall)
African Trypanosomiasis (Sleeping Sickness)	450,000	50,000	11%
Streptococcus pneumoniae (Pneumococcus)	7 million	1 million	10–30%
Rift Valley Fever	Less than 1,000 cases per year	<100	10–20%
Meningococcal Meningitis	500,000	50,000	10%
Legionnaire's Disease	10,000	<100	5–30%
West Nile Encephalitis	Less than 1,000 cases per year (Outbreak Disease)	<100	4–11%
Typhus Fever	12,000	550	4%
Diphtheria (Respiratory)	8,500	350	4%
Rocky Mountain Spotted Fever	Less than 1,000 cases per year	<100	3–5%
Cholera	155,000	5,000	3%
Typhoid Fever	17 million	600,000	3%
Relapsing Fever	Less than 1,000 cases per year	<100	2–10%, up to 50% in epidemics
Measles	35 million	750,000	2%
Human Papillomavirus	20 million	300,000	1.5%
Syphilis	12 million	125,000	1%
Lassa Fever	450,000	5,000	1%
Hepatitis B	2 billion	500,000	<1%
Tuberculosis (TB)	2 billion	2 million	<1%
Ascariasis	1.25 billion	60,000	<1%
Pertussis (Whooping Cough)	32 million	250,000	<1%
Influenza	1 billion	375,000	<1%
Malaria	300 million	1 million	<1%
Escherichia Coli (E-Coli)	210 million	380,000	<1%
Schistosomiasis	200 million	15,000	<1%
Hepatitis A	1.5 million	<100	<1%
Hepatitis C	185 million	600,000	<1%
Shigella	165 million	1.1 million	<1%
Rotavirus	125 million	740,000	<1%
Chagas	17 million	13,000	<1%
Dengue	50 million	22,000	<1%
Leishmaniasis	12 million	57,000	<1%
Rabies	10 million	45,000	<1%
Mumps	3,500	<100	<1%
Poliomyelitis	Less than 1,000 cases per year	<100	<1%
Buruli Ulcer	25,000	NA	NA

Continued

Table 5 Continued

Disease	Number of Cases (annual)	Number of Deaths (annual)	Mortality Rate (overall)
Helicobacter Pylori	4 billion	NA	NA
Hookworm	1 billion	NA	NA
Lymphatic Filariasis	120 million	NA	NA
Onchocerciasis (River Blindness)	18 million	NA	NA
Campylobacteriosis	2.4 million	NA	NA
Dracunculiasis	75,000	NA	NA
Leprosy	534,000	NA	NA

Note: Mortality figures are taken from WHO and CDC information on the specific diseases. Rates reported here are not necessarily the mathematical equivalent of the number of cases divided by the number of deaths because mortality is affected by treatment provided and the length of time the disease takes to kill its victim. NA stands for "Not Applicable."

APPENDIX B

SUMMARY DESCRIPTIONS OF DISEASES

The primary sources for the information on the diseases listed below are the World Health Organization (WHO) and the Centers for Disease Control and Prevention (CDC). The majority of the information found below came from WHO and CDC Fact Sheets, which are available at www.who.int/mediacentre/factsheets and http://www.cdc.gov/az.do respectively. To supplement certain sections, we also used the WHO World Health Reports, particularly those between 1996 and 2003, and the Institute of Medicine 2003 publication *Microbial Threats to Health*. Sources devoted to one specific disease are referenced in subsequent citations. In cases of conflicting information, we relied on WHO sources. The following descriptions of diseases are organized alphabetically.

African Trypanosomiasis (Sleeping Sickness)

African Trypanosomiasis, which is related to the Latin American disease Chagas, has two variants—East African and West African. They are caused by slightly different parasites, but both are transmitted to humans through the bite of tsetse flies. The disease causes serious fever, headaches, and a disturbed sleeping pattern. The East African variant leads to death within several weeks if it is untreated, whereas in the case of the West African variant death comes after several months or years. The WHO estimates that there are between 300,000 and 500,000 cases throughout the 36 African countries where the disease is endemic. (Actual reported cases numbers are much lower—only approximately 40,000—however, lack of effective surveillance means that the majority of cases go undetected and unreported.) The annual number of deaths is approximately 50,000. The disease kills all infected individuals if untreated. The drugs are very effective when administered soon after appearance of disease symptoms, but drug treatment should be followed up with visits to hospital for several years, making it difficult to treat for those in rural areas with little access to health care treatments. There are no vaccines for prevention of the illness.

African Trypanosomiasis was almost eradicated in the 1960s through the systematic screening and treatment of millions of at-risk people by mobile medical teams. Owing to the success of the program, however, surveillance and screening ceased. Because of this, the disease has re-established itself in many parts of Africa, and case rates have been in the hundreds of thousands since the 1970s. Since the early years of the twenty-first century, however, screening efforts have been re-established and the number of cases reported has been reduced through the actions of global health partnerships.

Anthrax

Anthrax is caused by the bacterium *Bacillus anthracis*. Although predominantly a disease of livestock, such as cows, sheep, and goats, Anthrax can be contracted by humans through contact with infected animals or through ingesting the meat of infected animals. A characteristic of the Anthrax bacteria is that it creates infectious spores. These spores can survive for years or even decades in the environment, until they are picked up by a host. Thus, another mode of human contraction is direct contact with anthrax spores. In fact, Anthrax gained significant notoriety as a terrorist biological weapon in October/November 2001, when anthrax spores were sent through the U.S. postal system.[1]

The disease has three forms: cutaneous, inhaled, and gastrointestinal. All three forms cause the victim to develop a high fever, chills, flu-like symptoms, cough, and sore throat. Cutaneous, the most common form among humans occurs when the bacteria enter the body through a wound or lesion. It is fatal in 20 percent of cases if the patient is untreated, but only 1 percent if proper treatment is provided. Inhaled Anthrax, which occurs when the victim breathes in anthrax spores, has a much higher fatality rate of approximately 75 percent of all cases. Gastrointestinal Anthrax is contracted through the ingestion of infected meat and its fatality rate ranges between 25 and 60 percent, depending on treatment. Effective drugs exist that can treat the disease, and there is also an effective vaccine.

Ascariasis

Ascariasis is the most common human worm infection. It can be found wherever sanitation is poor and/or human waste is used as fertilizer. The vast majority of cases are found in the developing world, with less than 1 percent occurring in industrialized countries. The parasitic roundworm ingested unknowingly with food or soil particles contaminated with infected human feces causes infection in the small intestine. There are approximately 1.25 billion cases of Ascariasis in the world and approximately 60,000 infected people die each year. It is estimated that 4 million cases of Ascariasis occur in the United States every year, predominantly in the southeast. The disease is almost never fatal outside the developing world.

Death can occur within several weeks or months after the initial infection, but there are medicines that can completely cure the disease by killing the worm. However, this disease occurs predominantly in rural areas, and access to medicine is very limited owing to cost and the lack of strong health care infrastructure. Despite the existence of simple prevention techniques, Ascariasis cases have remained relatively constant over the years. To lessen the active cases and thus decrease the disease burden on developing countries, it is imperative that clean water sources and improved health education be provided to those in need.

Avian Influenza

Avian Influenza was recognized as a severe and highly contagious disease that affects all species of birds more than a century ago. However, in the late 1990s the virus that causes the disease mutated allowing it to infect humans. The first reported case of human Avian Influenza occurred in Hong Kong in 1997. By the time the disease was contained, 18 people had fallen ill and 6 had died. To date, nine Asian countries have reported outbreaks of the disease, and it has spread to Russia, Central Asia, Eastern Europe, and Northern Africa. The most recent outbreak was in January 2004 in Hong Kong and by the autumn 2004, 44 cases had been reported with 32 fatalities, creating an exceptionally high mortality rate of more than 70 percent. As of February 2007, the total number of confirmed human cases of Avian Flu was 271, with 165 fatal infections.

To date, the disease is transmitted only through close contact with infected birds—not by human-to-human transmission. However, many scientists fear that the virus could change once again, and become communicable between humans. If that type of mutation occurred with such a deadly flu strain, a worldwide pandemic could result in millions of deaths. Case rates remain quite low, but the high mortality rate, the lack of drugs with proven efficacy, and difficulties in developing a vaccine have made Avian Flu a serious cause for concern. Furthermore, difficulty in containing Avian Influenza has been exacerbated by a flawed surveillance system. So far, the major control mechanism to limit the spread of the disease has been the mass culling of infected birds. The majority of these birds are owned by poor farmers in developing countries and the farmers have no motivation to report disease outbreaks to the authorities as they have no desire to have their entire flock killed.

Buruli Ulcer

Buruli Ulcer is a bacterial infection that produces a toxin that destroys tissue and suppresses the immune system. If left untreated, massive areas of skin and occasionally bone are destroyed by the toxin. Although not fatal, untreated victims can be left with severe disfigurement or disability. Little is known about the mode of transmission. A very rough estimate as to the number of active cases of Buruli Ulcer is 25,000; however, reliable data regarding the prevalence of the disease in developing countries is scarce. It is known that the disease predominantly affects women and children in wetland areas of West Africa, but the bacteria are endemic to approximately 30 countries in Africa, Latin America, Asia, and the Western Pacific. Surgery to remove the nodule on the skin, which is the source of infection, is the only effective treatment, although there is a generic vaccine that offers limited protection. Given the poor reporting of Buruli cases from rural areas, little useful information about the disease trend is currently available.

Campylobacteriosis

Campylobacteriosis is a very common bacterial disease among humans, with 2.4 million people infected in any given year. The disease is caused by bacteria that are present in contaminated, undercooked food, unclean water, or raw milk. It causes gastrointestinal infection, dysentery, and nausea. Although fatalities are rare, this disease can kill weak or immuno-compromised victims, making coinfection with HIV/AIDS patients a serious concern, particularly in Africa. It can be cured with proper medicines, but drugs are often unavailable in developing areas where the disease is most common.

Despite advances in medical technology, Campylobacteriosis is becoming a serious worldwide problem. Case numbers in the developed world have been rising for more than 20 years, particularly since 1990. New strains of the bacterium have been discovered, and previously known strains are developing resistance to the antibiotics traditionally prescribed for severe cases. Statistics from the WHO indicate that this disease still poses the most serious threat to children under the age of 5 in the developing world. Case rates for this group are thought to be between 40,000 and 60,000 per 100,000, whereas case rates for children under the age of 5 in the developed world are estimated at 300 per 100,000.

Chagas

Chagas disease, also known as American Trypanosomiasis, is a parasitic infection acquired by humans from certain bloodsucking insects. With some cases, shortly after infection, the victim develops fever, swelling of the lymph glands, and enlargement of the liver or spleen; death occurs occasionally in young children during this phase. More commonly, the infected person will remain asymptomatic for months or even years but will gradually fall ill as the parasite attacks and damages the victims' internal organs.

Chagas is endemic in 21 countries in Central and Southern America where there are between 16 and 18 million infected persons. The mortality rate is relatively low, but still results in 13,000 deaths per year. The disease can be treated effectively by medicines if they are administered soon after the appearance of symptoms, but there is no vaccine to prevent the disease. Disease transmission control programs, which target the insect that transmits the disease, have proved very successful in reducing the disease burden. Overall case numbers have been declining since the 1960s when the control programs began and WHO has targeted Chagas for complete eradication by 2010.

Cholera

Cholera posed one of the most serious health problems for Asia and Europe during the nineteenth century. In fact, it was the predominant catalyst for the first international health conferences of the late 1800s. There were six cholera pandemics between 1817 and the end of the century, all of which originated in India where the disease had been present for centuries. Most of the pandemics killed many millions of people in Asia and Europe along the paths of international commerce and migration. Major routes of migration that spread the disease were from India to Russia and from Russia to its Western European neighbors. The travel of Muslims to the holy sites in what is now Saudi Arabia was also a major influence in the spread of the disease.

The bacterium that causes cholera was isolated in the early 1880s. Shortly thereafter, it was learned that the bacterium is endemic to brackish water sources; humans become ill after ingesting contaminated water. Contamination can also occur by the entry of human feces into the water supply. Cholera causes an intestinal infection accompanied by vomiting and severe diarrhea, which can lead to fatal dehydration within days or even hours if untreated. Individuals with cholera can be cured through simple rehydration therapy, including Oral Rehydration Salts (ORS).

Certain antibiotics can be used to decrease the duration of the illness. Two oral vaccines, which are highly effective for a limited period, are available, and travelers to endemic areas are often advised to be vaccinated. Mass vaccination to control cholera outbreaks was attempted for the first time in January 2004 in a highly endemic region of Mozambique.

Before the twentieth century, 25 to 50 percent of cholera victims were expected to die. Nowadays, however, fatality rates can be as low as 1 percent, if proper and prompt treatment is provided. For example, during the 1991 cholera outbreak in Latin America, only 4,000 of the 400,000 infected persons died from the disease, whereas during the post-Rwanda crisis outbreak in 1994, there were 48,000 cases and 23,800 deaths in refugee camps in the Democratic Republic of the Congo.[2]

The El Tor strain of the cholera bacterium continues to cause fairly frequent outbreaks throughout the developing world and has spread to countries in West Africa and Latin America. Thanks to modern methods of sewage disposal, the advent of more effective treatment methods, and advances in transportation technology that allow health workers to reach cholera victims in a much timelier manner, preventing and treating the disease is easier than ever before. Nevertheless, cholera still poses a significant problem for poor countries without effective sewage treatment or health care systems. WHO reports indicate that there are between 110,000 and 200,000 cholera cases with 5,000 deaths each year. However, the organization estimates that this is only 5 to10 percent of the true figure.[3]

Dengue

Dengue is caused by four different but related viruses that are passed from human to human via the Aedes mosquito. Dengue fever causes severe flu-like symptoms, but rarely death. Dengue Haemorrhagic Fever (DHF) is a potentially fatal complication of an infection of the dengue virus. It can cause an extremely high fever, convulsions, and haemorrhagic bleeding. Estimates regarding the prevalence of dengue fever vary greatly; however, the majority of studies indicate that there are approximately 50 million individuals with the disease worldwide. The vast majority of the 22,000 annual fatal cases are from DHF. Mortality rates vary from 1 percent to 20 percent depending on the severity of the illness and the treatment provided. Death occurs, generally, within several weeks of contracting the disease. The disease can be treated effectively by rehydration therapy, but there is no vaccine.

Prevention is possible through elimination of the female *Aedes aegypti* mosquito—the primary vector that transmits the disease. This mosquito is an urban dweller. As more humans move into urban areas, contact with this type of mosquito increases. For this reason, dengue case rates have been consistently increasing throughout the twentieth and twenty-first centuries and serious outbreaks have been occurring in previously unaffected countries. The disease is now endemic in more than 100 countries in both the developed and developing worlds, although the highest case numbers are found in Southeast Asia and the Western Pacific.

Diphtheria (Respiratory)

Diphtheria is a bacterial infection that is passed among humans through respiratory droplets emitted via coughing or sneezing. There are two forms of the disease—respiratory and cutaneous—but only the former is a serious health problem. It causes sore throat and damage to the heart muscle and nerves. Today, an annual average of 8,500 people contract respiratory diphtheria and between 200 and 500 of them die; however, diphtheria is highly infectious so case rates can skyrocket during outbreaks. If it is untreated, the mortality rate can be close to 20 percent and death can come in a matter of weeks. Between 5 and 10 percent of patients die even with treatment, therefore, the very effective vaccine is the preferred method of disease control. The spread of the disease is limited to a relatively small population in the developing world and Eastern Europe where people have not been vaccinated. Diphtheria is part of the WHO Expanded Program on Immunization and as such only approximately 20 percent of the world's population remains unvaccinated and therefore at risk of catching this disease. Occasional serious outbreaks, with numbers in the hundreds of thousands, such as that in the former Soviet Union in 1994 and 1995 and in Laos and Thailand in 1996, occur among unvaccinated populations, but overall diphtheria rates have been falling since the mass vaccination programs of the 1940s and 1950s.

Dracunculiasis (Guinea Worm Disease)

Dracunculiasis is a nonfatal, but severely debilitating, parasitic infection that has affected humans for millennia. Humans contract the disease by consuming water contaminated with minute water fleas that are host to the parasite's larvae. Inside the human host, the larvae grow into worms that migrate through the victim's subcutaneous tissue, causing severe muscle and joint pain. When the worm exits from the infected person, usually through the foot about a year after the initial infection, it causes severe pain, as well as fever and vomiting. Currently, approximately 11,000 people in sub-Saharan African countries become infected each year (the majority of cases occur in Sudan and Ghana). Although there are no effective drugs or vaccines, Dracunculiasis is easily prevented by the use of an inexpensive mesh filter that removes infected fleas from community water sources. In addition, the water source can be treated with inexpensive pesticides that effectively destroy the larvae of the guinea worm.

Through the mid-1980s, there were millions of dracunculiasis victims in the Indian subcontinent, Southeast Asia, parts of the Middle East and Africa. Thanks to eradication efforts involving the Carter Center, the WHO, the CDC, and numerous other partners, the disease has been eliminated from all but a handful of countries in sub-Saharan Africa and case rates continue to decline rapidly.

Ebola Haemorrhagic Fever

The Ebola virus, which is related to Marburg, causes one of the deadliest known diseases for humankind. It produces violent haemorrhagic fever and profuse internal and external bleeding in its victims. Ebola kills between 50 and 90 percent of infected persons, regardless of treatment, within two to three weeks after the initial infection. It is believed that the virus is passed to humans via direct contact with an infected animal or through contact with the blood, bodily fluids, or tissue of an infected person. To date, the disease has been confined to a number of African countries, including the Democratic Republic of the Congo, Sudan, Gabon, Cote d'Ivoire, Uganda, and Zaire.[4] Owing to the highly infectious nature of the disease, infected persons must be isolated and health care workers must adopt the highest precautionary measures when dealing with patients.

The Ebola virus first appeared in 1976 in Sudan and the Democratic Republic of the Congo. Over the past 30 years, WHO has collected information on 17 outbreaks. Some outbreaks have been isolated cases with only one person becoming infected, however, the largest outbreak, which occurred between 2000 and 2001 in Uganda, caused 425 cases with 224 deaths. Since its discovery, the disease has caused 1,850 cases and more than 1,200 deaths. The lack of knowledge regarding the origin and natural reservoir of the disease, combined with the extremely high mortality rate and absence of effective medication makes the Ebola virus a major contemporary health concern. This is particularly true regarding the threat of bioterrorism. Not only would the disease itself cause mass causalities if it were to be released, but the gruesome nature of Ebola would also cause widespread panic and chaos if rumors regarding an outbreak were circulated. This is not an empty fear, as it is now known that the Japanese Aum Shinrikyo doomsday cult sent a team of doctors and nurses to Sudan in 1994 to attempt to locate the virus, bring it back to Japan, and turn it into a biological weapon. While their attempt was unsuccessful, this incident highlights the threat diseases such as Ebola pose to global health and security.[5]

Escherichia Coli (E. Coli)

Most strains of the E. Coli bacteria are relatively harmless. However, certain strains, such as E. Coli O157:H7, which are referred to as *enterohaemorrhagic E.coli* (EHEC), can cause serious illness. Humans contract the bacteria through consumption of undercooked meat, raw milk, or contaminated foods. It causes abdominal cramps, dysentery, and vomiting. Although most people who contract the illness recover without hospitalization or treatment, E. Coli infections can be extremely harmful and occasionally fatal to the very young and the very old. Severe cases can lead to death several weeks after the initial infection. E. Coli bacteria are endemic worldwide. They are thought to cause approximately 210 million bouts of illness and 380,000 deaths annually. Although the illness was first identified in the United States in 1982, most cases today are in the developing world. Case numbers are increasing worldwide. The disease can only be treated through rehydration therapy, which involves taking a number of drugs. There is no universally available vaccine.

Hantavirus Pulmonary Syndrome

Hantavirus pulmonary syndrome is caused by the Sin Nombre virus. The virus was isolated after an outbreak of the disease in 1993 in the southwestern United States. It attracted significant attention after a major outbreak in Peru in 1995. Humans contract the disease by inhaling aerosolized particles of the excrement of infected rodents, usually the deer mouse. The early stage of the disease brings fever, headache, and chills, and in the latter phase the lungs fill with fluid causing extreme respiratory distress.

The virus is found in many areas of the world, but the most notable outbreaks since the 1990s have occurred in North and South America. There are about 150 cases in the world annually, and 40 to 60 of these individuals die within days of contracting the disease. There is no specific treatment or vaccine for the disease, although certain drugs can be used to reduce the symptoms. Case rates have remained relatively low and constant since the discovery of the disease.

Helicobacter Pylori

Helicobacter Pylori, H. Pylori, is a bacterium that lives in the human stomach and and duodenum. It is the only known microorganism that can survive in the extremely acidic environment of the stomach. Within the past 20 years it has been learned that H. Pylori is the major cause of peptic ulcers, gastritis, and duodenitis, which result in symptoms such as severe stomach pain, nausea, and loss of appetite. It is estimated that two-thirds of the world's population, or about 4 billion people, are infected with H. Pylori, making it the most widespread infection known to humans. Fortunately, however, the majority—up to 70 percent—of infections are asymptomatic and self-immunizing. H. Pylori infections are not fatal in and of themselves; however, they can contribute to death in immuno-compromised victims, or in combination with other diseases, especially in countries where access to health care providers and antibiotics is difficult.

H. Pylori bacteria are found in humans around the globe, with an esti-mated prevalence of 70 percent of the population in developing countries and 25 to 30 percent in developed countries. In developed nations, infec-tions are most common among older segments of the population, but in poor countries, infections are found among all age groups. Transmission of the bacteria is from person to person, presumably via oral-oral or faecal-oral routes, thus good hygiene is an important preventative measure. In the absence of treatment, infection is potentially lifelong; however, effective treatment is available in the form of antibiotics. As with most diseases cur-rently treated by antibiotics, microbial resistance to existing first-line drugs is a growing problem in the treatment of this illness.

Hepatitis

The word "hepatitis" means inflammation of the liver. Thus, all five hepati-tis viruses (A, B, C, D, and E) cause liver damage in varying degrees. The five strains of the hepatitis virus cause similar symptoms: jaundice, fatigue, vomiting, and abdominal pain. However, they vary in mode of contraction and mortality rate. More people in the world have one of these forms of hepatitis than any other disease.[6]

Hepatitis A is contracted through consumption of water or food contam-inated with human feces. The disease is rarely fatal, and the majority of Hepatitis A infections are asymptomatic and self-immunizing, nevertheless, currently approximately 1.5 million people worldwide have symptomatic Hepatitis A. It predominantly affects developing regions with poor sanitary conditions. Four effective vaccines exist that can prevent the disease, but widespread vaccination is not recommended by WHO. This is because in areas where Hepatitis A is highly endemic, virtually all people contract the disease in childhood and develop lifelong immunity to it without ever experiencing symptoms. Adults who were not exposed to the virus in their childhood are at the highest risk of developing symptomatic Hepatitis A.

Therefore, vaccination is often recommended for travelers to endemic areas. No drugs are available that can cure the disease after infection. Hepatitis B is contracted via contact with bodily fluids, usually through sexual intercourse or needle sharing. In chronic cases, the virus can cause liver cancer. Approximately 2 billion people—one-third of the world's population—are Hepatitis B virus carriers; of this number, 350 million have symptomatic Hepatitis B. Approximately 500,000 people die of the disease each year. Chronic Hepatitis B occurs predominantly in Asia and Africa. Drugs exist that can treat the disease; however, the vaccine, available since 1982, is deemed a much more cost-effective method of control. As of the year 2000, 116 countries included Hepatitis B vaccinations to their mass immunization programs, and organizations affiliated with WHO are working to augment this number. Owing to these immunization programs, the new Hepatitis B cases has been on a sharp downward trend in recent years.

Hepatitis C is transmitted via contact with an infected person's blood, usually through unscreened blood transfusions, needle sharing among drug users, or the reuse of inadequately sterilized needles in health care organizations. Chronic Hepatitis C can lead to potentially fatal cirrhosis of the liver. An estimated 170 million people worldwide have Hepatitis C, and unlike those with Hepatitis B, the number of active cases is on an upward trend with approximately 3 to 4 million new cases each year. A comparatively high proportion—80 percent—of Hepatitis C carriers develop chronic Hepatitis, which causes death in approximately 1 percent of cases. Some medicines are available to treat the disease, but they are very expensive, negating their usefulness in the developing world, where approximately 65 percent of cases are found.

Hookworm

Hookworm infections are contracted when larvae in contaminated soil penetrate the skin. After maturing inside the human host, the worm attaches itself to the intestinal wall where it sucks blood from the victim. It causes anaemia, diarrhea, and weight loss but is rarely fatal. This is fortunate because there are more than 1 billion people with this parasitic infection in the developing world. Hookworms are endemic in tropical and subtropical regions and infected persons are found in Southern Europe, Northern Africa, Northern Asia, and parts of South America. There are effective drugs, but they are not available to many patients owing to poor health systems and lack of financial resources. Despite some attempts to reduce the prevalence of hookworms in the soil of endemic regions, case rates have remained relatively constant for the past several decades.

Human Immunodeficiency Virus/Acquired
Immune Deficiency Syndrome (HIV/AIDS)

It is now known that a few people died from acquired immune deficiency syndrome (AIDS) in Africa in the late 1950s, but it was not until 1981 that its existence was established. Extensive research over the past two decades has proven that AIDS is caused by the human immunodeficiency virus (HIV). The virus gradually destroys a type of blood cell that is an essential part of a strong immune system. Eventually the victim's immune system becomes too weak to ward off fatal diseases. HIV inevitably leads to AIDS; however, the advent of a powerful treatment called antiretroviral therapy (ART) has decreased the potency of the virus, and thus increased both patients' quality of life and the time lag between becoming HIV positive and developing AIDS.

HIV is transmitted via contact with bodily fluids. The most common modes of transmission are sexual intercourse, needle sharing, and blood transfusion. It can also be transmitted from mother to fetus during pregnancy. Despite attempts to reduce case rates through sex education, HIV/AIDS rates are still on an upward trend. Every year between 4 and 5 million people become HIV positive. Current research indicates that many of these new cases occur among children, who contract the disease from their mother. At present approximately 39.5 million people in the world are HIV positive, and 3 million die annually from AIDS-related illnesses.

Death rates alone do not provide an accurate picture of the toll this disease is taking around the world. Because HIV/AIDS gradually debilitates the segment of the population that is active work force for many years before proving fatal, the economic impacts of the disease are devastating to developing countries. Furthermore, AIDS is wreaking havoc on the social structure of developing countries because it has led to the creation of an entire generation of children termed "AIDS orphans." WHO, which defines AIDS orphans as children who have lost their mother or both parents to the disease before turning 15, predicts that there will be 41 million AIDS orphans worldwide by 2010.

The present global distribution of HIV/AIDS is approximately 66.5 percent of all cases in sub-Saharan Africa, 16 percent in South and Southeast Asia, 4 percent in Latin America, 3.8 percent in Eastern Europe and Central Asia, 2.5 percent in East Asia and the Pacific, 2.5 percent in North America, 1.5 percent in North Africa and the Middle East, 1.5 percent in Western Europe, 1.2 percent in the Caribbean, and 0.04 percent in Australia and New Zealand.[7] Although the proportions are thought to be relatively accurate, medical experts fear that the actual number of cases may be significantly higher because reporting and surveillance in many countries is often faulty.

Human Papillomavirus (HPV)

Human Papillomavirus (HPV) is the name of a group of viruses that includes more than 100 different strains or types. Some HPV types cause common and benign skin warts that are transmitted by casual skin-to-skin contact. Approximately 30 of the HPV viruses are sexually transmitted, and they can infect the genital area of men and women. Most people who come into contact with HPV will develop asymptomatic, self immunizing infections; however, some high-risk types of HPV can lead to cancer of the cervix, vulva, vagina, anus, or penis. Others, low-risk types, may cause genital warts that will disappear without treatment over time.

It is estimated that 20 million people worldwide are infected with at least one of the strains of HPV. It causes more than 500,000 cases of cervical cancer annually and is the second biggest cause of female cancer mortality worldwide with approximately 300,000 deaths. Nearly 80 percent of the cases of cervical cancer are thought to occur in developing countries. Treatment is available for all types of skin lesions caused by HPV, and cancer treatment is available as well, but it is more easily accessible for citizens of developed countries. A vaccine has recently been tested and approved; if distributed in a widespread fashion, it could greatly reduce overall caseloads.

Influenza

Influenza is a viral disease that comes in three major types—A, B, and C, each with many strains. Influenzas generally originate in the farmyards of southern China, where infections are transmitted from animals to humans; however, as this is a highly infectious, airborne illness influenza outbreaks can spread around the globe in a matter of weeks. The influenza virus generally causes high fever, headache, nausea, and weakness. Millions, if not billions, of people contract the flu every year, resulting in 3 to 5 million severe cases and between 250,000 and 500,000 deaths. The overall number of flu cases has remained constant over the years, with high peaks during flu-pandemics that occur approximately every three to four decades. For the most part, those who die are very young, very old, or seriously weakened by other illnesses. Major pandemics, which tend to occur several times per century, can cause extremely high fatality rates. For example, the most lethal flu pandemic in history occurred in 1918–1919 and killed more than 20 million people worldwide, making this the most deadly influenza outbreak in history.[8]

Influenza is a disease with a truly global spread and it can be found on virtually every country around the globe during an outbreak. Medicines exist that can mitigate the symptoms of the flu, but more widely recommended are vaccines. Unfortunately, however, a new vaccine is required every year, as the virus that causes the illness constantly mutates, so the vaccine used in the previous year is often entirely ineffective against the new strain. As such, research is constantly being done by the WHO Influenza Surveillance Network, which involves reporting by more than 100 medical centers throughout the world, to develop an effective vaccine.

Japanese Encephalitis

Japanese Encephalitis is caused by a virus, and it is transmitted from animals (specifically pigs and birds) to humans by mosquitoes. It causes fever, headaches, and possible brain damage in severe cases. Presently, there are 50,000 reported cases of the disease in Asia, Central Asia, the Indian subcontinent, and Australia annually. (WHO believes that the actual number of cases is significantly higher than this as many cases go unreported.) Japanese Encephalitis causes 15,000 reported deaths per year. Death occurs within weeks of contracting the disease. There are several vaccines now commercially available. Nevertheless, vaccination has not become universal because the available vaccines are prohibitively expensive. Research is being done to develop a safer, more cost-effective vaccine. More and more cases of Japanese Encephalitis are being reported each year as the virus increases its geographical range.

Lassa Fever

Lassa Fever is caused by a virus that is transmitted to humans by contact with rodent excreta in food or household items. It causes fever, vomiting, and diarrhea and, in severe cases, build-up of fluid in the lungs and brain dysfunction. There are between 300,000 and 500,000 people who contract the disease each year in West Africa, but the number of fatalities is only 5,000. In the case of those who die from the disease, death generally comes within several weeks of contracting it. There are reasonably effective drugs, but they must be administered soon after the contraction of the disease and, of course, this is often not possible in West Africa. The disease is geographically limited to West Africa. However, occasional cases, generally involving travelers to West Africa, have been reported in the developed world. Case rates have remained relatively constant since the disease was discovered in 1950.

Legionnaire's Disease (Legionelliosis)

Legionelliosis is caused by a bacterium that is transmitted to humans via mist from a contaminated water source, usually air conditioning systems. The symptoms include fever, chills, and cough. To date, the disease has largely been confined to developed countries, with occasional outbreaks on cruise ships. The bacterium causes outbreaks that usually affect 40 to 150 people per incident; however, global estimates indicate that roughly 10,000 Legionelliosis infections occur each year. The availability of very effective drugs that can cure the disease has significantly reduced the number of fatalities owing to Legionnaire's disease since it was first discovered in the 1960s. Without treatment, the mortality rate can be as high as 30 percent of all cases.

Leishmaniasis

Leishmaniasis is a parasitic infection that is transmitted to humans by the bite of infected sand fleas. There are four types of the disease, but only in the case of one—Visceral Leishmaniasis—is there a threat of serious illness. It can cause fever, enlargement of the spleen and liver, and anemia. There are presently approximately 12 million individuals with some form of the disease, and approximately 57,000 die annually—generally within several weeks of contracting the disease. (The vast majority of deaths are due to Visceral Leishmaniasis.) The effectiveness of available medicines for the disease is declining because the parasite is developing resistance to drugs. There is no vaccine to prevent the disease.

Leishmaniasis case rates have been on an upward trend for the past decade; approximately 500,000 new cases of Visceral Leishmaniasis alone are reported each year. Rural-urban migration combined with the environmental effects of projects such as dam building and deforestation have contributed to increased human contact with infected sand fleas as well as the geographical spread of the parasite, which is now endemic in 88 countries throughout Africa, Asia, Europe, North, and South America. The vast majority of Visceral Leishmaniasis occurs in just five countries: Bangladesh, Brazil, India, Nepal, and Sudan.

Leprosy (Hansen's Disease)

Leprosy, or Hansen's Disease, is caused by a bacteria that is transmitted to humans by droplets from the nose and mouth during close contact. Contrary to the views of many, Leprosy is not a particularly contagious disease. There are presently about half a million individuals with Leprosy, but it is rarely fatal. Leprosy is easily treated with a combination of drugs commonly referred to as Multidrug Therapy (MDT), which has replaced the traditionally used drug dapsone. The disease exists presently only in developing countries: more than 80 percent of cases occur in Southeast Asia; 8 percent in Africa; 6 percent in the Americas; and sporadic, occasional cases occur in the Eastern Mediterranean and Europe.

Donors (both NGOs and state governments) have been providing afflicted countries with sufficient drugs to treat all Leprosy patients for several years. Owing to this action, WHO estimates that over the past two decades approximately 12 million Leprosy victims have been cured. Effective treatment has led to the elimination of Leprosy from 108 out of the 122 countries where Leprosy was considered a public health problem in 1985. While the disease burden is decreasing every year, more education is necessary to eradicate the disease. Due to lack of knowledge regarding the disease, many victims in rural areas of the developing world are ashamed and afraid to seek medical treatment. Moreover, due to exaggerated fears of infection, many Leprosy victims are ostracized from their communities and denied access to treatment once the disease becomes obvious. Therefore, myths surrounding Leprosy must be dispelled before any eradication attempts could be made.

Lymphatic Filariasis (Elephantiasis)

Lymphatic Filariasis is a parasitic disease caused by microscopic worms that settle in the lymph system of an infected person. The disease is transmitted from person to person via mosquito bites. A prolonged infection can result in gross swelling of the limbs and genitals as well as damage to the lymph system and kidneys. There are approximately 120 million cases of elephantiasis in developing countries, about one-third of which occur in India, one-third in Africa, and the remainder spread across Southeast Asia, the Pacific, and the Americas. Although severely debilitating, the disease is rarely fatal. There is drug treatment, but it must be applied during early stages of the disease to be effective. Case rates are increasing as rural–urban migration increases human contact with the mosquitoes that transmit the disease.

Malaria

Malaria has been a health scourge for millennia, and it is responsible for the deaths of more humans than any other infectious disease. In fact, "since the beginning of history malaria has killed half of the men, women and children that have died on the planet. It has outperformed all wars, all famines and all other epidemics."[9] Malaria is caused by four different parasites that are transmitted to humans via Anopheles mosquito bites. It causes fatigue, headaches, vomiting, and fever. Presently, approximately 300 million people contract Malaria and 1 million die each year—generally within several weeks of contracting the illness. The disease exists throughout the developing world, but is concentrated in sub-Saharan Africa, where approximately 90 percent of all new cases and deaths from Malaria occur. The vast majority of deaths occur among young children in poor, rural areas.

The first medicine developed to treat the disease was quinine, which is derived from tree bark. It was brought to Europe by Western explorers in the sixteenth century. Quinine was superseded by a number of antimalarial drugs in the 1930s, and after World War II they were replaced by chloroquine; however, there are now serious problems regarding resistance of the malaria parasite to this drug. The invention of *dichlorodiphenyltrichloroethane* (DDT) in the 1940s was a very important development in the fight against Malaria as it could be used to kill the mosquitoes that transmitted the disease to humans. However, there is a current trend in many countries to ban the use or export of DDT because of potential damaging environmental impacts. Intensive research is currently being conducted in hopes of developing an effective vaccine. The main body of research on this is being carried out by the Malaria Vaccine Initiative and the Global Alliance for Vaccines and Immunization.

Marburg Hemorrhagic Fever

Marburg is one of the hemorrhagic fevers that originate in Africa. There have been very few occurrences of the disease, but because of its devastating and rapid effects, it has attracted considerable attention. This viral infection, which is related to Ebola, causes diarrhea, fever, vomiting of blood, and peeling of skin. It can cause death within weeks. There are no drugs available to treat Marburg Hemorrhagic Fever, but hospitalization and treatment can reduce symptoms. The virus is transmitted from primates to humans by direct contact and then from humans to humans via airborne respiratory droplets. There have been only two known significant outbreaks of the disease. In 1967, several African green monkeys were imported from Uganda to Germany and Yugoslavia as part of a polio vaccine research project. Thirty-seven people, who directly or indirectly came into contact with the monkeys, fell ill with the disease, and seven died. Then in 1999–2000, 18 individuals contracted the disease in the Democratic Republic of the Congo and 12 of them died. The first outbreak brought particular attention to the threat posed by the international trade in laboratory animals.

Measles

Measles was historically one of the most lethal diseases in the world. It is caused by a virus that is transmitted between humans by respiratory droplets, or by nasal or throat secretions. Symptoms include fatigue, fever, cough, and the characteristic rash of red, blotchy patches. Death can result from Measles in several weeks to months. There are presently 30 to 40 million individuals with the infection and in 2005 approximately 345,000 people died. The vast majority of mortal cases occur among children under the age of five. Measles remains one of the most deadly vaccine-preventable diseases in the world. Measles is currently confined almost solely to developing countries, with 99.6 percent of all cases occurring in Africa, although there are occasional cases in the developed world. There are medicines relatively effective in treating patients; particularly there has been a very effective vaccine since 1963. The vaccine is safe and inexpensive ($0.15 per dose), and mass vaccination has been deemed an extremely cost-effective way of managing the disease. However, there are serious barriers to mass immunization programs. Most importantly, highly skilled medical personnel are required to administer the injection of Measles vaccine, and there are serious concerns regarding the spread of other diseases, such as Hepatitis and HIV, if needles are reused. For this reason, the WHO is working in conjunction with CDC, the American Red Cross, and the Bill & Melinda Gates Foundation to develop and license an aerosolized vaccine, which would eliminate a major barrier to immunization by 2010.

Meningococcal Meningitis

Meningitis is an infection of the tissue surrounding the brain and spinal cord. It can result from both viral and bacterial infections. It is transmitted by droplets from the nose and throat, and the symptoms include high fever, headache, vomiting, and sensitivity to light. As these symptoms are very similar to influenza, misdiagnosis is a common problem and leads to higher fatality rates. Meningitis caused by a bacterial infection can result in brain damage and hearing loss. Between 5 and 10 percent of the people who contract the disease die within 24 to 48 hours. There are approximately 500,000 cases in the world and approximately 50,000 people die annually. Case rates have remained relatively steady for the past several decades, although occasional peaks have occurred owing to large outbreaks. It occurs everywhere in the world, but the large majority of cases occur in sub-Saharan Africa. There are medicines and very effective vaccines available.

Mumps

The Mumps is caused by the *rubulavirus*, which is passed from human to human via airborne droplets, direct contact, or saliva. Currently, between 1,500 and 5,000 contract the Mumps each year, but the disease is rarely fatal. Mumps used to be a much more serious health concern but the development of a safe and effective vaccine has drastically reduced annual case rates. To date, 500 million people have been vaccinated, and 120 countries administer the vaccine as part of their national immunization program. Such programs have led to a sharp downward trend in Mumps case rates.

Nipah Fever

Nipah Fever is contracted through a virus that is transmitted to humans from pigs or other humans. However, pigs and humans are thought to contract it from bats. The first outbreak was in Malaysia in 1999, and of the 265 cases, there were 105 deaths. (A handful of cases in Singapore were caused by pigs imported from Malaysia). A second outbreak in Bangladesh in 2004 of a Nipah-like virus resulted in 22 cases with 17 deaths. Death usually occurs within two to three weeks of the initial infection. There are no medicines or vaccines for the disease.

Noma (Cancrum Oris)

Noma is a horrific flesh-eating disease caused by a bacterium of unknown origin. The disease affects young children, between the ages of one and four. Early symptoms include gangrene of the mouth and bloody gums. This phase is followed by rapid destruction of both soft and hard facial tissue, as the bacteria destroys the victim's flesh, muscle, and bone.

Noma used to be found globally; however, advances in sanitation and hygiene caused the disease virtually to disappear from Europe and North America in the twentieth century. Nowadays, it is almost solely found among children in poor, rural areas of sub-Saharan Africa where hygiene and nutrition are substandard. It is estimated that approximately 500,000 cases of Noma occur each year; however, as this disease predominantly affects those with no access to health care, the reported number of cases is thought to be only a small percentage of the total. Noma has an extremely high mortality rate of approximately 90 percent if the disease is untreated. It is therefore thought to kill approximately 450,000 children each year, within weeks after contracting the initial infection. If caught during the early stages of the disease, effective and relatively inexpensive antibiotics can cure it. If the disease is allowed to progress, however, treatment becomes much more difficult with intensive dental surgery being the only options. At this stage, permanent and severe disfigurement is inevitable for the few surviving victims.

Onchocerciasis (River Blindness)

Onchocerciasis is caused by a parasitic worm that is passed between humans via black fly bites. Symptoms include an itchy rash, lesions, and visual impairment. There are 18 million cases in the world—99 percent in sub-Saharan Africa. Drugs exist that are effective if administered early. The main drug is *Ivermectin* that kills the larvae in the early stages of the disease. A major strategy of prevention involves the elimination of black flies in the areas of intensive infection in Africa. Overall case rates of Onchocerciasis are decreasing owing to the WHO-led African Programme for Onchocerciasis Control.

Pertussis (Whooping Cough)

Pertussis is a disease that has caused large numbers of deaths over recent centuries. It is caused by a bacterium and is spread from human to human through coughing. The disease causes frequent coughing and can cause pneumonia, seizures, and brain damage. In the developing world, 24 to 48 million people have the disease, and 200,000 to 300,000 die annually. Despite these high figures, mass vaccination programs have brought about a drastic decrease in the number of active Pertussis cases. Nearly 80 percent of the people in the world are vaccinated against whooping cough, and in addition, there is an antibiotic that eliminates the disease in its early stages.

Plague

The word "plague" is often inappropriately used to refer to any pestilential disease that kills large numbers of people. The fact that we use the term in a generic way for any outbreak that kills a significant number of people points to how devastating Plague was over the past two millennia. Plague is caused by a bacterium and has three major human forms: pneumonic, bubonic, and septicaemic. Pneumonic Plague is the most lethal; it is spread through the bites of fleas that have contracted the disease from infected rodents. It then spreads from person to person via respiratory droplets. Its symptoms are the swelling of glands, fever, headache, and weakness. It can kill infected individuals very quickly. Bubonic Plague is spread only by the bites of infected fleas. It causes similar symptoms, but it does not kill as quickly as Pneumonic Plague. Septicaemic Plague is caused by flea bites that deposit the plague bacillus directly into the victim's bloodstream. While this is the least common form of human Plague, it is the most deadly form and is almost always fatal. There are now only approximately 2,000 cases of Plague in the world, with 200 deaths, annually. It is found almost exclusively in developing countries, with approximately 90 percent of cases occurring in Africa. However, there are small numbers of cases and deaths in the developed world, including the United States. There is a vaccine that is generally given only to researchers or health care workers likely to come into contact with the disease. The vaccine is not generally prescribed as Plague has been geographically limited to only a very few locations around the globe. Furthermore, there are a number of antibiotics that are highly effective in curing the disease after exposure. The most important are streptomycin and tetracycline. In addition, pesticides now reduce the number of rats that are potential carriers of the Plague.

Plague was almost certainly a major cause of death in Europe and Asia before the fifth century AD, and cfrom the fifth to the seventeenth century, it was the major killer. It was responsible for the death of about one-third of the population of the Justinian Roman Empire in the fifth century AD. Then in the fourteenth century AD, it was responsible for 25 million deaths in Asia and another 25 million deaths in Europe (in just four years between 1346 and 1350). This latter epidemic, which is generally referred to as the Black Plague, killed about a third of the population of Europe. The last major Plague epidemic of Europe occurred in the mid-seventeenth century, and since then it has only been a minor health problem for the European countries.[10]

A recent, notable outbreak occurred in Surat, India in 1994. The outbreak caused widespread panic locally and widespread concern internationally, but fortunately the strain of Plague did not spread widely and did not kill large numbers. It resulted in approximately 500 cases with an estimated 50 deaths.

Poliomyelitis (Polio)

Poliomyelitis is a viral disease that is contracted through the consumption of water or food contaminated with human waste. Initial symptoms include high fever, headache, and vomiting; serious cases can lead to complete and permanent paralysis within hours to days of symptoms becoming apparent. The most severe cases, between 5 and 10 percent, result in death by asphyxiation. Historically, Poliomyelitis posed a serious global health problem with caseloads in the tens of thousands. Thanks, however, to a concentrated effort to eradicate the disease, case numbers dropped drastically during the last decades of the twentieth century. In fact, Polio case rates have decreased by

99 percent since 1988. In 2005, there were just 1,951 confirmed cases of Polio in the 4 countries that are still polio-endemic: Nigeria, India, Afghanistan, and Pakistan. This drastic reduction in disease prevalence is largely owing to the work of doctors Jonas Salk and Albert Sabin, who developed the first Polio vaccines in the 1950s. Thanks to mass vaccination programs, the Western Hemisphere was certified as Polio free in 1994; China, Europe, and the Western Pacific region followed within several years.

Rabies

Rabies is a viral disease that is transmitted to humans via bites from animals, specifically from the saliva of infected animals. Rabies is fatal to both animals and humans once symptoms appear. Exact case numbers are unknown because the disease is 100 percent fatal when symptomatic. Therefore, any one at risk of developing the disease is prescribed the antidote without waiting for confirmation of the presence of the virus. WHO reports that 10 million people per year are treated with antirabies medication. Nevertheless, it is estimated that 40,000 to 50,000 people die each year from Rabies, indicating that many people have no access to the necessary drugs. Rabies occurs globally, but fatal cases are predominantly restricted to Asia and Africa. Case rates have dropped drastically in the developed world owing to mass vaccination programs of the animal hosts of the disease, but case rates appear to have remained relatively constant throughout the developing world for the past several decades.

Relapsing Fever

Relapsing Fever is caused by a bacterium that is transmitted to humans by lice or ticks. Louse-borne Relapsing Fever is caused by *Borrelia recurrentis*, and tick-borne Relapsing Fever is caused by *Borrelia hermsii*. Symptoms are similar for both types of the disease: victims develop myalgia, nausea, headaches, and diarrhea and recurrent bouts of fever. Typically between 2 and 10 percent of those infected with the disease die if treatment is not provided, although the death rate has occasionally risen as high as 50 percent when outbreaks have occurred in areas with poor hygiene and lack of medical facilities. With appropriate treatment, however, the disease is not fatal. Louse-borne Relapsing Fever is often present in unsanitary areas such as slums, army camps, and refugee camps. As such, this variant of the disease is more prone to outbreaks with mass casualties than to its counterpart. It is geographically limited to a handful of countries in Africa, Asia, and the Americas. The tick-borne variant of the disease is found in western North America, where the tick-vector is endemic.

During the early part of the twenty-first century, Relapsing Fever posed a serious health concern with case rates in the tens of thousands. Thanks, however, to increased vector control and the development of highly effective drugs, the disease has become significantly less threatening. In fact, the WHO has reported no outbreaks of louse-borne Relapsing Fever since 1999. Although sporadic cases of tick-borne Relapsing Fever are reported in North America each year, case rates tend to range between one and six with no fatalities reported in recent years.

Rift Valley Fever

Rift Valley Fever is transmitted to humans from animals, either through direct contact with infected animals or from mosquito bites. It causes low-grade fever, abdominal pain, vomiting, diarrhea, and jaundice with liver and kidney dysfunction often progressing to death. Occasionally it leads to lesions of the eye, brain swelling, or haemorrhagic fever. It is found throughout sub-Saharan Africa and recently spread into the Middle East (probably from imported animals). There were two significant outbreaks in Saudi Arabia and Yemen in 2000. In the Saudi outbreak, there were 453 cases with approximately 95 deaths. In the Yemeni outbreak, there were 1087 cases with 121 deaths. In Kenya, in 1997/1998, a serious outbreak caused more than 300 deaths. The disease then spread to neighboring Somalia causing a relatively serious outbreak there as well. International concern over Rift Valley Fever derives from several factors: there is relatively high mortality rate, death comes quickly within a matter of days of showing symptoms, and there are no effective vaccines or medicines.

Rocky Mountain Spotted Fever

Rocky Mountain Spotted Fever is caused by a bacterium that is passed to humans via tick bites. Symptoms include fever, nausea, and a spotty rash. It was first identified in Idaho in 1896 and since then has spread throughout North and South America. The annual number of cases ranges between 250 and 1,200 and approximately 10 to 20 people die every year. In the case of those who die from the disease, death comes relatively quickly in a matter of days or weeks. There are effective antibiotics that can be given to those with the disease. Case rates have remained constant for the past several decades.

Rotavirus

Rotavirus is contracted by humans through ingesting water or food contaminated by human feces, or by respiratory droplets from people with the infection. It affects predominantly children, causing diarrhea, vomiting, and dehydration. In fact, rotaviruses are the leading cause of diarrheal disease and dehydration in children of both developed and developing countries. There are approximately 125 million cases of the disease and between 600,000 and 875,000 die every year. Death occurs within several days or weeks after contraction of the virus. It exists throughout the world, but the overriding majority of fatalities occur in developing countries. The Rotavirus Vaccine Program and the Global Alliance for Vaccines and Immunizations have been conducting promising research on developing an effective vaccine. Until such a vaccine is readily available, treatment consists of antibiotics and rehydration therapy.

Severe Acute Respiratory Syndrome (SARS)

SARS is caused by the *Coronavirus* that passes from human to human via respiratory droplets and close contact. The symptoms of the disease are high fever, coughing, and difficulty in breathing. In severe cases, pneumonia can develop. It originated in southern China in late 2002; humans are thought to have contracted it from civet cats and raccoon dogs. Between then and the end of the outbreak in July 2003, approximately 8,000 people contracted the disease and of these approximately 1,000 people died. Deaths from SARS are heavily concentrated in older people; and they generally occur within several weeks after the disease is contracted. A notable feature of the disease is its widespread geographical occurrence. People who contracted the disease in China and Hong Kong spread it to a number of Southeast Asian countries and Canada and from there it spread to other areas. Overall, SARS spread to 32 countries by the time the disease was contained. There are no medicines to cure the disease or vaccines to prevent it, but there are medicines that will reduce symptoms such as fever and coughing.[11]

Schistosomiasis (Bilharziasis)

Schistosomiasis is caused by the entry of parasitic worms into humans' intestines. The origin of these worms is snails that live in water and excrete larvae into the water. When humans bathe or swim in an infected water source, the larvae penetrates the skin and migrates into the internal organs. The disease comes in two forms—urinary and intestinal. Urinary Schistosomiasis causes painful, bloody urination and can cause bladder cancer. The intestinal variant causes enlargement of the liver and spleen and intestinal damage. Approximately 200 million people in the developing world have the disease, and approximately 15,000 of them die each year.

There is an effective medicine but it is often not available to infected people in developing countries. Schistosomiasis occurs predominantly in Africa.

Early in the twenty-first century, the cost of drugs to cure Schistosomiasis dropped sharply to just $0.20 per dose. In light of this, a number of organizations are working to treat those already infected with the worms and to create more sanitary latrine systems to slow and prevent the emergence of new cases.

Shigella

Shigella is caused by bacteria that are contracted by humans from contaminated food or direct contact with an infected person. It causes dysentery and dehydration. Approximately 165 million people in the developing world have the disease and about 1.1 million of them die each year. Death generally comes to infected people within several weeks after they contract the infection. There are antibiotics that can cure the disease, but they are having a decreasing impact because of resistance of the pathogen to the drugs. This resistance is causing the overall number of cases to rise, as new cases continue to occur and existing cases cannot be cured.

Smallpox

Smallpox was one of the major killers of humans in past millennia. It is the only major disease that has been eliminated as a result of the progress of medical science over the past two centuries. It is caused by the *variola* virus that comes in two forms. The *variola* major virus kills approximately 30 percent of those who are infected, and the *variola* minor virus kills less than 1 percent of its victims. It was a particularly lethal disease between the sixteenth and eighteenth centuries; it killed approximately 20 percent of the European population, and it was a major contributor to the killing of 90 percent of the Indian population from Mexico through South America.

The disease is transmitted between humans through direct contact or respiratory droplets and it causes a fever, coughing, damage to internal organs, blindness, and often death. It also causes a characteristic rash that develops into scabby sores; when the scabs fall away, the victim is left with deep, pock marked permanent scars.

In 1796, a British doctor, Edward Jenner, developed a cowpox vaccine that proved to be highly effective in preventing contraction of the disease. This vaccine was in use for a full century before vaccines for other diseases were developed. In the twentieth century, the utilization of the smallpox vaccine increased steadily; this was facilitated by the invention of the icebox that allowed for the storage of the vaccine. Between the 1950s and 1970s, considerable international cooperation led to the complete elimination of smallpox in 1977. The virus that causes the disease now only exists in laboratories in the United States and in Russia; it has been completely eliminated from nature. A major contributor to the success of the eradication drive was the fact that there is no vector for the disease. The existence of a reservoir, or vector, such as an animal, insect, or parasitic worm increases tremendously the obstacles to the elimination of a disease.[12]

Streptococcus Pneumoniae (Pneumococcus)

Diseases caused by the bacteria streptococcus pneumoniae constitute a major global public health problem. Pneumococcus can cause mild illnesses, such as sinus and ear infections, but it also causes several life-threatening infections including pneumonia, Meningitis, osteomyelitis, and brain abscesses. Roughly estimated, 7 million people each year become infected with Streptococcus Pneumoniae. A relatively large proportion carry the bacteria and remain healthy, however, as it causes approximately 1 million deaths per year, it falls into the category of a severe threat to global public health. Children in developing countries, especially under the age of five, are most likely to die from the infection; however, the elderly in developed countries are also susceptible to serious and potentially fatal bouts of the disease.

Traditionally, antibiotics (especially penicillin) were successfully used to treat diseases caused by Streptococcus Pneumoniae. Nowadays, however, drug resistance on the part of the bacteria is increasing at a dramatic rate and therefore widespread use of the effective vaccine is recommended.

Syphilis

Syphilis is a sexually transmitted viral disease. The first stage of the disease is the appearance of a single sore within several weeks of infection. The second stage, which can take anywhere from three to twelve months to develop, manifests in a rash, fever, swollen lymph glands, headaches, and muscle aches. The third stage, which occurs after a year from the initial infection, is characterized by blindness and dementia. There are now approximately 12 million people with the disease, and between 100,000 and 150,000 die of it each year. Since the invention of penicillin in 1943, a highly effective drug has existed for curing the disease. Most cases of the disease occur in developing countries, but there are still a significant number of cases in the industrialized world.

It is generally accepted that Syphilis was transmitted from the Caribbean to Europe in the sixteenth century, from where it spread rapidly into

Eastern Europe and Asia. It is now a worldwide health concern. Case rates in North America have been on a relatively steady decline for the past several years. However, case rates in Russia and other areas of the former Soviet Union have been increasing.

Tuberculosis (TB)

TB is a bacterial disease caused by the bacillus *Mycobacterium tuberculosis*. The bacillus is passed from human to human via respiratory droplets that travel through the air. Symptoms include chest pain, fever, and a persistent, severe cough. Approximately 2 billion people, or one-third of the world's population, are carriers of the bacillus. A relatively small proportion of this number— 8 million people per year—develop symptomatic, or "active" TB at some point in their lives, 2 million of whom die annually. Death generally comes several years after the development of symptoms. There is a vaccine for TB, Bacille Calmette Guerin (BCG), but owing to serious side effects and a questionable level of effectiveness, it has not been universally adopted.

TB is found predominantly in the developing world, but it is also present in relatively small numbers in the industrialized countries, particularly in Eastern Europe. Historically, this disease was a major killer of humans in the industrialized world, as indicated by the fact that up to a quarter of all deaths in the United States and Europe were attributable to TB throughout the nineteenth century. This disease is particularly associated today with economically poor areas and insanitary conditions such as those that exist in slums and refugee camps. As such, TB rates in the developed world dropped significantly during the twentieth century as living conditions improved. Nowadays, however, case rates are rising once again—in both developed and developing countries—for two reasons.

First, many TB bacilli have become resistant to commonly administered drugs, making it harder to treat and cure. The standard remedial treatment for TB is a multidrug therapy called "Direct Observation Treatment— Short-course" or DOTS. DOTS must be followed over a six to eight month period. Drug resistant strains of TB have emerged in part because patients have not complied with the DOTS regimen by ceasing to take the medication after symptoms subside and not completing the full six to eight month course of medication. Partial noncompliance leaves a number of TB bacilli still living in the infected person, and these bacilli become resistant to the prescribed drug. In the developing countries and particularly among inmates of prisons throughout the former Soviet Union, resistance is growing generally because victims do not have access to the necessary medicine for the required period. The two types of drug resistant TB are MDR-TB and XDR-TB. MDR-TB stands for multidrug resistant TB; this variant resists treatment from the "first-line" TB medicines, but can still be treated and cured with "second-line" drugs, although second-line drugs need to be taken for a longer period of time, are more expensive and have more side effects. XDR-TB, which develops if drugs prescribed for TB and MDR-TB are not taken properly, stands for extreme or extensive drug resistant TB and this variant of the disease is resistant to both first- and second-line drugs, making treatment options extremely limited and difficult. XDR-TB is currently found in 27 countries, including developed countries such as Canada, Japan, and Norway.

The second factor behind the increase in TB cases is HIV/AIDS. A relatively healthy person can contract TB but not fall ill; however, if they contract HIV and their immune system becomes weakened, their body can no longer ward off TB, resulting in a highly lethal combined illness. Thus, people infected with HIV/AIDS are particularly prone to developing active TB, making HIV/TB coinfection a serious contemporary health concern, especially in Africa where both diseases are rampant.

Typhoid Fever

Typhoid fever results from a bacterial infection that people contract from drinking water that has been infected with *salmonella typhi*. It causes serious fever, headache, and nausea. There are presently approximately 17 million cases in the world, and approximately 600,000 die from it every year. If infected people are not treated with the proper drugs, 10 percent of them die; but if they are properly treated, less than 1 percent dies. The possibility of death occurs several weeks to months after the disease is contracted. The disease presently exists solely in developing countries, but this was not the case in the past when it was a major problem in unsanitary conditions in the Western world. Interestingly, in the Boer War the British army suffered 13,000 deaths owing to Typhoid Fever, compared to 8,000 battlefield deaths. The major medical development that reduced the number of deaths was the invention of the antibiotic *chloramphenicol*. However, the emergence of drug-resistant strains since the 1970s has caused serious problems. There is an available vaccine, but it is of limited efficacy, as it only protects people for approximately two years. There are now new vaccines that are given to people in endemic areas, but they only prevent contraction of the disease in 35 to 45 percent of vaccinated individuals.

Typhus Fever

Typhus Fever (which is not related to Typhoid Fever) is a bacterial infection that is transferred to humans by infected body lice. It causes fever, muscle pain, and the appearance of a dark spot that eventually spreads to cover almost the entire body. It tends to appear in areas where there is severe poverty and cramped living conditions. For this reason, it is often associated with army encampments or refugee camps. There are presently between 7,000 and 17,000 cases in the world varying with the occurrence of epidemic outbreaks, and many hundreds die each year. Typhus Fever now exists only in Africa, particularly in Rwanda, Burundi, and Ethiopia. There is no vaccine for Typhus Fever, but there are very effective sulfa drugs available for treatment. Whereas the death rate for untreated Typhus Fever can be as high as 20 percent, if properly treated the mortality rate drops to less than 1 percent. Case rates have been declining, as the geographical spread of Typhus Fever has been limited to the three countries mentioned earlier.[13]

West Nile Encephalitis

West Nile Encephalitis is caused by the West Nile virus. Birds are the primary reservoir for the virus, which is transmitted to humans via mosquitoes. It usually results in a mild flu-like illness; however, serious cases can lead to meningitis, encephalitis, coma, and death. The mortality rate of the disease ranges between 4 and 11 percent, and death occurs weeks to months after the initial infection.

The first case of West Nile Encephalitis was identified in Uganda in 1937. Until the late twentieth century, the disease did not arouse significant alarm as it tended to cause only asymptomatic or mild infections. Since 1996, however, the virus has spread beyond Africa and caused outbreaks in Congo, the Czech Republic, France, Israel, Romania, and Russia. These outbreaks usually involved between 50 and 100 cases, with some deaths. In 1999, the disease was discovered in the United States and caused an outbreak of 149 cases and 18 deaths. Since the late 1990s, West Nile virus has become a global problem increasingly causing serious illness and death on almost every continent. Medication exists only to treat symptoms of the illness and there is no vaccine to prevent the disease.

Yellow Fever

Yellow Fever is a viral infection that is transmitted to humans from mosquito bites, who themselves contract it from biting infected humans or monkeys. It causes fever, vomiting, and backache. It sometimes develops into jaundice and causes bleeding from the mouth, nose, and eyes. There are now approximately 200,000 cases in the world and 30,000 deaths annually. Death generally occurs within several weeks after the disease is contracted.

The disease was originally brought from Africa to the Western Hemisphere by the slave trade, and from the seventeenth through the nineteenth century, it spread throughout much of Latin America, the Caribbean, and the United States where it caused numerous serious outbreaks.

In 1900, research proved that Yellow Fever was transmitted by mosquitoes. This led to programs to reduce and control the mosquito population. In the 1930s, the first vaccine against Yellow Fever was developed; since that time better and more effective ones have superseded it. The currently used vaccine provides effective protection for a 10-year period. Thanks to mass vaccination campaigns, Yellow Fever case rates have decreased significantly at the global level. Nevertheless, the disease continues to pose a serious health risk in agricultural and forested areas of Africa and Central and South America.

NOTES

Chapter 1   Overview of Infectious Diseases and Analytical Framework

1. Infectious diseases are defined as diseases caused by the actions of a living organism. Communicable infectious diseases are contagious, which means that they can be transmitted directly from human to human. Noncommunicable infectious diseases are diseases that are contracted by humans either through direct contact with an infected animal or bird, or through contact with disease vectors (or intermediaries), such as ticks, mosquitoes, and rodents.

2. William H. McNeill, *Plagues and People* (Garden City: Anchor Books, 1976), 108–110.

3. Hans Zinsser, *Rats, Lice, and History* (New York: Black Dog and Leventhal Publishers, 1934), 119; Frederick F. Cartwright and Michael D. Biddiss, *Disease and History* (New York: Barnes and Noble, 1972), 6–8.

4. W. Hobson, *World Health and History* (Bristol: John Wright and Sons, 1963), 16.

5. Jonathan B. Tucker, *Scourge: The Once and Future Threat of Smallpox* (New York: Atlantic Monthly Press, 2001), 5–6; Michael B. A. Oldstone, *Viruses, Plagues, and History* (Oxford: Oxford University Press, 1998), 81.

6. Zinsser, *Rats, Lice, and History*, 94.

7. Zinsser, *Rats, Lice, and History*, 155.

8. McNeill, *Plagues and People*, 146; 199.

9. Norman Cantor, *In the Wake of the Plague: The Black Death and the World It Made* (New York: Perennial Books, 2002), 13–16.

10. Cantor, *In the Wake of the Plague*, 6; Mark Harrison, *Disease and the Modern World: 1500 to Present Day* (Cambridge, MA: Polity, 2004), 22–23; Sheldon Watts, *Epidemics and History: Disease, Power, and Imperialism* (New Haven, CT: Yale University Press, 1997), Chap. 1.

11. Harold E. Hinman, *World Eradication of Infectious Diseases* (Springfield: Charles C. Thomas, 1966), 33; R. Berkov, *The World Health Organization: A Study in Decentralized International Administration* (Geneva: Librairie E. Droz, 1957), 36; Harrison, *Disease and the Modern World*, 26; 43.

12. Berkov, *The World Health Organization*, 36.

13. Neville Goodman, *International Health Organizations and Their Work* (London: Churchill Livingston, 1971), 27–36.

14. McNeill, *Plagues and People*, 306.

15. A. Karlen, *Man and Microbes: Diseases and Plagues in History and Modern Times* (New York: Simon and Schuster, 1995), 104; Jared Diamond, *Guns, Germs, and Steel: The Fates of Human Societies* (New York: W.W. Norton, 1999), 210–212.

16. Cartwright and Biddiss, *Disease and History*, 145; Harrison, *Disease and the Modern World*, 72–82.

17. Folke Henschen, *The History and Geography of Diseases* (New York: Seymour Lawrence, 1966), 36–39.

18. Cartwright and Biddiss, *Disease and History*, 54–81; Watts, *Epidemics and History*, Chap. 4; Harrison, *Disease and the Modern World*, 35–38.

19. Cartwright and Biddiss, *Disease and History*, 82–112; Zinsser, *Rats, Lice, and History*, 159.

20. Cartwright and Biddiss, *Disease and History*, 83; 133; 145.

21. McNeill, *Plagues and People*, 154.

22. McNeill, *Plagues and People*, 212.

23. Hobson, *World Health and History*, 32; Zinsser, *Rats, Lice, and History*, 163–164; Cartwright and Biddiss, *Disease and History*, 82–112.

24. McNeill, *Plagues and People*, 233; Charles Winslow, *The Conquest of Epidemic Diseases* (Princeton, NJ: Princeton University Press, 1943), 277; Watts, *Epidemics and History*, Chap. 5.

25. In 1843, the Alexandria Health Council was superseded by the Egyptian Sanitary Council.

26. Oleg Schepin and Waldeermar Yermakov, *International Quarantine* (Madison, WI: International University Press, 1991), 37–62.

27. Richard N. Cooper, "International Cooperation in Public Health as a Prologue to Macroeconomic Cooperation," in *Can Nations Agree? Issues in International Economic Cooperation*, ed. Richard N. Cooper, Barry Eichengreen, C. Randall, Henning Gerald Holtham, and Robert D. Putnam. (Washington, DC: Brookings Institution, 1989), 183–190; Norman Howard-Jones, *International Public Health between the Two World Wars: The Organizational Problems* (Geneva: WHO, 1978).

28. Goodman, *International Health Organizations and Their Work*, 46–68; David P. Fidler, *International Law and Infectious Diseases* (Oxford: Clarendon Press, 1999), Chap. 2.

29. McNeill, *Plagues and People*, 277.

30. Sheldon Watts, *Disease and Medicine in World History* (New York: Routledge, 2003), xii; Zinsser, *Rats, Lice, and History*, 290; Oldstone, *Viruses, Plagues, and History*, Chap. 2; Harrison, Disease and the Modern World, Chaps. 5–6.

31. McNeill, *Plagues and People*, 344.

32. Fidler, *International Law and Infectious Diseases*, 55.

33. McNeill, *Plagues and People*, 246.

34. Laurie Garrett, *The Coming Plague: Newly Emerging Diseases in a World Out of Balance* (New York: Farrar, Strauss and Giroux, 1994), 66–70; Cartwright and Biddiss, *Disease and History*, 145–150.

35. Gina Kolata, *Flu: The Story of the Great Influenza Pandemic of 1918 and the Search for the Virus That Caused It* (New York: Farrar, Strauss, and Giroux, 1999), 7.

36. Cartwright and Biddiss, *Disease and History*, 80.

37. Watts, *Disease and Medicine in World History*, 135.

38. Carol Lancaster, "The Chinese Aid System," *Center for Global Development* June 2007: 497–498, http://www.cgdev.org/content/publications/detail/13953/.

39. Cartwright and Biddiss, *Disease and History*, 223; Harrison, *Disease and the Modern World*, 149–150.

40. The first passenger planes could carry up to 20 people.

41. James E. Vance, *Capturing the Horizon: The Historical Geography of Transportation since the Transportation Revolution of the Sixteenth Century* (New York: Harper and Row, 1986), 57–65.

42. Goodman, *International Health Organizations and Their Work*, 107–137; Howard-Jones, *International Public Health between the Two World Wars*, 21–28; Fidler, *International Law and Infectious Diseases*, 50–51.

43. Watts, *Disease and Medicine in World History*, 27.

44. Quoted in Garrett, *The Coming Plague*, 33.

45. Watts, *Epidemics and History*, Chap. 3; Fenner, F., D. A. Henderon, I. Arita, Z. Jezek, and I. D. Ladnyi, *Smallpox and Its Eradication* (Geneva: WHO, 1988); Tucker, *Scourge*, 125–127.

46. Harrison, *Disease and the Modern World*, 167–168.

47. Judith Miller, Stephen Engelberg, and William Broad, *Germs: Biological Weapons and America's Secret War* (New York: Simon and Schuster, 2001), 37.

48. David Heymann, "Evolving Infectious Disease Threats to National and Global Security," in *Global Health Challenges for Human Security*, ed. Lincoln Chen, Jennifer Leaning, and Vasant Narasimhan (Cambridge, MA: Harvard University Press, 2003), 118.

49. World Health Organization, *Global Defense against the Infectious Disease Threat* (Geneva: WHO, 2002), 176.

50. World Bank, World Development Report, 1993: Investing in Health (Washington, DC: World Bank, 1993), 1.

51. WHO, *Global Defense against the Infectious Disease Threat*, Chap. 1.

52. WHO, *Global Defense against the Infectious Disease Threat*, Chap. 1.

53. WHO, *Global Defense against the Infectious Disease Threat*, Chap. 2.

54. Heymann, "Evolving Infectious Disease Threats to National and Global Security," 118.

55. C. J. L. Murray, "Quantifying the Burden of Disease: The Technical Basis for Disability Adjusted Life Years," *Bulletin of the World Health Organization* 72: 3 (1994): 429–445, http://whqlibdoc.who.int/bulletin/1994/Vol72-No3/bulletin_1994_72(3)_429–445.pdf; C. J. L. Murray and A. D. Lopez, "Quantifying Disability: Data, Methods and Results," *Bulletin of the World*

Health Organization 72: 3 (1994): 481–494, http://whqlibdoc.who.int/bulletin/1994/Vol72-No3/bulletin_1994_72(3)_481–494.pdf; Sudhir Anand and Kara Hansen, "DALYs: Efficiency versus Equity," *World Development* 26: 2 (1998): 309; World Health Organization, *The World Health Report 2002: Reducing Risks, Promoting Health Life* (Geneva: WHO, 2002), Annex 3.

56. Commission on Macroeconomics and Health, *Macroeconomics and Health: Investing in Health for Economic Development*, 1, 16.

57. Richard Holbrooke, "Battling the AIDS Pandemic," *AIDS: The Threat to World Security.* (Electronic Journal of the U.S. Department of State) 5: 2 (July 2000), http://usinfo.state.gov/journals/itgic/0700/ijge/gj01.htm.

58. Laurie Garrett, "Microbial Threats and the Global Society," *Emerging Infectious Diseases* 2 (1996): 73; WHO, *Global Defense against the Infectious Disease Threat*, 175.

59. The World Tourism Organization is a specialized branch of the United Nations that is concerned with the promotion, regulation, and governance of international tourism. The organization estimates that in 1950 there were 25 million international arrivals; by 2020, it estimates that that number will have increased more than hundred fold to approximately 1.56 billion.

60. World Tourism Organization, "Facts and Figures," http://www.world-tourism.org/facts/menu.html.

61. Institute of Medicine, Microbial Threats to Health: Emergence, Detection, and Response (Washington, DC: National Academies Press, 2003), 107.

62. B. D. Gushulak and D. W. MacPherson, "Population Mobility and Infectious Diseases: The Diminishing Impact of Classical Infectious Diseases and New Approaches for the 21st Century," *Clinical Infectious Diseases* 31 (2000): 777.

63. Garrett, "Microbial Threats and the Global Society," 73.

64. Laurie Garrett, *Betrayal of Trust: the Collapse of Global Public Health* (New York: Hyperion Books, 2000), Chap. 1.

65. All descriptions of diseases are intended to provide necessary background information for the volume, not for medical treatment purposes. Similarly, all figures and statistics are approximate and subject to change.

66. James N. Rosenau, "Governance, Order and Change in World Politics," in *Governance without Government: Order and Change in World Politics Vol. 20: Cambridge Studies in International Politics*, ed. James N. Rosenau (Cambridge: Cambridge University Press, 1992), 4.

67. John G. Ruggie, "American Exceptionalism, Exemptionalism and Global Governance," in *American Exceptionalism and Human Rights*, ed. Michael Ignatieff (Princeton, NJ: Princeton University Press, 2005), 307.

68. Ruggie, "American Exceptionalism, Exemptionalism and Global Governance," 308.

69. Robert O. Keohane and Joseph S. Nye, "Introduction." in *Governance in a Globalizing World*, ed. Joseph Nye and John Donahue (Washington, DC: Brookings Institution Press, 2000), 12.

70. A study that classifies the functions of international organizations in a comparable fashion is described in Robert W. Cox, Harold K. Jacobson, Gerard and Victoria Curzon, Joseph S. Nye, Lawrence Scheinman, James P. Sewell, and Susan Strange, *The Anatomy of Influence: Decision Making in International Organization* (New Haven, CT: Yale University Press, 1973).

71. Roy Widdus, "Public-Private Partnerships for Health: Their Main Targets, Their Diversity, and Their Future Directions," *Bulletin of the World Health Organization* 79: 8 (2001): 713–720; Kent Buse and Gill Walt, "Globalisation and Multilateral Public-Private Health Partnerships: Issues for Health Policy," in *Health Policy in a Globalising World*, ed. Kelley Lee, Kent Buse, and Suzanne Fustikian (Cambridge: Cambridge University Press, 2002), 41–62; Michael Reich, "Introduction: Public-Private Partnerships for Public Health," in *Public-Private Partnerships for Public Health*, ed. Michael R. Reich (Cambridge, MA: Harvard Center for Population and Development Studies, 2002), 1–16.

72. Jonathan L. Charney, "Commentary: Compliance with International Soft Law," in *Commitment and Compliance: The Role of Non-binding Norms in the International Legal System*, ed. Dinah Helton (Oxford: Oxford University Press, 2000), 117–119; Kenneth Abbott and Duncan Snidal, "Hard and Soft Law in International Governance," *International Organization* 54: 3 (2000): 421–456.

73. Oran R. Young, *Governance in World Affairs* (London: Cornell University Press, 1999), 1; Robert O. Keohane and Joseph S. Nye, *Power and Interdependence: World Politics in Transition* (Boston: Little Brown, 1989), Chap. 1; Obijiofor Aginam, *Global Health Governance: International Law and Public Health in a Divided World* (Toronto: University of Toronto Press, 2005), 27–70.

74. Robert O. Keohane, *After Hegemony: Cooperation and Discord in the World Global Economy* (Princeton, NJ: Princeton University Press, 1984); Abram Chayes and Antonia Handler, "On Compliance," in *International Institutions: An International Organizations Reader*, ed. Lisa L. Martin and Beth A Simmons (Cambridge, MA: MIT Press, 1993), 248–277; Andrew Hurrell, "International Society and the Study of Regimes," in *Regime Theory and International Relations*, ed. Volker Rittberger (Oxford: Clarendon Press, 1993), 49–72; Keohane and Nye, "Introduction," 1–41; Barbara Koremenos, Charles Lipson, and Duncan Snidal, "Rational Design: Looking Back to Move Forward," *International Organization* 55: 4 (2001): 1051–1082.

75. Peter M. Haas, "Epistemic Communities," in *Handbook of International Environmental Law*, ed. Daniel Bodansky, Jutta Brunee, and Ellen Hey (Oxford: Oxford University Press, 2007), 791–806.

76. James N. Rosenau, *The Study of Global Interdependence* (London: Frances Pinter, 1980), 39, 51.

77. Richard N. Cooper, *The Economics of Interdependence: Economic Policy in the Atlantic Community* (New York: McGraw-Hill, 1968), 183–190; Edward L.

Morse, *Modernization and the Transformation of International Relations* (New York: Free Press, 1976).

78. External Committee on Smart Regulation, *Smart Regulation: A Regulatory Committee for Canada* (Ottawa: Government of Canada, 2004), 17.
79. Cooper, "International Cooperation in Public Health as a Prologue to Macroeconomic Cooperation," 183–189.
80. Ruggie, "American Exceptionalism, Exemptionalism and Global Governance," 313.
81. Richard Price, "Transnational Civil Society and Advocacy in World Politics," *World Politics* 55 (July 2003): 584, 587; Keohane, *After Hegemony*, Chap. 1; Margaret Keck and Kathryn Sikkink, *Activists beyond Borders: Advocacy Networks in International Politics* (Ithaca, NY: Cornell University Press, 1999); Ann M. Florini, "Lessons Learned," in *The Third Force: The Rise of Transnational Civil Society*, ed. Ann M. Florini (Washington, DC: Carnegie Endowment for International Peace, 2000), 211–240; Michael Barnett and Martha Finnemore, *Rules for the World: International Organizations in Global Politics* (Ithaca, NY: Cornell University Press, 2004), Chap. 4.
82. See Miles Kahler and David Lake, "Globalization and Changing Patterns of Political Authority," in *Governance in a Global Economy: Political Authority in Transition*, ed. Miles Kahler and David Lake (Princeton, NJ: Princeton University Press, 2003), 412–438; Robert Keohane, *Neoliberal Institutionalism: A Perspective on State Politics*. Boulder, CO: Westview, 1989; David P. Fidler, "Emerging Trends in International Law Concerning Global Infectious Diseases Control," *Emerging Infectious Diseases* 9: 3 (2003): 285–290; David P. Fidler, "Constitutional Outlines of Public Health's 'New World Order,' " *Temple Law Review* 77: 1 (2004): 247–272.

Chapter 2   Global Health Governance in the Twentieth Century

1. Daniel R. Headrick, *The Tools of Empire: Technology and European Imperialism in the Nineteenth Century* (Oxford: Oxford University Press, 1981), 167.
2. A. G. Kenwood and A. L. Lougheed, *Growth of the International Economy 1820–1900 3rd Edition* (London: Routledge, 1992), 11–12.
3. Headrick, *The Tools of Empire*, 155; Daniel R. Headrick, *The Tentacles of Progress: Technology Transfer in the Age of Imperialism, 1850–1940* (Oxford: Oxford University Press, 1988), 26.
4. Andre Siegfried, Trans., *Routes of Contagion* (New York: Harcourt Press, 1965), 16.
5. Seigfried, *Routes of Contagion*, 32–33.
6. James Foreman-Peck, *A History of the World Economy: International Economic Relations since 1850* (London: FT Prentice Hall, 1983), 3.
7. Yellow fever was also a concern at this time, but it was more of a problem for the Western Hemisphere, specifically the United States, than it was for Europe.

8. Neville Goodman, *International Health Organizations and Their Work* (London: Churchill Livingston, 1971), 31–35; Oleg Schepin and Waldeermar Yermakov, *International Quarantine* (Madison, WI: International University Press, 1991), 9–25.

9. Schepin and Yermakov, *International Quarantine*, 47–61.

10. Conference Sanitaire Internationale de Paris, Proces-verbaux. Paris: Imprimerie Nationale, 1851; Obijiofor Aginam, *Global Health Governance: International Law and Public Health in a Divided World* (Toronto: University of Toronto Press, 2005), 61–66.

11. Goodman, *International Health Organizations and Their Work*, 42–50; Schepin and Yermakov, *International Quarantine*, 63–73; Norman Howard-Jones, *The Scientific Background to the International Sanitary Conferences 1851–1938* (Geneva: WHO, 1975), 12–16; Richard N. Cooper, "International Cooperation in Public Health as a Prologue to Macroeconomic Cooperation," in *Can Nations Agree? Issues in International Economic Cooperation*, ed. Richard N. Cooper, Barry Eichengreen, C. Randall, Henning Gerald Holtham, and Robert D. Putnam (Washington, DC: Brookings Institution, 1989), 193–196.

12. Howard-Jones, *The Scientific Background to the International Sanitary Conferences 1851–1938*, Chap. 2; Cooper, "International Cooperation in Public Health as a Prologue to Macroeconomic Cooperation," 185–186.

13. Goodman, *International Health Organizations and Their Work*, 43.

14. Conference Sanitaire Internationale, Paris, 1859.

15. Goodman, *International Health Organizations and Their Work*, 54; Howard-Jones, *The Scientific Background to the International Sanitary Conferences 1851–1938*, 20–22; Schepin and Yermakov, *International Quarantine*, 74–77.

16. Conference Sanitaire Internationale, Paris, 1866.

17. Goodman, *International Health Organizations and Their Work*, 54–58; Howard-Jones, *The Scientific Background to the International Sanitary Conferences 1851–1938*, 23–34; Cooper, "International Cooperation in Public Health as a Prologue to Macroeconomic Cooperation," 198–200.

18. Conference Sanitaire Internationale, Paris, 1874.

19. Goodman, *International Health Organizations and Their Work*, 58–60; Howard-Jones, *The Scientific Background to the International Sanitary Conferences 1851–1938*, 35–41.

20. Conference Sanitaire Internationale, Rome, 1885.

21. Schepin and Yermakov, *International Quarantine*, 111–121; Cooper, "International Cooperation in Public Health as a Prologue to Macroeconomic Cooperation," 208–209; Goodman, *International Health Organizations and Their Work*, 64–66; Howard-Jones, *The Scientific Background to the International Sanitary Conferences 1851–1938*, 46–57.

22. Schepin and Yermakov, *International Quarantine*, 118.

23. Conference Sanitaire International de Paris, 1892; Conventions Sanitaires Internationales 1892–1897.

24. Goodman, *International Health Organizations and Their Work*, 66–67; Howard-Jones, *The Scientific Background to the International Sanitary Conferences 1851–1938*, 58–66; Schepin and Yermakov, *International Quarantine*, 131–133.

25. Conventions Sanitaires Internationales, 1892–1897.

26. Howard-Jones, *The Scientific Background to the International Sanitary Conferences 1851–1938*, 66–70; Goodman, *International Health Organizations and Their Work*, 67–68; Schepin and Yermakov, *International Quarantine*, 136–144.

27. Conference Sanitaire Internationale, Paris, 1894; Conventions Sanitaires Internationales, 1892–1897.

28. The Ottoman Empire had formal legal jurisdiction over the Hejaz region, although the Hashimid Sharifs had effective control until 1924 when the Saudis established control.

29. Schepin and Yermakov, *International Quarantine*, 146–150; Goodman, *International Health Organizations and Their Work*, 68; Howard-Jones, *The Scientific Background to the International Sanitary Conferences 1851–1938*, 71–75.

30. Howard-Jones, *The Scientific Background to the International Sanitary Conferences 1851–1938*, 42–45; Goodman, *International Health Organizations and Their Work*, 61–63; Cooper, "International Cooperation in Public Health as a Prologue to Macroeconomic Cooperation," 204–207; Conference Sanitaire Internationale, Paris, 1881.

31. Conference Sanitaire Internationale Paris, 1897; Conventions Sanitaires Internationales, 1892–1897.

32. Michael B. A. Oldstone, *Viruses, Plagues, and History* (Oxford: Oxford University Press, 1998), 8–13.

33. Schepin and Yermakov, *International Quarantine*, 158.

34. Goodman, *International Health Organizations and Their Work*, 68–69; Howard-Jones, *The Scientific Background to the International Sanitary Conferences 1851–1938*, 78–80; Cooper, "International Cooperation in Public Health as a Prologue to Macroeconomic Cooperation," 212–213.

35. Ann Beck, *A History of the British Medical Administration of East Africa, 1900–1950* (Cambridge, MA: Harvard University Press, 1970), 7.

36. Goodman, *International Health Organizations and Their Work*, 70; Howard-Jones, *The Scientific Background to the International Sanitary Conferences 1851–1938*, Chap. 3; Cooper, "International Cooperation in Public Health as a Prologue to Macroeconomic Cooperation," 182.

37. Goodman, *International Health Organizations and Their Work*, 79–106.

38. Goodman, *International Health Organizations and Their Work*, 318–326.

39. Alexandra Minna Stern and Howard Markel, "International Efforts to Control Infectious Diseases, 1851 to the Present," *Journal of the American Medical Association* 292: 12 (2004): 1476.

40. Goodman, *International Health Organizations and Their Work*, 389; David P. Fidler, *International Law and Infectious Diseases* (Oxford: Clarendon Press, 1999), 19.

41. Conference Sanitaire Internationale, Paris, 1904, Arts. 52–180.
42. Norman Howard-Jones, *International Public Health between the Two World Wars: The Organizational Problems* (Geneva: WHO, 1978), 17.
43. Stern and Markel, "International Efforts to Control Infectious Diseases, 1851 to the Present," 1475; Fidler, *International Law and Infectious Diseases*, 9.
44. Goodman, *International Health Organizations and Their Work*, 79–106.
45. Green Williams, *The Plague Killers* (New York: Charles Scribner's Sons, 1969), Chap. 3; Armando Solorzano, "Sowing the Seeds of Neo-imperialism: The Rockefeller Foundation's Yellow Fever Campaign." *International Journal of Health Service* 22: 3 (1992): 529–554; Rockefeller Foundation, *Official Website*, "The Rockefeller Foundation Timeline," 2006, http://www.rockfound.org/about_us/history/timeline.shtml.
46. Anne Marie Moulin, "The Pasteur Institutes between the Two World Wars: The Transformation of the International Sanitary Order," in *International Health Organizations and Movements 1918–1939*, ed. Paul Weindling (Cambridge: Cambridge University Press, 1995), 259.
47. Goodman, *International Health Organizations and Their Work*, 20–25; David M. Leive, *International Regulatory Regimes: Case Studies in Health, Meteorology, and Food Volumes I & II* (Lexington, MA: Lexington Books, 1976), 25.
48. Goodman, *International Health Organizations and Their Work*, 74–75.
49. International Sanitary Convention, 1926; Goodman, *International Health Organizations and Their Work*, 71–74; Howard-Jones, *International Public Health between the Two World Wars*, 142–145.
50. International Sanitary Regulations, 1926, Art. 15; Leive, *International Regulatory Regimes*, 20; Howard-Jones, *International Public Health between the Two World Wars*, 32.
51. Howard-Jones, *International Public Health between the Two World Wars*, 13; Fidler, *International Law and Infectious Diseases*, 46.
52. Goodman, *International Health Organizations and Their Work*, 94–95.
53. David Arnold, "Medicine and Colonialism," in *Companion Encyclopedia of the History of Medicine Vol. 2*, ed. W. F. Bynum and R. Porter (London: Routledge, 1993), 1393–1416; Mark Harrison, *Public Health in British India: Anglo-American Preventive Medicine 1859–1914* (New York: Cambridge University Press, 1994), 3; Moulin, "The Pasteur Institutes between the Two World Wars," 259.
54. Williams, *The Plague Killers*, 47–50; Solorzano, "Sowing the Seeds of Neo-imperialism," 530.
55. Richard E. Brown, *Rockefeller Medicine Men* (Los Angeles: University of California Press, 1979), 116–117.
56. Marta Aleksandra Balinska, "Assistance and Not Mere Relief: The Epidemic Commission of the League of Nations, 1920–1923," in *International Health Organizations and Movements, 1918–1939*, ed. Paul Weindling (Cambridge: Cambridge University Press, 1995), 92.
57. Balinska, "Assistance and Not Mere Relief," 78–90.
58. Goodman, *International Health Organizations and Their Work*, 138–150.

59. Fidler, *International Law and Infectious Diseases*, 13.
60. This left just three officially reportable diseases in the IHRs—cholera, plague, and yellow fever.
61. WHO Resolution, 9:48 (1956); Michel Bélanger, *Droit International de la Santé* (Paris: Economica, 1983), 96–97.
62. WHO Doc. Epid/44 (1950): 16, 34–35; Leive, *International Regulatory Regimes*, 33.
63. World Health Organization. *International Health Regulations (Revised 1981)* (Geneva: WHO, 1983), Arts. 23, 29, 91.
64. Bélanger, *Droit International de la Santé*, 98–99.
65. *Weekly Epidemiological Report*, "Functioning of the International Health Regulations from the Period 1 January to 31 December 1981," 57: 48 (1982): 369; *Weekly Epidemiological Report*, "Functioning of the International Health Regulations from the Period 1 January to 31 December 1981 (Continued from No 49)," 58: 50 (1983): 386; *Weekly Epidemiological Report*, "Functioning of the International Health Regulations from the Period 1 January to 31 December 1985," 61: 50 (1986): 386.
66. *Weekly Epidemiological Report*, "Cholera," 56: 49 (1981): 387.
67. WHO Doc. IQ/26 (1956), 25, 31; IQ/61 (1957), 405.
68. Leive, *International Regulatory Regimes*, 102.
69. Leive, *International Regulatory Regimes*, 42–55, 62–64; Bélanger, *Droit International de la Santé*, 112–113.
70. Goodman, *International Health Organizations and Their Work*, 214–224; David Koplow, *Smallpox: The Fight to Eradicate a Global Scourge* (Berkeley: University of California Press, 2003), 139–144.
71. WHO, *International Health Regulations*. Arts. 20, 21. 1983; Fidler, *International Law and Infectious Diseases*, 60.
72. Fidler, *International Law and Infectious Diseases*, 112–115.

Chapter 3 Disease Containment: Surveillance Systems, Emergency Responses, and Transborder Regulations

1. David Heymann and Guenael Rodier, "Hot Spots in a Wired World: WHO Surveillance of Emerging and Re-emerging Infectious Diseases," *Lancet* 1: December (2001): 347.
2. Institute of Medicine, *Microbial Threats to Health: Emergence, Detection, and Response* (Washington, DC: National Academies Press, 2003), 32. (See Chap. 3 of publication for a description of factors driving the emergence of new diseases and resurgence of old diseases. The list includes microbial adaptation and change; human susceptibility to infection; climate and weather; changing ecosystems; economic development and land use; human demographics and behavior; technology and industry; international travel and commerce; breakdown of public health measures; poverty and social inequality; war and famine; lack of political will; and intent to harm.)

3. Institute of Medicine, *Microbial Threats to Health*, 14.

4. Laurie Garrett, "The Next Pandemic," *Foreign Affairs* 84: 3 (2005): 3; 10–13.

5. Marc L. Ostfield, "Bioterrorism as a Foreign Policy Issue," *SAIS* 24 (Winter–Spring 2004): 132, http://muse.jhu.edu/journals/sais_review/ v024/24.1ostfield01.pdf.

6. Kyle B. Olson, "Aum Shinrikyo: Once and Future Threat," *Emerging Infectious Diseases* 5: 4 (1999): 514; Institute of Medicine, *Microbial Threats to Health*, 130.

7. Institute of Medicine, *Microbial Threats to Health*, 46.

8. Michael Stebbins, "Is the U.S. Prepared for a Bioterrorist Attack?" *Technology for Training against Terror. Federation of American Scientists*, February 17, 2006, http://www.fas.org/main/content.jsp?formAction= 297&contentId=343.

9. Institute of Medicine, *Microbial Threats to Health*, 131.

10. Institute of Medicine, *Emerging Infections: Microbial Threats to Health in the United States* (Washington, DC: National Academies Press, 1992), 115.

11. World Health Organization, *International Health Regulations (Revised 1981)* (Geneva: WHO, 1983), Arts. 3, 5, 6, 10.

12. Heymann and Rodier, "Hot Spots in a Wired World," 345.

13. David Heymann and Guenael Rodier, "Global Surveillance, National Surveillance and SARS," *Emerging Infectious Diseases* 10: 2 (2004): 1, http://www.cdc.gov/ncidod/EID/vol10no2/03-1038.htm.

14. Between 1951 and 1969 the International Sanitary Regulations specified that states should report outbreaks of cholera, plague, yellow fever, small-pox, relapsing fever, and typhus. The Regulations were amended in 1969 (when the name was changed to the International Health Regulations), 1973, and 1981 to remove relapsing fever, typhus, and smallpox from the list, leaving only cholera, plague, and yellow fever as reportable diseases until the IHR underwent major revision in 2005.

15. WHO, *Official Website*, "WHO Global Influenza Surveillance Network," 2007, http://www.who.int/csr/disease/influenza/surveillance/en/.

16. ProMed, *Official Website*, "About ProMed Mail," http://www.promedmail. org/pls/promed/f?p=2400:1950:14756322966045941699::NO:::

17. Deborah MacKenzie, "Don't Let It Die," *New Scientist*, February 6, 1999, 50; Martin Hugh-Jones, "Global Awareness of Disease Outbreaks: The Experience of ProMED-Mail," *Public Health Reports* 116: 6 (2001): 27–32; Stephen S. Morse, Barbara Hatch-Rosenberg, and Jack Woodall, "ProMED Global Monitoring of Emerging Diseases" Health Policy 38 (December 1996): 135–153.

18. GPHIN, *Official Website*, "Information," http://www.phac-aspc.gc.ca/ media/nr-rp/2004/2004_gphin-rmispbk_e.html; National Advisory Committee on SARS and Public Health, *Learning from SARS: Renewal of Public Health in Canada* (Ottawa: Health Canada, 2003), 198; WHO, *Global Defense against the Infectious Disease Threat* (Geneva: WHO, 2002), 5–6.

19. Jennifer Brower and Peter Chalk, *The Global Threat of New and Reemerging Infectious Diseases: Reconciling U.S. National Security and Public Health Policy* (Arlington, VA: Rand Corporation, 2003), 92.

20. GEIS, *Official Website*, "About DOD-GEIS," http://www.geis.fhp.osd. mil/; Brower and Chalk, *The Global Threat of New and Reemerging Infectious Diseases*, 110–111.

21. Institute of Medicine, *Microbial Threats to Health*, 154.

22. This fear is not unfounded. Thailand was estimated to have lost more than $1 billion in poultry exports after the outbreak was discovered and publicized. See "A Shot of Transparency," *Economist*, August 12, 2006, 65.

23. "A Shot of Transparency," *Economist*, August 12, 2006, 65.

24. William Karesh and Robert Cook, "The Human-Animal Link," *Foreign Affairs* 84: 3 (2005): 49.

25. Karesh and Cook, "The Human-Animal Link," 40.

26. Heymann and Rodier, "Hot Spots in a Wired World," 351.

27. Brower and Chalk, *The Global Threat of New and Reemerging Infectious Diseases*, 92.

28. Although USAMRIID is predominantly a research facility, on several occasions in the past it has offered its services during outbreaks at least in part because it is the only Department of Defense body that has the medical capacity to study highly hazardous infectious agents that require maximum containment at biosafety level 4. Importantly, it also has a maximum-containment treatment facility where individuals exposed to lethal infectious agents can be quarantined.

29. The Red Cross is made up of the Red Cross/Red Crescent groups, the International Federation of Red Cross and Red Crescent Societies, and the International Committee of the Red Cross. For information on the similarities and differences between these groups see John Hutchinson, "Custodians of the Sacred Fire: The ICRC and the Postwar Reorganisation of the International Red Cross," in *International Health Organizations and Movements 1918–1939* ed. Paul Weindling (Cambridge: Cambridge University Press, 1995), 17–35.

30. Medecins Sans Frontieres (International), *Official Website*, "About MSF," 2007, http://www.msf.org/msfinternational/aboutmsf/.

31. United Nations Children's Fund (UNICEF), *Official Website*, "What We Do," 2007, http://www.unicef.org/whatwedo/index.html.

32. GOARN operated informally from 1997 until 2000.

33. WHO, *Official Website*, "Global Outbreak Alert & Response Network," 2007, www.who.int/csr/outbreaknetwork/en.

34. Institute of Medicine, *Microbial Threats to Health*, 157.

35. The criteria that GOARN uses in determining what constitutes an outbreak of international concern are the following points: it is unknown; it might spread beyond borders; it has high rates of morbidity and mortality; it could provoke interference with international trade; the country where the outbreak occurs has inadequate capabilities to manage it; and/or it emanated from an accidental or deliberate discharge.

36. Thomas W. Grein, Kande-Bure O. Kamara, Guenael Rodier, Aileen J. Plant, Patrick Bovier, Michael J. Ryan,et al., "Rumors of Disease in the Global Village: Outbreak Verification," *Emerging Infectious Diseases* 6: 2 (2000): 97–102; Institute of Medicine, *Microbial Threats to Health*, 154–161; WHO, "Global Outbreak Alert & Response Network," www.who.int/csr/outbreaknetwork/en.

37. David P. Fidler, *International Law and Infectious Diseases* (Oxford: Clarendon Press, 1999), 234; Maire Connolly, M. Gayer, M. J. Ryan, P. Spiegel, P. Salama, and D. L. Heymann. "Communicable Diseases in Complex Emergencies: Impact and Challenges," *Lancet* 364: 9449 (2004): 1978.

38. Food and Agriculture Organization of the United Nations (FAO), "FAO: Import Ban on Fish Products from Africa 'Not the Most Appropriate Answer,'" Press Release 98/21, 1998, http://www.fao.org/waicent/ois/press_ne/presseng/1998/PREN9821.htm.

39. Kelley Lee and Richard Dodgson, "Globalization and Cholera: Implications for Global Governance," *Global Governance: A Review of Multilateralism and International Organizations* 6: 2 (2000): 222–226.

40. WHO, *Official Website*, "Cholera." 2007, http://www.who.int/csr/disease/cholera/impactofcholera/en/.

41. Laurie Garrett, *Betrayal of Trust: The Collapse of Global Public Health* (New York: Hyperion Books, 2000), 21.

42. Garrett, *Betrayal of Trust*, 16.

43. WHO, Press Release 71. (September 28, 1994); WHO, Press Release 76. (October 11, 1994).

44. Garrett, *Betrayal of Trust*, 18; 36; 89.

45. Garrett, *Betrayal of Trust*, 104.

46. Heymann and Rodier, "Hot Spots in a Wired World," 347–351; WHO, *Global Defense against the Infectious Disease Threat*, 67.

47. Christopher Woods, Adam M. Karpati, Thomas Grein, Noel McCarthy, Peter Gaturuku, Eric Muchiri et al. "An Outbreak of Rift Valley Fever in Northeastern Kenya, 1997–1998," *Emerging Infectious Diseases* CDC 8: 2 (2002): 138–144.

48. Although most sources accept that the pandemic killed between 40 and 50 million people, Gina Kolata argues that estimates in the chaotic years following the pandemic ranged from 20 million to more than 100 million. If the low end of the range is more accurate, the Spanish Flu would still have killed more people than were in World War I or World War II. In fact, there were enough fatal cases of flu that in the United States alone "the average life span . . . fell by twelve years in 1918." [Gina Kolata, *Flu: The Story of the Great Influenza Pandemic of 1918 and the Search for the Virus that Caused It* (New York: Farrar, Strauss, and Giroux, 1999), 7].

49. Laurie Garrett, "The Next Pandemic," *Foreign Affairs* 84:3 (2005), 3,5; Gina Kolata, *Flu: The Story of the Great Influenza Pandemic of 1918 and the Search for the Virus That Caused It* (New York: Farrar, Strauss, and Giroux, 1999).

50. Kolata, *Flu*, 219–241.

51. John S. Tam, "Influenza A (H5N1) in Hong Kong: An Overview," *Vaccine* 20 (2002): S81.

52. The victim, who was from Beijing, was initially thought to have contracted SARS. In August 2006, it was confirmed that he died of avian influenza. See WHO, *Official Website*, H5N1 Avian Influenza Timeline, 2005, http://www.who.int/csr/disease/avian_influenza/Timeline_28_10a.pdf.

53. After the case in China, an outbreak was confirmed in Vietnam (2004), followed by Thailand (2004); Cambodia (2005); Indonesia (2005); Turkey (2006); Iraq (2006); Azerbaijan (2006); Egypt (2006); Djibouti (2006); and Lao PDR (2007). See WHO *Official Website*, H5N1 Avian Influenza Timeline, 2005, http://www.who.int/csr/disease/avian_influenza/Timeline_ 28_10a.pdf.

54. David P. Fidler, "Constitutional Outlines of Public Health's 'New World Order,'" *Temple Law Review* 77: 1 (2004): 267–268.

55. Ronald J. Glasser, "We are not Immune: Influenza, SARS, and the Collapse of Public Health." *Harper's Magazine* 309 (2004): 41.

56. David P. Fidler, *SARS, Governance, and the Globalization of Disease* (London: Palgrave Macmillan, 2004), 4.

57. United States General Accounting Office (US-GAO). *Emerging Infectious Diseases: Asian SARS Outbreak Challenged International and National Responses* (Washington, DC: US-GAO, 2004), 32–33; 56–58; Adel A. F. Mahmoud and Stanley M. Lemon, "Summary and Assessment," in *Learning from SARS: Preparing for the Next Disease Outbreak*, ed. Stacey Knobler, et al. (Washington, DC: National Academies Press, 2004), 11–12.

58. National Advisory Committee, *Learning from SARS*, 205.

59. Fidler, *SARS, Governance, and the Globalization of Disease*, 105.

60. Mahmoud and Lemon, "Summary and Assessment," 2–3.

61. Fidler, *SARS, Governance, and the Globalization of Disease*, 269.

62. WHO, *Severe Acute Respiratory Syndrome (SARS): Status of the Outbreak and Lessons for the Immediate Future* (Geneva: WHO, 2003); Mahmoud and Lemon, "Summary and Assessment," 6–15.

63. Fidler, *SARS, Governance, and the Globalization of Disease*, 79.

64. WHO, *Severe Acute Respiratory Syndrome*, 6.

65. Guenael R. M. Rodier, "Why Was Toronto Included in the World Health Organization's SARS-Related Travel Advisory?" *Journal of Canadian Medical Association* 168: 11 (2003): 1434.

66. Fidler, *SARS, Governance, and the Globalization of Disease*, 91–99.

67. US-GAO, *Emerging Infectious Diseases*, 14–15.

68. Centers for Disease Control and Prevention (CDC), "CDC Tele-Briefing Transcript: CDC's Response to Atypical Pneumonia in Southeast Asia and Canada," Atlanta: CDC, March 15, 2003, 1.

69. US-GAO, *Emerging Infectious Diseases*, 12–13.

70. US-GAO, *Emerging Infectious Diseases*, 17; Mahmoud and Lemon, "Summary and Assessment," 13.

71. David L. Heymann and Guenael Rodier, "SARS: Lessons from a New Disease," in *Learning from SARS: Preparing for the Next Disease Outbreak*,

ed. Stacey Knobler, Adel Mahmoud, Stanley Lemon, Alison Mack, Laura Sivitz, and Katherine Oberholtzer. (Washington, DC: National Academies Press, 2004), 237.

72. US-GAO, *Emerging Infectious Diseases*, 14.

73. Fidler, *SARS, Governance, and the Globalization of Disease*, 97; Mahmoud and Lemon, "Summary and Assessment," 14.

74. WHO, *Severe Acute Respiratory Syndrome*, 8.

75. Fidler, *SARS, Governance, and the Globalization of Disease*, 101–102.

76. World Health Assembly, Res. 56.28; 56.29. (2003).

77. WHO, *International Health Regulations: Provisional Draft* (Geneva: WHO, 1998), page 3.

78. WHO, *International Health Regulations, Draft*: Arts. 11–39. 1998.

79. WHO, *International Health Regulations, Draft*: Art. 1, Art. 2.1, and Annex III. 1998.

80. World Health Assembly, Res. 58.3 (2005).

81. Grein, Kamara, Rodier et al., "Rumors of Disease in the Global Village," 97–102.

82. World Health Assembly, Res. 54.14 (2001); 56.28 (2003); 56.29 (2003).

83. WHO, "Constitution," Arts. 19–21; 60. 2006.

84. David M. Leive, *International Regulatory Regimes: Case Studies in Health, Meteorology, and Food Volumes I & II* (Lexington, MA: Lexington Books, 1976), 58–64.

85. WHO, *International Health Regulations:* Art. 47. 2005.

86. WHO, *International Health Regulations:* Arts. 48–49. 2005.

87. WHO, *International Health Regulations:* Arts. 50–53. 2005.

88. WHO, *International Health Regulations:* Arts. 54–56. 2005.

89. WHO, *International Health Regulations:* Arts. 59–62. 2005.

90. David P. Fidler, "From International Sanitary Conventions to Global Health Security: The New International Health Regulations," *Chinese Journal of International Law* 4: 2 (2005): 342; 335–336.

91. WHO, *International Health Regulations: Provisional Draft* (1998).

92. Fidler, "From International Sanitary Conventions to Global Health Security," 337; 344.

93. WHO, *International Health Regulations:* Arts. 2, 5. 2005.

94. WHO, *International Health Regulations:* Art. 3. 2005.

95. WHO, *International Health Regulations:* Art. 9. 2005.

96. WHO, *International Health Regulations:* Art. 5. 2005.

97. WHO, *International Health Regulations:* Art. 4. 2005.

98. WHO, *International Health Regulations:* Art. 5; Arts. 12–13. 2005.

99. WHO, *International Health Regulations:* Art. 6. 2005.

100. WHO, *International Health Regulations:* Art. 7. 2005.

101. WHO, *International Health Regulations* Art. 7. 2005; Fidler, "From International Sanitary Conventions to Global Health Security," 352; 365–367.

102. Fidler, "From International Sanitary Conventions to Global Health Security," 370–374.

103. WHO, *International Health Regulations*: Art. 46. 2005.
104. WHO, *International Health Regulations*: Arts. 23–39. 2005.
105. WHO, *International Health Regulations*: Arts. 42–43. 2005.
106. David P. Fidler, "Emerging Trends in International Law Concerning Global Infectious Diseases Control," *Emerging Infectious Diseases* 9: 3 (2003): 286.
107. International Maritime Organization, *Official Website*, "IMO Documents," 2007, http://www.imo.org/.
108. International Civil Aviation Organization (ICAO), *Official Website*, "Convention on International Civil Aviation" 9th Edition, 2006. Doc 7300. Paragraphs: 2.22, 3.25, 6.C, and 8.2, http://www.icao.int/icaonet/dcs/7300.html.

Chapter 4   Disease Control: Transformation of Health Assistance Programs

1. According to the official Organization for Economic Cooperation and Development (OECD) definition, Official Development Assistance (ODA) consists of "Grants or Loans to countries and territories on Part I of the DAC List of Aid Recipients (developing countries) which are (a) undertaken by the official sector; (b) with promotion of economic development and welfare as the main objective; (c) at concessional financial terms [if a loan, having a Grant Element (q.v.) of at least 25 percent]. In addition to financial flows, Technical Co-operation (q.v.) is included in aid. Grants, Loans and credits for military purposes are excluded. Transfer payments to private individuals are in general not counted." OECD, *Official Website*, "Glossary," 2006, http://www.oecd.org/glossary/0,3414, en_2649_33721_1965693 _1_1_1_1,00. html#1965586.
2. Pablo Gottret and George Schieber, *Health Financing Revisited: A Practitioner's Guide* (Washington, DC: IBRD and World Bank, 2006), 125–126; International Development Association (IDA), *Report 38750: Aid Architecture: An Overview of the Main Trends in Official Development Assistance Flows* (Washington, DC: IDA, February 23, 2007), 2, http://go.worldbank.org/JM00RQYL00.
3. Only five countries—Denmark, Luxembourg, the Netherland, Norway, and Sweden—currently achieve this target. Six other countries have set dates to achieve it: Belgium (2010), Finland (2010), France (2012), Ireland (2007), Spain (2012), and the United Kingdom (2013). See Robert Hecht and Raj Shah, "Recent Trends in Innovations in Development Assistance," in *Disease Control Priorities in Developing Countries*, 2nd Edition, ed. Dean T. Jamison, Joel G. Breman, and Anthony R. Mesham. (Washington, DC: World Bank and Oxford University Press, 2006), 243–244.
4. Gottret and Schieber, *Health Financing Revisited*, 125–126.

5. Hecht and Shah, "Recent Trends in Innovations in Development Assistance," 245.

6. Numerous writers and scholars on this issue, including Hecht and Shah (2006) and Sridhar and Batniji (2007) bemoan the lack of comprehensive and organized data on DAH. Furthermore, the difficulty of avoiding double-counting multilateral aid is particularly hard to avoid in matters of health assistance as so much of it is fungible. Because of this, all numbers should be taken as estimated educated guesses.

7. Gottret and Schieber, *Health Financing Revisited*, 133; Devi Sridhar and Rajaie Batniji, "Global Health Institutions: Financing and Accountability," *Global Economic Governance Programme, University of Oxford*, 2006, www. globaleconomicgovernance.org/health/research.php, 1.

8. Laurie Garrett, "The Challenge of Global Health," *Foreign Affairs* 86: 1 (2007): 14.

9. Hecht and Shah, "Recent Trends in Innovations in Development Assistance," 243.

10. Hecht and Shah, "Recent Trends in Innovations in Development Assistance," 244.

11. World Bank spending on health reached $3.4 billion in 2003 then dropped to $2.1 billion in 2007; $87 million of that figure was allocated to HIV/AIDS, TB, and malaria programs; $250 million was allocated to child and maternal health. See Garrett, "The Challenge of Global Health," 20.

12. IDA, *Report 38750*, 19.

13. The majority of development aid has traditionally been channeled through the Development Assistance Committee (DAC) of the (OECD). It is the principal body through which the OECD deals with issues related to cooperation with developing countries. See OECD, *Official Website*, "Development Cooperation Directorate," http://www.oecd.org/searchResult/0,3400,en_2649_33721_1_1_1_1_1,00.html.

14. IDA, *Report 38750*, 19; Hecht and Shah, "Recent Trends in Innovations in Development Assistance," 249; Gottret and Schieber, *Health Financing Revisited*, 125.

15. Nicolaus Lorenz, "Effectiveness of Global Health Partnerships: Will the Past Repeat Itself?" *Bulletin of WHO* 85: 7 (2007): 567.

16. The Indicators of Progress include a requirement for aid to be more predictable and untied. The indicators also call for increased ownership over spending plans on the part of developing countries and better alignment of aid goals. See Paris Declaration, *Paris Declaration on Aid Effectiveness: Ownership, Harmonization, Alignment, Results and Mutual Accountability* (Paris: High Level Forum on Aid Effectiveness, 2005).

17. Steve Radelet, "Grants for the World's Poorest: How the World Bank Should Distribute Its Funds," Center for Global Development, 2005, http://www.cgdev.org/content/publications/detail/2681; Paris Declaration, 2005; Romily Greenhill and Patrick Watt, "Real Aid: An Agenda for Making Aid Work," Action Aid International, 2005, http://www.actionaid.org.uk/doc_lib/69_1_real_aid.pdf.

18. DALYs are Disability Adjusted Life Years and are an attempt to quantify the economic burden of illness and diseases; while many experts have found it useful, others have criticized the methods used to calculate the disease burden. DALYs is discussed in more detail in chapter 1, pages 9–10.

19. Richard Holbrooke, "Battling the AIDS Pandemic," *AIDS: The Threat to World Security* 5: 2 (July 2000), http://usinfo.state.gov/journals/itgic/0700/ijge/gj01.htm; Sandra Thurman, "The Shared Struggle Against AIDS," *AIDS: The Threat to World Security* 5: 2 (July 2000), http://usinfo.state.gov/journals/itgic/0700/ijge/gj01.htm.

20. Kelley Lee, Gill Walt, and Andy Haines, "The Challenge to Improve Global Health: Financing the Millennium Development Goals," *Journal of the American Medical Association* 291: 2 (2004): 2636.

21. The goals are (1) To eradicate extreme poverty and hunger; (2) To achieve universal primary education; (3) To promote gender equality and empower women; (4) To reduce child mortality; (5) To improve maternal health; (6) To combat HIV/AIDS, malaria, and other major diseases; (7) To ensure environmental sustainability; (8) To create a global partnership for development. For more details, see United Nations Millennium Project, *Official Website*, "About MDGs: What They Are," 2006, http://www.unmillenniumproject.org/goals/index.htm.

22. United Nations Millennium Project, "About MDGs: What They Are."

23. Hecht and Shah, "Recent Trends in Innovations in Development Assistance," 244.

24. Gottret and Schieber, *Health Financing Revisited*, 124; Lee, Walt and Haines, "The Challenge to Improve Global Health," 2636–2637.

25. Joint United Nations Programme on HIV/AIDS (UNAIDS), *Official Website*, "About UNAIDS," 2007, http://www.unaids.org/en/AboutUNAIDS/default.asp.

26. United Nations, *Official Website: The Secretary General*, "Message on the Occasion of World AIDS Day," December 1, 2006, http://data.unaids.org/pub/PressStatement/2006/SG-worldaidsday2006.pdf.

27. Hecht and Shah, "Recent Trends in Innovations in Development Assistance," 244.

28. Landis MacKeller, "Priorities in Global Health Assistance for Health, AIDS, and Population," *Working Paper 244 OECD Development Centre* (Paris: OECD, 2005), 7.

29. MacKeller, "Priorities in Global Health Assistance for Health AIDS, and Population," 4.

30. Gordon Conway, "Re-imagining Philanthropy: Partnerships and Poverty in the Global Age," Speech at the Global Philanthropy Forum, Stanford University, March 4, 2004, http://www.rockfound.org/display.asp?context=1&Collection=1&DocID=652&Preview=0&ARCurrent=1.

31. Lorenz, "Effectiveness of Global Health Partnerships, 567.

32. Bill & Melinda Gates Foundation and McKinsey & Company, "Global Health Partnerships: Assessing Country Consequences," 2005, http://www.who.int/healthsystems/gf16.pdf, 1.
33. Australia, Austria, Belgium, Canada, Denmark, the EU, Finland, France, Germany, Greece, Ireland, Italy, Japan, Luxembourg, the Netherlands, New Zealand, Norway, Portugal, Spain, Sweden, and Switzerland are all members of the DAC.
34. OECD and World Health Organization (WHO), *Poverty and Health: DAC Guidelines and Reference Series*. (Geneva: WHO, 2003) 25.
35. OECD, *Official Website*, "Aid Statistics—Donor Aid Charts" 2007, http://www.oecd.org/countrylist/0,3349,en_2649_34447_1783495_1_1_1_1,00.html.
36. Kent Buse and Gill Walt, "An Unruly Melange? Coordinating External Resources to the Health Sector: A Review," *Social Science Medicine* 45 (1997): 455–460.
37. IDA, *Report 38750*, 4, 15.
38. Carol Lancaster, "The Chinese Aid System," Essay for Center for Global Development, June 27, 2007, http://www.cgdev.org/content/publications/detail/13953/, 20–25; Sridhar and Batniji, "Global Health Institutions," 10.
39. President's Emergency Plan for AIDS Relief (PEPFAR), *Official Website*, "About PEPFAR," 2006, http://www.pepfar.gov/about/.
40. As the UNFPA does not deal with infectious diseases it is not discussed here.
41. WHO, *Official Website*, "WHO Proposed Programme Budget 2004–2005," 2002, http://www.who.int/gb/e/e_ppb2003.html, 5–7.
42. United Nations, *Official Website*, "UNDP Budget Estimates for the Biennium 2004–2005," 2003, http://www.undp.org/execbrd/pdf/dp03-28e.pdf.
43. United Nations Development Programme (UNDP), *Official Website*, "About UNDP," 2007, http://www.undp.org/about/.
44. United Nations Children's Fund (UNICEF), *Official Website*, "The 2002 UNICEF Annual Report," 2002, http://www.unicef.org/publications/pub_ar02_en.pdf.
45. UNICEF, *Official Website*, "What We Do," 2007, http://www.unicef.org/whatwedo/index.html.
46. World Bank, *World Bank Group: Working for a World Free of Poverty* (Washington, DC: World Bank Group, 2004), 10–11.
47. World Bank, *World Bank Group*, 12–15.
48. World Bank, *World Bank Group*, 19.
49. World Bank, *Official Website*, "Sector Strategy: Health Nutrition and Population." 2002, http://wbln0018.worldbank.org/HDNet/hddocs.nsf/c840b59b6982d2498525670c004def60/6fafece74ab8f0c6852568f0007054 2d?OpenDocument.
50. World Bank, *Official Website*, "Communicable Diseases," 2004, http://go.worldbank.org/QAM90WR0A0.
51. World Bank, "Communicable Diseases," 2004.

52. Inter-American Development Bank (IDB), *Official Website*, "About the IDB," 2007, http://www.iadb.org/aboutus/index.cfm?language=English.

53. IDB, *Official Website*, "Basic Facts," 2007, http://www.iadb.org/exr/basicfacts/.

54. IDB, "Basic Facts," 22.

55. Philip E. English and Harris M. Mule, "The African Development Bank Volume I," in *The Multilateral Development Banks* (Ottawa: North-South Institute and Lynne Rienner Publishers, 1995).

56. Nihal Kappagod, *The Asian Development Bank (The Multilateral Development Banks, Vol. 2)* (Ottawa: North-South Institute and Lynne Rienner Publishers, 1995).

57. Kent Buse, Nick Drager, Suzanne Fustukian, and Kelley Lee, "Globalisation and Health Policy: Trends and Opportunities," in *Health Policy in a Globalising World*, ed. Kelley Lee, Kent Buse, and Suzanne Fustikian (Cambridge: Cambridge University Press, 2002), 268–269; WHO, *Official Website*, "WHO's Interaction with Civil Society and Nongovernmental Organizations," 2002, http://www.who.int/civilsociety/documents/en/RevreportE.pdf.

58. International Committee of the Red Cross, *Official Website*, "About the ICRC," http://www.icrc.org/web/eng/siteeng0.nsf/iwpList2/About_the_ICRC?OpenDocument; John F. Hutchinson, "Custodians of the Sacred Fire: The ICRC and the Postwar Reorganisation of the International Red Cross," in *Intern ational Health Organizations and Movements 1918–1939*, ed. Paul Weindling (Cambridge: Cambridge University Press, 1995), 16–17.

59. Hutchinson, "Custodians of the Sacred Fire," 17–35.

60. Medecins Sans Frontieres (International), *Official Website*, "About MSF," 2007, http://www.msf.org/msfinternational/aboutmsf/.

61. People's Health Movement, *Official Website*, "About PHM," 2007, http://www.phmovement.org/en/about.

62. Davidson R Gwatkin, Abbas Bhuiya, and Cesar G Victora, "Making Health Systems more Equitable," *Lancet* 364 (2004): 1273–1280.

63. Gwatkin, Bhuiya, and Victora, "Making Health Systems more Equitable," 1273–1280.

64. Christian Children's Fund, *Official Website*, "What We Do," 2007, http://www.christianchildrensfund.org/content.aspx?id=144; Toni Radler, ed. "Christian Children's Fund 2003 Annual Report," 2007, http://www.christianchildrensfund.org/uploadedFiles/Publications/Annual_Report_2003.pdf.

65. The fourth pillar of Islam, known as Zakat or almsgiving, requires that Muslims donate a certain percentage—usually 2.5 percent—of their income to charity each year.

66. Aga Khan Foundation, *Official Website*, "About Us." 2007, http://www.akfc.ca/en/about_us/.

67. Carter Center, *Official Website*, "About the Center," 2007, http://www.cartercenter.org/about/index.html.

68. Rockefeller Foundation, *Official Website*, "About Us," 2007, http://www.rockfound.org/about_us/about_us.shtml.
69. Bill & Melinda Gates Foundation, *Official Website*, "Global Health." 2007, http://www.gatesfoundation.org/GlobalHealth/.
70. The Nippon Foundation, *Official Website*, "Supported Projects" 2006, http://www.nippon-foundation.or.jp/eng/projects/index.html.
71. United Nations Foundation, *Official Website*, "About Us," 2007, http://www.unfoundation.org/about/index.asp.
72. William J. Clinton Foundation, *Official Website*, "HIV/AIDS Initiative," 2007, http://www.clintonfoundation.org/cf-pgm-hs-ai-home.htm.
73. PhRMA, "Global Partnerships: Humanitarian Programs of the Pharmaceutical Industry in Developing Nations," 2003: 1, http://world.phrma.org/global.partnership.2003.pdf.
74. International Federation of Pharmaceutical Manufacturers Associations (IFPMA), "Building Healthier Societies through Partnerships," (2004): 5, http://www.ifpma.org/site_docs/Health/Health_Initiatives_Brochure_May04.pdf.
75. PhRMA. "Global Partnerships," 3–4.
76. Roy Widdus, "Public-Private Partnerships for Health: Their Main Targets, Their Diversity, and Their Future Directions," *Bulletin of the World Health Organization* 79: 8 (2001): 717.
77. IFPMA, "Building Healthier Societies through Partnerships," 13.
78. Roy Widdus and Katherine White, *Combating Diseases Associated with Poverty: Financing Strategies for Product Development and the Potential Role of Public-Private Partnerships*. Workshop Report (London: Initiative on Public Private Partnerships for Health, 2004); also see Michael Reich, "Introduction: Public-Private Partnerships for Public Health," in *Public-Private Partnerships for Public Health*, ed. Michael Reich (Cambridge, MA: Harvard Center for Population and Development Studies, 2002) 1; 8–9.
79. IDA, *Report 38750*, 4.
80. IDA, *Report 38750*, 12.
81. IDA, *Report 38750*, 12.
82. IDA, *Report 38750*, 13.
83. AidWatch, *Official Website*, "Tied Aid Briefing Paper," 2002, https://www.aidwatch.org.au/index.php?current=24&display=aw00443&display_item=1;Paris Declaration, *Paris Declaration on Aid Effectiveness*, 2005.
84. Sridhar and Batniji, "Global Health Institutions," 10.
85. Sridhar and Batniji, "Global Health Institutions," 10.
86. It should be noted here that remittances, which are private financial transfers between diasporas and their communities of origin, have recently been recognized as a major source of development assistance. In fact, some World Bank estimates suggest that recorded remittances total between two and three times ODA and unrecorded remittances may increase that by another 50 percent. Evidence as to the scope and impact of remittances is only just now emerging but this area of development aid will undoubtedly be a key area for future studies. See Carlo Dade, "The Privatization of

Foreign Development Assistance," Focal Policy Paper (July 2006), http://www.focal.ca/pdf/focal_privatization_jul06.pdf and Sanjeev Gupta et al., Impact of Remittances on Poverty and Financial Development in Sub-Saharan Africa. IMF Working Paper. (WP 07/38), http://www. imf.org/external/pubs/ft/wp/2007/wp0738.pdf.

87. Nicolaus Lorenz, "Effectiveness of Global Health Partnerships: Will the Past Repeat Itself?" *Bulletin of WHO* 85: 7 (2007). 567.

88. Karin Caines, Kent Buse, Cindy Carlson, Rose marie de Loor, Nel Druce, Cheri Grace, Mark Pearson, Jennifer Sancho, and Rajeev Sadanandan, *Assessing the Impact of Global Health Partnerships. DFID Health Resource Centre* (London: DFID, 2004), 9.

89. Widdus, "Public-Private Partnerships for Health," 713.

90. Drugs for Neglected Diseases Initiative (DNDi), *Official Website*, "About DNDi," 2003, http://www.dndi.org/cms/public_html/insidearticleListing. asp?CategoryId=87&ArticleId=288&TemplateId=1.

91. Merck & Co, *Official Website*, "The Merck MECTIZAN Donation Program," 2007, http://www.merck.com/cr/enabling_access/developing_ world/mectizan/; Yves Beigbeder, *International Public Health: Patients Rights vs. the Protection of Patents* (Aldershot: Ashgate Inc, 2004), 87–94.

92. Beigbeder, *International Public Health*, 87.

93. Donald R. Hopkins, Ernesto Ruiz-Tiben, Nwando Diallo, P. Craig Withers Jr. and James H. Maguire, "Dracunculiasis Eradication: And Now, Sudan," *American Journal of Tropical Medicine and Hygiene* 67: 4 (2002): 421.

94. Chris Greenaway, "Dracunculiasis (Guinea worm disease)," *Canadian Medical Association Journal* 170: 4 (2004): 495; *Weekly Epidemiological Record*, "Dracunculiasis Eradication Programme: Status During January–July 2004," 79: 38 (2004): 342–343.

95. Greenaway, "Dracunculiasis," 499–500.

96. UNAIDS, *Official Website*, "Goals," 2006, http://www.unaids.org/en/ Goals/default.asp.

97. UNAIDS, *Official Website*, "About UNAIDS" 2006, http://www.unaids. org/en/.

98. Lee, Walt, and Haines, "The Challenge to Improve Global Health," 2637; David H. Banta, "WHO Meeting Targets Global Concerns," *Journal of the American Medical Association* 290: 2 (2003): 183; Clare Kapp, "Global Fund Faces Uncertain Future as Cash Runs Low," *Lancet* 360: 9341 (2002): 1225.

99. Global Fund to Fight AIDS, Tuberculosis, and Malaria, *Official Website*, "How the Global Fund Works." 2007, http://www.theglobalfund.org/ en/about/how/.

100. Caines et al., *Assessing the Impact of Global Health Partnerships*, 4.

101. Widdus, "Public-Private Partnerships for Health," 718.

102. Widdus, "Public-Private Partnerships for Health," 718.

103. Sonja Bartsch. "Accountability of Global Public-Private Partnerships for Health." Paper prepared for the sixth Pan-European Conference on International Relations (Turin) September 2007, http://www.sgir.org/ archive/turin/uploads/Bartsch-bartschsonja.pdf.

Chapter 5   Disease Cures: International Patent
Law and Access to Essential Medicines

1. The first WHO Model List of Essential Medicines (EML) identified just
   more than 200 drugs that fit the accepted definition of "essential." The EML
   has been updated every two years since 1977 by a panel of doctors and global
   public health experts brought together by WHO. The current, or fourteenth, EML identifies 312 medicines, 12 of which are antiretrovirals for
   treating AIDS patients. Most antiretrovirals are under patent protection. The
   list is broken down into two categories: core and complementary. Core
   drugs are deemed the most basic and fundamental drugs that a functioning
   health care system requires. Drugs on the complementary list include drugs
   that are used to treat specific priority diseases. Although the list is not legally
   binding, WHO recommends that the drugs on the EML should be available
   in adequate amounts and at an affordable price from member states' health
   providers at all times. To date, the list has been adopted by more than 150
   countries in various manifestations. It has been lauded by many as an important revolution in international public health; however, the pharmaceutical
   industry is strongly opposed to its existence as they argue that the EML is
   restrictive and that focusing on a limited list of specific medicines could hinder the development of new drugs.
2. Jillian Clare Cohen, Monique F Mrazek, and Loraine Hawkins,
   "Corruption and Pharmaceuticals: Strengthening Good Governance to
   Improve access," in *The Many Faces of Corruption: Tracking Vulnerabilities at
   the Sector Level*, ed. Edgardo Campos and Sanjay Pradhan (Washington, DC:
   World Bank, 2007), 29.
3. In their recent piece "Corruption and Pharmaceuticals," Cohen, Mrazek and
   Hawkins describe in detail the nature and scope corruption at six identified
   points within the pharmaceutical sector. These points are manufacturing, reg-
   istration and market authorization, selection, procurement, distribution, and
   drug prescribing and dispensing (34–50). They note the specific gravity of the
   corruption issue as "the consequences of corruption within the pharmaceutical system are unfortunately fairly easy to identify . . . At an extreme, unsafe
   counterfeit drugs can lead to server health consequences including death." (29)
4. Ellen t'Hoen, "TRIPS, Pharmaceutical Patents, and Access to Essential
   Medicines: A Long Way from Seattle to Doha," *Chicago Journal of
   International Law* Spring 3: 1 (2002): 28.
5. Ramesh Govindaraj, Michael Riech, and Jillian C. Cohen, "HNP Discussion
   Paper: World Bank Pharmaceuticals," 2000: 8, http://www1.worldbank.
   org/hnp/Pubs_Discussion/Govindaraj-WBPharmacuetical-whole.pdf.
6. Graham Dukes, "Interim Report of Task Force 5 Working Group on
   Access to Essential Medicines," *Millennium Project*, February 2004: 33, www.
   unmillenniumproject.org/documents/tf5ateminterim.pdf.
7. Michael Westerhaus and Arachu Castro, "How Do Intellectual Property
   Law and International Trade Agreements Affect Access to Antiretroviral
   Therapy," *PLoS Medicine* 3: 8 (2006): 1232; Adam Mannan and Alan Story,

"Abolishing the Product Patent: A Step Forward in Global Access to Drugs," in *The Power of Pills: Social, Ethical, and Legal Issues in Drug Development, Marketing & Pricing*, ed. Jillian Clare, Patricia Illingworth, and Udo Schuklenk (Ann Arbor, MI: Pluto Press, 2006), 179–180.

8. Govindaraj, Reich, and Cohen, "HNP Discussion Paper," 12–13; Nathan Ford, "The Enduring Crisis in Neglected Diseases," in *The Power of Pills: Social, Ethical, and Legal Issues in Drug Development, Marketing & Pricing*, ed. Jillian Clare, Patricia Illingworth and Udo Schuklenk (Ann Arbor, MI: Pluto Press, 2006), 110.

9. Kent Ranson, Robert Beaglehole, Carlos Correa, Zafar Mirza, Kent Buse, and Nick Drager, "The Public Health Implications of Multilateral Trade Agreements," in *Health Policy in a Globalizing World*, ed. Kelley Lee, Kent Buse, and Suzanne Fustukian (Cambridge: Cambridge University Press, 2002), 29; t'Hoen, "TRIPS, Pharmaceutical Patents, and Access to Essential Medicines," 29.

10. Pierre Chirac, "Global Framework on Essential Health R&D," *Lancet* 367 (2006): 1560.

11. Ford, "The Enduring Crisis in Neglected Diseases," 109.

12. David B. Resnik, "Access to Medications and Global Justice," in *The Power of Pills: Social, Ethical, and Legal Issues in Drug Development, Marketing & Pricing*, ed. Jillian Clare, Patricia Illingworth, and Udo Schuklenk (Ann Arbor, MI: Pluto Press, 2006), 89.

13. Graham Dukes, "Interim Report of Task Force 5 Working Group on Access to Essential Medicines," *Millennium Project*, February 2004. www.unmillenniumproject.org/documents/tf5ateminterim.pdf, 6.

14. James Orbinski and Barry Burciul, "Moving Beyond Charity for R&D for Neglected Diseases," in *The Power of Pills: Social, Ethical, and Legal Issues in Drug Development, Marketing & Pricing*, ed. Jillian Clare, Patricia Illingworth, and Udo Schuklenk (Ann Arbor, MI: Pluto Press, 2006), 117–119.

15. It ought to be noted that the existence of the loopholes in and of themselves is insufficient; to benefit public health, the loopholes must be made more clear and functional. The loopholes are complex and many developing countries have not been able to exploit them owing to bureaucratic, legal, and technical stumbling blocks.

16. Number accurate as of September 2007. The largest country not part of the WTO is Russia, which is currently negotiating terms of membership. Virtually all other rich states are members of the Organization.

17. David P. Fidler, *International Law and Infectious Diseases* (Oxford: Clarendon Press, 1999), 123–132.

18. Fidler, *International Law and Infectious Diseases*, 114–115.

19. Susan Sell and Aseem Prakash, "Using Ideas Strategically: The Contest between Business and NGO Networks in Intellectual Property Rights," *International Studies Quarterly* 48 (2004): 154.

20. The majority of patent-holding pharmaceutical companies are located in the United States, with a large number located in the United Kingdom, Germany, Japan, and Switzerland. Frederick M. Abbott, "The WTO

Medicines Decision: World Pharmaceutical Trade and the Protection of Public Health," *American Journal of International Law* 99 (2005): 324.

21. Sell and Prakash, "Using Ideas Strategically," 156.

22. Sell and Prakash, "Using Ideas Strategically," 156; Susan Sell, "Books, Drugs and Seeds: The Politics of Access," Paper presented at the annual meeting of the International Studies Association, San Diego. March 22, 2006, http://www.allacademic.com/meta/p98118_index.html, 23.

23. Sell and Prakash, "Using Ideas Strategically," 157.

24. Although the 1995 TRIPS Agreement applies to all types of intellectual property, it is particularly germane to pharmaceutical products. This is demonstrated by the fact that during the negotiation of the TRIPS Agreement a coalition of pharmaceutical firms "provided the technical and legal expertise and advocacy skills on which US trade negotiators based their strategies." Duncan Matthews, "Is History Repeating Itself? The Outcome of Negotiations on Access to Medicines, the HIV/AIDS Pandemic and Intellectual Property Rights in the World Trade Organization." *Law, Social Justice & Global Development Journal* (2004): 1, http://elj.warwick.ac.uk/global/04-1/matthews.html; also see Michael P. Ryan, *Knowledge Diplomacy: Global Competition and the Politics of Intellectual Property* (Washington, DC: Brookings Institution, 1998), Chaps. 1 and 4.

25. Jillian C. Cohen and Patricia Illingworth, "The Dilemma of Intellectual Property Rights for Pharmaceuticals," *Developing World Bioethics* 3 (2003): 33.

26. Duncan Matthews, *Globalizing Intellectual Property Rights: The TRIPS Agreement* (London: Routledge, 2002), 44; Duncan Matthews, "Is History Repeating Itself?" 2.

27. Matthews, "Is History Repeating Itself?" 2–5.

28. Sell and Prakash, "Using Ideas Strategically," 160.

29. Jillian C. Cohen, "Civilizing Drugs: Intellectual Property Rights in Global Pharmaceutical Markets," in *Global Standards of Market Civilization*, ed. Brett Bowde and Leonard Seabrooke (London: Routledge, 2006), 179.

30. World Trade Organization and World Health Organization, *WTO/WHO Joint Study: WTO Agreements and Public Health* (Geneva: WHO/WTO, 2002), 39; see Art. 7 of TRIPS.

31. WTO/WHO, *WTO/WHO Joint Study*, 38.

32. Mannan and Story, "Abolishing the Product Patent," 181–182.

33. According to the Tufts Center for the Study of Drug Development (2001), a new drug costs more than $800 million to research and produce. This figure, however, has been contested by some scholars, including Marcia Angell, who, in a 2004 publication, argued that the amount spent on R&D per new drug is significantly lower than $800 million, but the actual amount is unknown because the financial records of drug companies are too opaque to glean a clear understanding of the breakdown of R&D costs.

34. Susan Sell, "Post-TRIPS Developments: The Tension between Commercial and Social Agendas in the Context of Intellectual Property," *Florida Journal of International Law* Spring (2002): 211.

35. Alan O. Sykes, "TRIPS, Pharmaceuticals, Developing Countries and the Doha 'Solution,'" *Chicago Journal of International Law* 3: 1 (2002): 47.
36. This extreme price differential between patented and generic drugs has led to a criticism of The President's Emergency Plan for AIDS Relief (PEPFAR), which was announced by George W. Bush at the 2003 State of the Union Address. PEPFAR, which calls for the provision of $15 billion for AIDS prevention and treatment over a five-year period, was initially welcomed as a major contribution to the global fight against AIDS. However, the plan has been severely critiqued because PEPFAR money can only be used to purchase antiretroviral drugs that are approved for use by the U.S. Food and Drug Administration. In practice, this means that recipient governments must buy the patented versions of ART drugs made by U.S. companies, rather than the generic versions of ART drugs. (PEPFAR is also discussed in chapter 4).
37. Ranson, Beaglehole, Correa, Mirza, Buse, and Drager, "The Public Health Implications of Multilateral Trade Agreements," 29.
38. WTO/WHO, *WTO/WHO Joint Study*, 42.
39. Sell, "Post-TRIPS Developments," 193.
40. Cohen, "Civilizing Drugs," 180–181.
41. World Trade Organization, *Official Website*, "Agreement on Trade-Related Aspects of Intellectual Property Rights," 1994, http://www.wto.org/english/tratop_e/trips_e/trips_e.htm.
42. World Trade Organization, *Official Website*, "Declaration on the TRIPS Agreement and Public Health," November 20, 2001, http://www.wto.org/english/thewto_e/minist_e/min01_e/mindecl_trips_e.htm, Arts. 5(b) and 6.
43. t'Hoen, "TRIPS, Pharmaceutical Patents, and Access to Essential Medicines," 32.
44. Jane Galvro, "Access to antiretroviral drugs in Brazil," *Lancet* 360: (2002): 862; Sykes, "TRIPS, Pharmaceuticals, Developing Countries and the Doha 'Solution,'" 55.
45. Galvro, "Access to antiretroviral drugs in Brazil," 1864.
46. J. P. Wogart and G. Calcagnotto, "Brazil's Fight against AIDS and Its Implications for Global Health Governance," *World Health and Population* January (2006): 8.
47. "Brazil Points to Way Ahead in AIDS battle," BBC News, January 7, 2004, http://news.bbc.co.uk/2/hi/business/3306345.stm.
48. t'Hoen, "TRIPS, Pharmaceutical Patents, and Access to Essential Medicines," 30; Sell, "Post-Trips Developments," 209.
49. Caroline Thomas, "Trade Policy, the Politics of Access to Drugs and Global Governance for Health," in *Health Impacts of Globalization*, ed. Kelley Lee (London: Palgrave MacMillian, 2003), 182–183.
50. "Court Battle over AIDS drugs," *BBC News*, March 5, 2001, http://news.bbc.co.uk/1/hi/world/africa/1202402.stm.
51. Thomas, "Trade Policy, the Politics of Access to Drugs and Global Governance for Health," 183.

52. t'Hoen, "TRIPS, Pharmaceutical Patents, and Access to Essential Medicines," 35.

53. Presidential Documents, United States Government, *Access to HIV/AIDS Pharmaceuticals and Medical Technologies.* Executive Order No 13155 May 10, 2000, http://frwebgate.access.gpo.gov/cgi-bin/getdoc.cgi?dbname= 2000_register&docid=fr12my00-170.pdf.

54. Sell, "Post-TRIPS Developments," 213.

55. "Drugs firms drop AIDS case," BBC News, April 19, 2001, http://news. bbc.co.uk/1/hi/world/africa/1284633.stm.

56. Sell, "Post-TRIPS Developments," 209–210.

57. Carlos M. Correa, "Implications of the Doha Declaration on the TRIPS Agreement and Public Health," *Health Economics and Drugs EDM Series* 12 (2002), http://www.who.int/medicines/library/par/who-edm-par-2002-3/ doha-implications.pdf. Accessed Fall 2004, 1–2.

58. Karl Vick, "African AIDS Victims Losers of a Drug War: US Policy Keeps Prices Prohibitive," *Washington Post*, December 4, 1999, A01.

59. Correa, "Implications of the Doha Declaration on the TRIPS Agreement and Public Health," I.

60. t'Hoen, "TRIPS, Pharmaceutical Patents, and Access to Essential Medicines," 28.

It should be noted that not all experts were in support of the Doha Declaration and the support it provided for compulsory licenses. Alan O. Sykes, for example, argues that allowing developing countries exceptions to TRIPS rules will hinder their long-term health goals, by continuing not to provide any incentive on the part of pharmaceutical companies to invest in R&D for new drugs to treat the diseases that are most commonly found in developing countries. Sykes, "TRIPS, Pharmaceuticals, Developing Countries and the Doha 'Solution,'" 47–68.

61. The anthrax attacks are also significant because they highlight the fact that no nation, even the richest and most powerful, is immune to health crises. Some access advocates have used this incident to emphasize the fact that in a pandemic situation, such as a virulent influenza outbreak or biological attack, even countries with a developed pharmaceutical industry will not be able to produce or purchase necessary supplies of drugs. Abbott, "The WTO Medicines Decision 334–336; also see Sell and Prakash, "Using Ideas Strategically," 149; Sell, "Books, Drugs and Seeds," 30–31.

62. WTO/WHO, *WTO/WHO Joint Study*, 45; Correa, "Implications of the Doha Declaration on the TRIPS Agreement and Public Health," i.

63. World Trade Organization, *Official Website*, "Implementation of paragraph 6 of the Doha Declaration on the TRIPS Agreement and public health" (Document: WT/L/540) September 1, 2003, http://www.wto.org/english/ tratop_e/trips_e/implem_para6_e.htm, Art. 2.

64. WTO, "Implementation of paragraph 6 of the Doha Declaration on the TRIPS Agreement and public health," Art. 2(a).

65. WTO, "Implementation of paragraph 6 of the Doha Declaration on the TRIPS Agreement and public health," Art. 2; "The Right Fix?" *Economist*, September 1, 2003.

66. Matthews, "Is History Repeating Itself?" 5.
67. "The Right Fix?" *Economist*, September 1, 2003.
68. "Letter from CPTech, Oxfam, MSF, HAI to WTO delegates regarding December 16, 2002 Chairman's Text for 'solution' to Paragraph 6 of the Doha Declaration on TRIPS and Public Health," December 19, 2002, http://www.accessmed-msf.org/prod/publications.asp?scntid=6120031111255&contenttype=PARA&.
69. MSF, "Joint NGO Statement on TRIPS and Public Health WTO Deal on Medicines: A 'Gift' Bound in Red Tape," MSF Press Release, September 10, 2003, http://www.accessmed-msf.org/prod/publications.asp?scntid=1292003916443&contenttype=PARA&.
70. Abbott, "The WTO Medicines Decision," 349.
71. Sell, "Books, Drugs and Seeds," 10.
72. Abbott, "The WTO Medicines Decision," 349–350; Brook K. Baker, "Placing Access to Essential Medicines on the Human Rights Agenda," in *The Power of Pills: Social, Ethical, and Legal Issues in Drug Development, Marketing & Pricing*, ed. Jillian Clare, Patricia Illingworth, and Udo Schuklenk (Ann Arbor, MI: Pluto Press, 2006), 243–246.
73. David P. Fidler, "Fighting the Axis of Illness: HIV/AIDS, Human Rights, and US Foreign Policy," *Harvard Human Rights Journal* 17: Spring (2004), 108, http://www.law.harvard.edu/students/orgs/hrj/iss17/fidler.shtml.
74. Fidler, "Fighting the Axis of Illness," 110.
75. WHO, "Constitution of the World Health Organization," 45th Edition, Supplement, October 2006, http://www.who.int/governance/eb/who_constitution_en.pdf.
76. These and other multilateral initiatives are discussed in detail in chapter 4.
77. The contribution made by philanthropic foundations cannot be overemphasized. For example, in 2004, the Bill & Melinda Gates Foundation provided $159 million—almost 10 times the amount of financial support—than did states for various public-private partnerships. Ford, "The Enduring Crisis in Neglected Diseases" in *The Power of Pills: Social, Ethical, and Legal Issues in Drug Development, Marketing & Pricing*, ed. Jillian Clare, Patricia Illingworth, and Udo Schuklenk (Ann Arbor: Pluto Press) 113.
78. Ford, "The Enduring Crisis in Neglected Diseases," 113.
79. Ford, "The Enduring Crisis in Neglected Diseases," 113.
80. In March 2007, DNDi and its partner Sanofi-aventis announced the development and release of a new treatment regime for malaria. The drugs, ASAQ, will be distributed throughout sub-Saharan Africa at a "no profit no loss" cost of $0.50 for children under the age of five, and $1 for older children and adults.
81. It should, however, be noted that the power of WHO, and similar international organizations, to "name and shame" states into submitting to their guidelines has increased significantly since the advent of mass communication technology. This power was noted most dramatically in the case of the 2003 SARS outbreak, and the influence WHO had on the government of China in forcing it to release information to other governments

and international medical officials. This event is further discussed in specific detail in chapter 3.

82. Mary Ellen O'Connell, "The Role of Soft Law in a Global Order," in *Commitment and Compliance: The Role of Non-Binding Norms in the International Legal System*, ed. Dinah Shelton (Oxford: Oxford University Press, 2000), 110.

83. To date, compulsory licenses have been used only four times: by Malaysia, Indonesia, Zambia, and Mozambique for ARV products in 2004. Michael Westerhaus and Arachu Castro, "How Do Intellectual Property Law and International Trade Agreements Affect Access to Antiretroviral Therapy," 1231.

Chapter 6   Health and Global Governance: Concluding Perspectives

1. Oran R. Young, *International Governance: Protecting the Environment in a Stateless Society* (Ithaca, NY: Cornell University Press, 1994), 1.

2. WHO, *Official Website*, "Global Outbreak Alert & Response Network," 2007. www.who.int/csr/outbreaknetwork/en.

3. Charles Pannenborg, *A New International Health Order: An Inquiry into the International Relations of World Health and Medical Relations* (Boston: Brill, 1979), 183; Charles Allen, "World Health and World Politics," *International Organization* 4: 27 (1950): 29.

4. Specific examples of successful GHPs, including the Dracunculiasis Eradication Initiative and the Drugs for Neglected Diseases Initiative, are discussed in chapter 4.

5. Roy Widdus, "Public-Private Partnerships for Health: Their Main Targets, their Diversity, and their Future Directions," *Bulletin of the World Health Organization* 79: 8 (2001): 717; Karin Caines et al., *Assessing the Impact of Global Health Partnerships. DFID Health Resource Centre* (London: DFID, 2004), 9; Bill & Melinda Gates Foundation and McKinsey & Company, "Global Health Partnerships: Assessing Country Consequences," 2005.

6. PEPFAR is the President's Emergency Plan for AIDS Relief. Its characteristics and goals are described in chapters 3 and 4.

7. Young, *International Governance*, 27.

8. Confidential Interview: Government Representative to the World Health Organization (2005).

9. Collaborating Centers are laboratories or research institutions that are affiliated with the World Health Organization. They "participate in the strengthening of country resources, in terms of information, services, research and training, in support of national health development." WHO, *Official Website*, "WHO Collaborating Centers General Information," 2006, http://www.who.int/kms/initiatives/whoccinformation/en/index1.html.

10. David P. Fidler, *SARS, Governance, and the Globalization of Disease* (London: Palgrave Macmillan, 2004); David P. Fidler, "Constitutional Outlines of

Public Health's 'New World Order.'" *Temple Law Review* 77: 1 (2004): 252–259.

11. Obijiofor Aginam, *Global Health Governance: International Law and Public Health in a Divided World* (Toronto: University of Toronto Press, 2005), 46–89.

12. Mark W. Zacher, "The Decaying Pillars of the Westphalian Temple: Implications for International Order and Governance," in James Rosenau, ed., *Governance without Government* (Cambridge: Cambridge University Press, 1992), 58–101; Fidler, "Constitutional Outlines of Public Health's 'New World Order,'" 247–272.

13. P. J. Simmons and Chantal de Jonge Oudraat, *Managing Global Issues: Lessons Learned* (Washington, DC: Carnegie Endowment for International Peace, 2001), 664.

14. J. F. Richard, *High Noon: Twenty Global Problems, Twenty years to Solve Them* (New York: Basic Books, 2002), 48.

15. Ann M. Florini, "Lessons Learned," in *The Third Force: The Rise of Transnational Civil Society*, ed. Ann Florini (Washington, DC: Carnegie Endowment for International Peace, 2000), 228–229.

16. Harold K. Jacobson, *Networks of Interdependence: International Organizations and the Global Political System* (New York: Knopf, 1984), 418.

17. Robert Keohane. "International Institutions: Two Perspectives," *International Studies Quarterly* 32 (1988): 386.

18. "Child Mortality 'At Record Low'" BBC Article, September 13, 2007, http://news.bbc.co.uk/2/hi/health/6992401.stm.

Appendix B   Summary Descriptions of Diseases

1. "Publishing the Anthrax Genome," *Economist*, May 1, 2003.

2. WHO, *Global Epidemics and Impact of Cholera*, (Geneva: WHO, 2001) http://www.who.int/topics/cholera/impact/en/.

3. Kelley Lee and Richard Dodgson, "Globalization and Cholera: Implications for Global Governance," Global Governance: A Review of Multilateralism and International Organizations 6: 2 (2000): 213–236.

4. The disease was found in Reston, Virginia, United States in 1989 in a batch of monkeys imported for medical research purposes. Fortunately, the Reston strain of the Ebola virus proved not to cause illness in humans. Richard Preston, *The Hot Zone: A Terrifying True Story*, (New York: Random House, 1995).

5. Kyle B. Olson, "Aum Shinrikyo: Once and Future Threat," *Emerging Infectious Diseases*. 5: 4 (1999): 514.

6. Hepatitis D and E cause comparatively few instances of illness and so are not discussed here.

7. WHO, *World Health Report 2004: Changing History* (Geneva: WHO, 2004) Chapter 1.

8. Estimates as to how many people died during the 1918 influenza outbreak vary dramatically from 20 million to 100 million. While the exact casualty

figure will never likely be known, even the low end of the scale is shockingly high; more than the total number of death in World War I (15 million), World War II (16 million combat deaths). Gina Kolata, *Flu: The Story of the Great Influenza Pandemic of 1918 and the Search for the Virus That Caused It*, (New York: Farrar, Strauss, and Giroux, 1999), 7–9.

9. Andrew Nikiforuk, *The Fourth Horseman: A Short History of Epidemics, Plagues, Famine and Other Scourges* (Toronto: Viking Press, 2001), 25.
10. Norman F. Cantor, *In the Wake of the Plague: The Black Death and the World It Made* (New York: Perennial Books, 2002); Frederick F. Cartwright and Michael D. Biddiss, *Disease and History* (New York: Barnes and Noble, 1972), 29.
11. David P. Fidler, *SARS, Governance, and the Globalization of Disease* (London: Palgrave Macmillan, 2004); National Advisory Committee on SARS and Public Health. *Learning from SARS: Renewal of Public Health in Canada* (Ottawa: Health Canada, 2003).
12. Sheldon Watts, *Epidemics and History: Disease, Power, and Imperialism* (New Haven, CT: Yale University Press, 1997), chapter 3; Donald Hopkins, *Princes and Peasants: Smallpox in History* (Chicago: University of Chicago Press, 1983).
13. Cartwright and Biddiss, *Disease and History*, 82; Hans Zinsser, *Rats, Lice, and History* (New York: Black Dog and Leventhal Publishers, 1934).

BIBLIOGRAPHY

Abbott, Frederick M. "The Doha Declaration on the TRIPS Agreement and Public Health: Lighting a Dark Corner at the WTO." *Journal of International Economic Law* 5: 1 (2002): 469–505.

———. "The WTO Medicines Decision: World Pharmaceutical Trade and the Protection of Public Health." *American Journal of International Law* 99 (2005): 317–358.

Abbott, Kenneth and Duncan Snidal. "Hard and Soft Law in International Governance." *International Organization* 54: 3 (2000): 421–456.

African Development Bank Group. *Official Website.* "About Us" 2006. http://www.afdb.org/portal/page?_pageid=473,968615&_dad=portal&_schema=PORTAL.

Aga Khan Foundation. *Official Website.* "About Us." 2007. http://www.akfc.ca/en/about_us/.

Aginam, Obijiofor. *Global Health Governance: International Law and Public Health in a Divided World.* Toronto: University of Toronto Press, 2005.

AidWatch. *Official Website.* "Tied Aid Briefing Paper." 2002. https://www.aidwatch.org.au/index.php?current=24&display=aw00443&display_item=1.

Allen, Charles. "World Health and World Politics." *International Organization* 4: 27 (1950): 27–43.

Anand, Sudhir and Kara Hansen. "DALYs: Efficiency versus Equity." *World Development* 26: 2 (1998): 307–310.

Angell, Marcia. *The Truth about the Pharmaceutical Industry. How They Deceive Us and What to Do About It.* New York: Random House Ltd, 2004.

Arai-Takahashi, Y. "The World Health Organization and the Challenges of Globalization: A Critical Analysis of the Proposed Revision to the International Health Regulations." *Law, Social Justice & Global Development Journal (LGD)* June (2004). http://elj.warwick.ac.uk/global/issue/2004-1/arai.html.

———. "The World Health Organization and the Challenges of Monitoring of Emerging Diseases: Design for a Demonstration Program." *Health Policy* 38 (2004): 135–153.

Arnold, David. "Introduction: Disease, Medicine and Empire." In *Imperial Medicine and Indigenous Societies*, edited by David Arnold, 1–27. Manchester: Manchester University Press, 1998.

Baker, Brook K. "Placing Access to Essential Medicines on the Human Rights Agenda." In *The Power of Pills: Social, Ethical, and Legal Issues in Drug*

Development, Marketing & Pricing, edited by Jillian Clare, Patricia Illingworth, and Udo Schuklenk, 239–248. Ann Arbor, MI: Pluto Press, 2006.

Balinska, Marta Aleksandra. "Assistance and Not Mere Relief: The Epidemic Commission of the League of Nations, 1920–1923." In *International Health Organizations and Movements, 1918–1939*, edited by Paul Weindling, 81–108. Cambridge: Cambridge University Press, 1995.

Ban, J. *Health, Security, and US Global Leadership*. Washington, DC: Chemical and Biological Arms Control Institute, 2001.

Banta, David H. "WHO Meeting Targets Global Concerns." *Journal of the American Medical Association* 290: 2 (2003): 183–197.

Barnett, Michael and Martha Finnemore. *Rules for the World: International Organizations in Global Politics*. Ithaca, NY: Cornell University Press, 2004.

Bartsch, Sonja. "Accountability of Global Public-Private Partnerships for Health." Paper prepared for the 6th Pan-European Conference on International Relations (Turin) September, 2007. http://www.sgir.org/archive/turin/uploads/Bartsch-bartschsonja.pdf.

Basch, Paul. *Textbook of International Health*. New York: Oxford University Press, 1990.

Beck, Ann. *A History of the British Medical Administration of East Africa, 1900–1950*. Cambridge, MA: Harvard University Press, 1970.

Beigbeder, Yves. *International Public Health: Patients Rights vs. the Protection of Patents*. Aldershot: Ashgate Inc, 2004.

Bélanger, Michel. *Droit International de la Santé*. Paris: Economica, 1983.

Berkov, R. *The World Health Organization: A Study in Decentralized International Administration*. Geneva: Librairie E. Droz, 1957.

Bill & Melinda Gates Foundation. *Official Website*. "Global Health." 2007. http://www.gatesfoundation.org/GlobalHealth/.

Bill & Melinda Gates Foundation and McKinsey & Company. "Global Health Partnerships: Assessing Country Consequences." 2005. http://www.who.int/healthsystems/gf16.pdf.

"Brazil Points to Way Ahead in AIDS Battle." BBC News, January 7, 2004. http://news.bbc.co.uk/2/hi/business/3306345.stm.

Brower, Jennifer and Peter Chalk. *The Global Threat of New and Reemerging Infectious Diseases: Reconciling U.S. National Security and Public Health Policy*. Arlington, VA: Rand Corporation, 2003.

Brown, E. Richard. *Rockefeller Medicine Men*. Los Angeles: University of California Press, 1979.

Brown Weiss, Edith. "Conclusions: Understanding Compliance with Soft Law." In *Commitment and Compliance: The Role of Non-Binding Norms in the International Legal System*, edited by Dinah Helton, 535–554. Oxford: Oxford University Press, 2000.

Buse, Kent and Gill Walt. "Globalisation and Multilateral Public-Private Health Partnerships: Issues for Health Policy." In *Health Policy in a Globalising World*, edited by Kelley Lee, Kent Buse, and Suzanne Fustikian, 41–62. Cambridge: Cambridge University Press, 2002.

————. "An Unruly Melange? Coordinating External Resources to the Health Sector: A Review." *Social Science Medicine* 45 (1997): 449–463.

Buse, Kent, Nick Drager, Suzanne Fustukian, and Kelley Lee. "Globalisation and Health Policy: Trends and Opportunities." In *Health Policy in a Globalising World*, edited by Kelley Lee, Kent Buse, and Suzanne Fustikian, 251–280. Cambridge: Cambridge University Press, 2002.

Bush, George W. *The White House Official Site.* "State of the Union Address 2003." January 28, 2003. http://www.whitehouse.gov/news/releases/2003/01/20030128-19.html.

Caines, Karin, Kent Buse, Cindy Carlson, Rose marie de Loor, Nel Druce, Cheri Grace, Mark Pearson, Jennifer Sancho, and Rajeev Sadanandan. *Assessing the Impact of Global Health Partnerships. DFID Health Resource Centre.* London: DFID, 2004.

Cantor, Norman F. *In the Wake of the Plague: The Black Death and the World It Made.* New York: Perennial Books, 2002.

Carter Center. *Official Website.* "About the Center," 2007. http://www.cartercenter.org/about/index.html.

————. *Official Website.* "2002–2003 Annual Report." August 31, 2003. http://www.cartercenter.org/documents/1625.pdf.

Cartwright, Frederick F. and Michael D. Biddiss. *Disease and History.* New York: Barnes and Noble, 1972.

Centers for Disease Control and Prevention (CDC). "CDC Tele-briefing Transcript: CDC's Response to Atypical Pneumonia in Southeast Asia and Canada." Atlanta: CDC, March 15, 2003.

Chapman, Audrey R. "The Human Rights Implications of Intellectual Property Protection." *Journal of International Economic Law* 5: 4 (2002): 861–882.

Charney, Jonathan L. "Commentary: Compliance with International Soft Law." In *Commitment and Compliance: The Role of Non-binding Norms in the International Legal System*, edited by Dinah Helton, 115–120. Oxford: Oxford University Press, 2000.

Chayes, Abram and Antonia Handler. "On Compliance." In *International Institutions: An International Organizations Reader*, edited by Lisa L. Martin and Beth A. Simmons, 248–277. Cambridge, MA: MIT Press, 1993.

"Child Mortality 'At Record Low'" BBC Article, September 13, 2007. http://news.bbc.co.uk/2/hi/health/6992401.stm.

Chirac, Pierre. "Global Framework on Essential Health R&D," *Lancet* 367 (2006): 1560–1561.

Christian Children's Fund. *Official Website.* "What We Do." 2007. http://www.christianchildrensfund.org/content.aspx?id=144.

Cohen, Jillian C. "Civilizing Drugs: Intellectual Property Rights in Global Pharmaceutical Markets." In *Global Standards of Market Civilization*, edited by Brett Bowde and Leonard Seabrooke, 175–187. London: Routledge, 2006.

Cohen, Jillian C. and Kristina M. Lybecker. "AIDS Policy and Pharmaceutical Patents: Brazil's Strategy to Safeguard Public Health." *The World Economy* 28: 2 (2005): 211–230.

Cohen, Jillian C. and Patricia Illingworth. "The Dilemma of Intellectual Property Rights for Pharmaceuticals." *Developing World Bioethics* 3 (2003): 27–48.

Cohen, Jillian C., Monique F. Mrazek, and Loraine Hawkins. "Corruption and Pharmaceuticals: Strengthening Good Governance to Improve access." In *The Many Faces of Corruption: Tracking Vulnerabilities at the Sector Level* edited by Edgardo Campos and Sanjay Pradhan, 29–62. Washington, DC: World Bank, 2007.

Commission on Macroeconomics and Health. *Macroeconomics and Health: Investing in Health for Economic Development.* Geneva: WHO, 2001.

Conference Sanitaire Internationale de Paris. Proces-verbaux. Paris: Imprimerie Nationale. 1851.

———. Proces-verbaux. Paris: Imprimerie Nationale. 1859.

———. Proces-verbaux. Paris: Imprimerie Nationale. 1866.

———. Proces-verbaux. Vienna: Imprimerie Nationale. 1874.

———. Proces-verbaux. Vienna: Imprimerie Nationale. 1881.

———. Proces-verbaux. Rome: Imprimerie Nationale. 1885.

———. Proces-verbaux. Paris: Imprimerie Nationale. 1892.

———. Proces-verbaux. Paris: Imprimerie Nationale. 1894.

———. Proces-verbaux. Paris: Imprimerie Nationale. 1897.

———. Proces-verbaux. Paris: Imprimerie Nationale. 1904.

———. Proces-verbaux. Paris: Imprimerie Nationale. 1926.

Connolly, Maire, M. Gayer, M. J. Ryan, P. Spiegel, P. Salama, and D. L. Heymann "Communicable Diseases in Complex Emergencies: Impact and Challenges." *Lancet* 364: 9449 (2004): 1974–1983.

Convention Sanitaire Internationale de Paris. Paris: Ministere des Affaires Etrangeres. 1926.

Conway, Gordon. "Re-imagining Philanthropy: Partnerships and Poverty in the Global Age." Speech at the Global Philanthropy Forum, Stanford University. March 4, 2004. http://www.rockfound.org/display.asp?context=1&Collection=1&DocID=652&Preview=0&ARCurrent=1.

Cooper, Richard N. *The Economics of Interdependence: Economic Policy in the Atlantic Community.* New York: McGraw-Hill, 1968.

———. "International Cooperation in Public Health as a Prologue to Macroeconomic Cooperation." In *Can Nations Agree? Issues in International Economic Cooperation,* edited by Richard N. Cooper, Barry Eichengreen, C. Randall, Henning Gerald Holtham, and Robert D. Putnam, 183–190. Washington, DC: Brookings Institution, 1989.

Correa, Carlos M. "Implications of the Doha Declaration on the TRIPS Agreement and Public Health." *Health Economics and Drugs EDM Series* 12 (2002). http://www.who.int/medicines/library/par/who-edm-par-2002-3/doha-implications.pdf Accessed Fall 2004.

"Court Battle over AIDS Drugs." *BBC News*, March 5, 2001. http://news.bbc.co.uk/1/hi/world/africa/1202402.stm.

Cox, Robert W., Harold K. Jacobson, Gerard and Victoria Curzon, Joseph S. Nye, Lawrence Scheinman, James P. Sewell, and Susan Strange. *The Anatomy of Influence: Decision Making in International Organization.* New Haven, CT: Yale University Press, 1973.

Dade, Carlo. "The Privatization of Foreign Development Assistance." Focal Policy Paper. FPP 06/05 (July, 2006). http://www.focal.ca/pdf/focal_privatization_jul06.pdf.

Diamond, Jared. Guns, Germs, and Steel: The Fates of Human Societies. New York: W.W. Norton, 1999.

Drechsler, Denis and Felix Zimmermann. OECD Development Centre Policy Brief 33: New Actors in Health Financing: Implications for Donor Darlings. Paris: OECD, 2006.

"Drugs Firms Drop AIDS Case." BBC News, April 19, 2001. http://news.bbc.co.uk/1/hi/world/africa/1284633.stm.

Drugs for Neglected Diseases Initiative (DNDi). Official Website. "About DNDi." 2003. http://www.dndi.org/cms/public_html/insidearticleListing.asp?CategoryId=87&ArticleId=288&TemplateId=1.

Dukes, Graham. "Interim Report of Task Force 5 Working Group on Access to Essential Medicines." Millennium Project, February 2004. www.unmillennium project.org/documents/tf5ateminterim.pdf.

English, Philip E. and Harris M. Mule. The Multilateral Development Banks: Volume I: The African Development Bank (Ottawa: North-South Institute, 1995; and Boulder, Colorado: Lynne Rienner 1995).

External Committee on Smart Regulation. Smart Regulation: A Regulatory Committee for Canada. Ottawa: Government of Canada, 2004.

Farmer, Paul. Infections and Inequalities: The Modern Plagues. Berkeley: University of California Press, 1999.

Fenner, F., D. A. Henderon, I. Arita, Z. Jezek, and I. D. Ladnyi. Smallpox and Its Eradication. Geneva: World Health Organization, 1988.

Fidler, David P. "Constitutional Outlines of Public Health's 'New World Order.'" Temple Law Review 77: 1 (2004): 247–272.

———. "Emerging Trends in International Law Concerning Global Infectious Diseases Control." Emerging Infectious Diseases 9: 3 (2003): 285–290.

———. "Fighting the Axis of Illness: HIV/AIDS, Human Rights, and US Foreign Policy." Harvard Human Rights Journal 17 (Spring, 2004): 99–136. http://www.law.harvard.edu/students/orgs/hrj/iss17/fidler.shtml.

———. "From International Sanitary Conventions to Global Health Security: The New International Health Regulations." Chinese Journal of International Law 4: 2 (2005): 325–392.

———. International Law and Infectious Diseases. Oxford: Clarendon Press, 1999.

———. "Public Health and National Security in the Global Age: Infectious Diseases, Bioterrorism, and Realpolitik." George Washington International Law Review 35: 4 (2003): 787–856.

———. "Racism or Realpolitik? U.S. Foreign Policy and the HIV/AIDS Catastrophe in Sub-Saharan Africa." Journal of Gender, Race, and Justice 7: (2003): 97–146.

———. "Revision of World Health Organization's International Health Regulations." American Society of International Law (2004). http://www.asil.org/insights/insigh132.htm.

———. SARS, Governance, and the Globalization of Disease. London: Palgrave Macmillan, 2004.

Finnemore, Martha and Kathryn Sikkink. "International Norm Dynamics and Political Change." International Organization 52: 4 (1998): 887–918.

Florini, Ann M., ed. "Lessons Learned." In *The Third Force: The Rise of Transnational Civil Society*, edited by Ann M. Florini, 211–240. Washington, DC: Carnegie Endowment for International Peace, 2000.

———. *The Third Force: The Rise of Transnational Civil Society*. Washington, DC: Carnegie Endowment for International Peace, 1999.

Florini, Ann M. and P.J. Simmons. "What the World Needs Now?" In *The Third Force: The Rise of Transnational Civil Society*, edited by Ann M. Florini, 1–15. Washington, DC: Carnegie Endowment for International Peace, 2000.

Food and Agriculture Organization of the United Nations (FAO). "FAO: Import Ban on Fish Products from Africa 'Not the most Appropriate Answer.'" Press Release 98/21, 1998. http://www.fao.org/waicent/ois/press_ne/presseng/1998/PREN9821.htm.

Ford, Nathan. "The Enduring Crisis in Neglected Diseases." In *The Power of Pills: Social, Ethical, and Legal Issues in Drug Development, Marketing & Pricing*, edited by Jillian Clare, Patricia Illingworth, and Udo Schuklenk, 109–116. Ann Arbor, MI: Pluto Press, 2006.

Foreman-Peck, James. *A History of the World Economy: International Economic Relations since 1850*. London: FT Prentice Hall, 1983.

Galvro, Jane. "Access to Antiretroviral Drugs in Brazil." *Lancet* 360 (2002): 1862–1865.

Garrett, Laurie. *Betrayal of Trust: The Collapse of Global Public Health*. New York: Hyperion Books, 2000.

———. "The Challenge of Global Health." *Foreign Affairs* 86: 1 (2007): 14–38.

———. *The Coming Plague: Newly Emerging Diseases in a World Out of Balance*. New York: Farrar, Strauss and Giroux, 1994.

———. "The Lessons of Wildlife Health." *Foreign Affairs* 84: 3 (2005): 51–61.

———. "Microbial Threats and the Global Society." *Emerging Infectious Disease* 2 (1996): 62–83.

———. "The Next Pandemic." *Foreign Affairs* 84: 3 (2005): 3–23.

Glasser, Ronald J. "We Are Not Immune: Influenza, SARS, and the Collapse of Public Health." *Harper's Magazine* 309 (2004): 35–44.

Global Emerging Infections Surveillance and Response System (GEIS). *Official Website*. "About DOD-GEIS." 2006. http://www.geis.fhp.osd.mil/.

Global Forum for Health Research (GFHR). *The 10/90 Report on Health Research 2001–2002*. Geneva: Global Forum for Health Research, 2002.

Global Fund to Fight AIDS, Tuberculosis and Malaria. *Official Website*. "How the Global Fund Works." 2007. http://www.theglobalfund.org/en/about/how/.

Global Partnership to Stop TB (GPSTB). *Official Website*. "About the Stop TB Partnership." 2007. http://www.stoptb.org/stop_tb_initiative/.

Global Polio Eradication Initiative (GPEI). *Official Website*. "Spearheading Partners." 2007. http://www.polioeradication.org/partners.asp.

Global Public Health Intelligence Network (GPHIN). *Official Website*. "Information." 2007. http://www.phac-aspc.gc.ca/media/nr-rp/2004/2004_gphin-rmispbk_e.html.

Goldstein, Judith, Timothy Josling, and Richard Steinberg. *The Evolution of the Trade Regime*. Princeton, NJ: Princeton University Press, 2006.

Goodman, Neville. *International Health Organizations and Their Work*. London: Churchill Livingston, 1971.

Gostin, Lawrence O. "International Infectious Disease Law: Revision of the World Health Organization's International Health Regulations." *Journal of the American Medical Association* 291: 21 (2004): 2623–2627.

Gottret, Pablo and George Schieber. *Health Financing Revisited: A Practitioner's Guide*. Washington, DC: IBRD and World Bank, 2006.

Govindaraj, Ramesh, Michael Riech, and Jillian C. Cohen. "HNP Discussion Paper: World Bank Pharmaceuticals." 2000. http://www1.worldbank.org/ hnp/Pubs_Discussion/Govindaraj-WBPharmacuetical-whole.pdf.

Greenaway, Chris. "Dracunculiasis (Guinea Worm Disease)." *Canadian Medical Association Journal* 170: 4 (2004): 495–500.

Greenhill, Romily and Patrick Watt. "Real Aid: An Agenda for Making Aid Work." ActionAid International, Aid and Accountability Team. June 2005. http://www.actionaid.org.uk/doc_lib/69_1_real_aid.pdf.

Grein, Thomas W., Kande-Bure O. Kamara, Guenael Rodier, Aileen J. Plant, Patrick Bovier, Michael J. Ryan, et al. "Rumors of Disease in the Global Village: Outbreak Verification." *Emerging Infectious Diseases* 6: 2 (2000): 97–102.

Gupta, Sanjeev, Catherine Pattillo, and Smita Wagh. "Impact of Remittances on Poverty and Financial Development in Sub-Saharan Africa." IMF Working Paper. (WP 07/38). 2007. http://www.imf.org/external/pubs/ft/wp/2007/ wp0738.pdf.

Gushulak B. D. and D. W. MacPherson. "Population Mobility and Infectious Diseases: The Diminishing Impact of Classical Infectious Diseases and New Approaches for the 21st Century." *Clinical Infectious Diseases* 31 (2000): 776–780.

Gwatkin, Davidson, Abbas Bhuiya, and Cesar G Victora. "Making Health Systems More Equitable." *Lancet* 364 (2004): 1273–1280.

Haas, Ernst B. *When Knowledge Is Power*. Berkeley: University of California Press, 1990.

Haas, Peter M. "Epistemic Communities." In *Handbook of International Environmental Law*, edited by Daniel Bodansky, Jutta Brunee, and Ellen Hey, 791–806. Oxford: Oxford University Press, 2007.

———., ed. *Knowledge, Power, and International Policy Coordination*. Columbia: University of South Carolina Press, 1997.

———. "Policy Knowledge: Epistemic Communities." In *The International Encyclopedia of the Social and Behavioral Sciences*, edited by N. J. Smelser and P. B. Baltes, 11578–11586. Amsterdam: Elsevier, 2001.

Harrison, Mark. *Disease and the Modern World: 1500 to Present Day*. Cambridge, MA: Polity, 2004.

———. *Public Health in British India: Anglo-American Preventive Medicine 1859–1914*. New York: Cambridge University Press, 1994.

Headrick, Daniel R. *The Tentacles of Progress: Technology Transfer in the Age of Imperialism, 1850–1940*. Oxford: Oxford University Press, 1988.

———. *The Tools of Empire: Technology and European Imperialism in the Nineteenth Century*. Oxford: Oxford University Press, 1981.

Hecht, Robert and Raj Shah. "Recent Trends in Innovations in Development Assistance." In *Disease Control Priorities in Developing Countries*, 2nd Edition, edited by Dean T. Jamison, Joel G. Breman, and Anthony R. Mesham, 243–257. Washington, DC: World Bank and Oxford University Press, 2006.

Henschen, Folke. *The History and Geography of Diseases*. New York: Seymour Lawrence, 1966.

Heymann, David. "Evolving Infectious Disease Threats to National and Global Security." In *Global Health Challenges for Human Security*, edited by Lincoln Chen, Jennifer Leaning, and Vasant Narasimhan, 105–124. Cambridge, MA: Harvard University Press, 2003.

———. "The Microbial Threat in Fragile Times: Balancing Known and Unknown Risks." *Bulletin of the World Health Organization* 80: 3 (2002): 179–180.

Heymann, David and Guenael Rodier. "Global Surveillance, National Surveillance and SARS." *Emerging Infectious Diseases* 10: 2 (2004). http://www.cdc.gov/ncidod/EID/vol10no2/03-1038.htm.

———. "Global Surveillance of Communicable Diseases." *Emerging Infectious Diseases* 4: 3 (1998): 362–365.

———. "Hot Spots in a Wired World: WHO Surveillance of Emerging and Re-emerging Infectious Diseases." *Lancet* December 1 (2001): 345–353.

———. "SARS: Lessons from a New Disease." In *Learning from SARS: Preparing for the Next Disease Outbreak*, edited by Stacey Knobler, Adel Mahmoud, Stanley Lemon, Alison Mack, Laura Sivitz, and Katherine Oberholtzer, 234–246. Washington, DC: National Academies Press, 2004.

Hinman, E. Harold. *World Eradication of Infectious Diseases*. Springfield, IL: Charles Thomas, 1966.

Hobson, W. *World Health and History*. Baltimore: John Wright and Sons, 1963.

Holbrooke, Richard. "Battling the AIDS Pandemic." *AIDS: The Threat to World Security* 5: 2 (July, 2000). http://usinfo.state.gov/journals/itgic/0700/ijge/gj01.htm.

Hopkins, Donald. *Princes and Peasants: Smallpox in History*. Chicago: The University of Chicago Press, 1983.

Hopkins, Donald R., Ernesto Ruiz-Tiben, Nwando Diallo, P. Craig Withers Jr., and James H. Maguire. "Dracunculiasis Eradication: And Now, Sudan." *American Journal of Tropical Medicine and Hygiene* 67: 4 (2002): 415–422.

Howard-Jones, Norman. *International Public Health between the Two World Wars: The Organizational Problems*. Geneva: WHO, 1978.

———. *The Scientific Background to the International Sanitary Conferences 1851–1938*. Geneva: WHO, 1975.

Hugh-Jones, Martin. "Global Awareness of Disease Outbreaks: The Experience of Pro-MED-Mail." *Public Health Reports* 116: 6 (2001): 27–32.

Hurrell, Andrew. "International Society and the Study of Regimes." In *Regime Theory and International Relations*, edited by Volker Rittberger, 49–72. Oxford: Clarendon Press, 1993.

Hutchinson, John F. "Custodians of the Sacred Fire: The ICRC and the Postwar Reorganisation of the International Red Cross." In *International Health*

Organisations and Movements 1918–1939, edited by Paul Weindling, 17–35. Cambridge: Cambridge University Press, 1995.

Institute of Medicine. *America's Vital Interest in Global Health: Protecting Our People, Enhancing Our Economy, and Advancing Our International Interests.* Washington, DC: National Academies Press, 1997.

———. *Emerging Infections: Microbial Threats to Health in the United States.* Washington, DC: National Academies Press, 1992.

———. *Microbial Threats to Health: Emergence, Detection, and Response.* Washington, DC: National Academies Press, 2003.

Inter-American Development Bank (IDB). *Official Website.* "Basic Facts." 2007. http://www.iadb.org/exr/basicfacts/.

International Civil Aviation Organization (ICAO). *Official Website.* "Convention on International Civil Aviation," 9th Edition, 2006. Doc 7300. Paragraphs: 2.22, 3.25, 6.C, and 8.2. http://www.icao.int/icaonet/dcs/7300.html.

International Committee of the Red Cross (ICRC). *Official Website.* "About the ICRC." 2007. http://www.icrc.org/web/eng/siteeng0.nsf/iwpList2/About_the_ICRC?OpenDocument.

International Development Association (IDA). *Report 38750: Aid Architecture: An Overview of the Main Trends in Official Development Assistance Flows.* Washington, DC: IDA, February 23, 2007. http://go.worldbank.org/JM00RQYL00.

International Federation of Pharmaceutical Manufacturers Associations (IFPMA). "Building Healthier Societies through Partnerships." May 4, 2004. http://www.ifpma.org/site_docs/Health/Health_Initiatives_Brochure_May04.pdf.

International Federation of Red Cross and Red Crescent Societies (IFRCS). *Official Website.* "Health Activities." 2007. http://www.ifrc.org/what/health/index.asp?navid=04_04.

International Maritime Organization (IMO). *Official Website.* "IMO Documents." 2007. http://www.imo.org/.

International Red Cross and Red Crescent Movement. *Official Website.* "Our History." 2007. http://www.redcross.int/en/history/.

International Sanitary Convention, 1911–1912. London: His Majesty's Stationery Office, 1919.

International Sanitary Convention, 1926. London: His Majesty's Stationery Office, 1928.

International Sanitary Convention, 1944. Washington, DC: U.N. Relief and Rehabilitation Administration, 1945.

International Sanitary Convention for Aerial Navigation. The Netherlands: The Hague, 1933.

Jackson, John. *Sovereignty, the WTO and Changing Fundamentals of International Law.* Cambridge: Cambridge University Press, 2006.

Jacobson, Harold K. *Networks of Interdependence: International Organizations and the Global Political System.* New York: Knopf, 1984.

Joint United Nations Programme on HIV/AIDS (UNAIDS). *Official Website.* "About UNAIDS." 2007. http://www.unaids.org/en/AboutUNAIDS/default.asp.

Kahler, Miles and David Lake. "Globalization and Changing Locations of Governance." In *Governance in a Global Economy: Political Authority in Transition*, edited by Miles Kahler and David Lake, 1–32. Princeton, NJ: Princeton University Press, 2003.

———. "Globalization and Changing Patterns of Political Authority." In *Governance in a Global Economy: Political Authority in Transition*, edited by Miles Kahler and David Lake, 412–438. Princeton, NJ: Princeton University Press, 2003.

Kapp, Clare. "Global Fund Faces Uncertain Future as Cash Runs Low." *Lancet* 360: 9341 (2002): 1225.

Kappagod, Nihal. *The Asian Development Bank (The Multilateral Development Banks, Vol. 2)*. Ottawa: North-South Institute and Lynne Rienner Publishers, 1995.

Karesh, William and Robert Cook. "The Human-Animal Link." *Foreign Affairs* 84: 3 (2005): 38–50.

Karlen, A. *Man and Microbes: Diseases and Plagues in History and Modern Times*. New York: Simon and Schuster, 1995.

Keck, Margaret and Kathryn Sikkink. *Activists beyond Borders: Advocacy Networks in International Politics*. Ithaca, NY: Cornell University Press, 1999.

Kenwood, A.G. and A.L. Lougheed. *Growth of the International Economy 1820–1900 3rd Edition*. London: Routledge, 1992.

Keohane, Robert O. *After Hegemony: Cooperation and Discord in the World Global Economy*. Princeton, NJ: Princeton University Press, 1984.

———. "International Institutions: Two Perspectives." *International Studies Quarterly* 32 (December, 1988): 379–396.

———. *Neoliberal Institutionalism: A Perspective on State Politics*. Boulder, CO: Westview, 1989.

Keohane, Robert O. and Joseph S. Nye. "Introduction." In *Governance in a Globalizing World*, edited by Joseph Nye and John Donahue, 1–41. Washington, DC: Brookings Institution Press, 2000.

———. *Power and Interdependence: World Politics in Transition*. Boston: Little Brown, 1989.

Kickbusch, Ilona. "Global Health Governance: Some Theoretical Considerations on the New Political Space." In *Health Impacts of Globalization: Towards Global Governance*, edited by Kelley Lee, 192–203. London: Palgrave Macmillan, 2003.

Kiovusalo, Meri. "Assessing the Health Policy Implications of WTO Trade and Investment Agreements." In *Health Impacts of Globalization*, edited by Kelley Lee, 161–176. London: Palgrave MacMillian, 2003.

Knobler, Stacey, Adel Mahmoud, Stanley Lemon, Alison Mack, Laura Sivitz, and Katherine Oberholtzer, eds., *Learning from SARS: Preparing for the Next Disease Outbreak*. Washington, DC: National Academies Press, 2004.

Kolata, Gina. *Flu: The Story of the Great Influenza Pandemic of 1918 and the Search for the Virus That Caused It*. New York: Farrar, Strauss, and Giroux, 1999.

Koplow, David. *Smallpox: The Fight to Eradicate a Global Scourge*. Berkeley: University of California Press, 2003.

Koremenos, Barbara, Charles Lipson, and Duncan Snidal. "Rational Design: Looking Back to Move Forward." *International Organization* 55: 4 (2001): 1051–1082.

Laing, Richard, Brenda Waning, Andy Gray, Nathan Ford, and Ellen t'Hoen. "25 Years of the WHO Essential Medicines List: Progress and Challenges." *Lancet* 361 (2003): 1723–1729.

Lancaster, Carol. "The Chinese Aid System." Essay for Center for Global Development. June 27, 2007. http://www.cgdev.org/content/publications/detail/13953/.

Lee, Kelley and Richard Dodgson. "Globalization and Cholera: Implications for Global Governance." *Global Governance: A Review of Multilateralism and International Organizations* 6: 2 (2000): 213–236.

Lee, Kelley, Gill Walt, and Andy Haines. "The Challenge to Improve Global Health: Financing the Millennium Development Goals." *Journal of the American Medical Association* 291: 2 (2004): 2636–2638.

Leive, David M. *International Regulatory Regimes: Case Studies in Health, Meteorology, and Food Volumes I & II.* Lexington, MA: Lexington Books, 1976.

"Letter from CPTech, Oxfam, MSF, HAI to WTO Delegates Regarding December 16, 2002 Chairman's Text for 'Solution' to Paragraph 6 of the Doha Declaration on TRIPS and Public Health." December 19, 2002. http://www.accessmed-msf.org/prod/publications.asp?scntid=6120031111255&contenttype=PARA&.

Lorenz, Nicolaus. "Effectiveness of Global Health Partnerships: Will the Past Repeat Itself?" *Bulletin of WHO* 85: 7 (2007): 567–568.

Lucas, Adetokunbo O. "Public-Private Partnerships: Illustrative Examples." In *Public-Private Partnerships for Public Health*, edited by Michael R. Reich, 19–39. Cambridge, MA: Harvard Center for Population and Development Studies, 2002.

MacKeller, Landis. "Priorities in Global Health Assistance for Health, AIDS, and Population." *Working Paper 244 OECD Development Centre*. Paris: OECD, 2005.

MacKenzie, Deborah. "Don't Let It Die." *New Scientist*. February 6, 1999, 5050–5051.

Mahmoud, Adel A. F. and Stanley M. Lemon. "Summary and Assessment." In *Learning from SARS: Preparing for the Next Disease Outbreak*, edited by Stacey Knobler, Adel Mahmoud, Stanley Lemon, Alison Mack, Laura Sivitz, and Katherine Oberholtzer, 1–39. Washington, DC: National Academies Press, 2004.

Mannan, Adam and Alan Story. "Abolishing the Product Patent: A Step Forward in Global Access to Drugs." In *The Power of Pills: Social, Ethical, and Legal Issues in Drug Development, Marketing & Pricing*, edited by Jillian Clare, Patricia Illingworth, and Udo Schuklenk, 179–189. Ann Arbor, MI: Pluto Press, 2006.

Martin, Lisa L. and Beth Simmons. "Theories and Empirical Studies of International Institutions." *International Organization* 54: 4 (1998): 729–758.

Matthews, Duncan. *Globalizing Intellectual Property Rights: The TRIPS Agreement*. London: Routledge, 2002.

———. "Is History Repeating Itself? The Outcome of Negotiations on Access to Medicines, the HIV/AIDS Pandemic and Intellectual Property Rights in the World Trade Organization." *Law, Social Justice & Global Development Journal* 1 (2004). http://elj.warwick.ac.uk/global/04-1/matthews.html.

Matthews, Duncan. "WTO Decision on Implementation of Paragraph 6 of the Doha Declaration on the TRIPS Agreement and Public Health: A Solution to the Access to Essential Medicines Problem?" *Journal of International Economic Law* 7: 1 (2004): 73–107.

McNeill, William H. *Plagues and People*. Garden City, NY: Anchor Books, 1976.

Measles Initiative. *Official Website*. "What is the Measles Initiative." August 1, 2007. http://www.measlesinitiative.org/mip2.asp.

Medicines for Malaria Venture (MMV). *Official Website*. "About MMV." 2007. http://www.mmv.org/rubrique.php3?id_rubrique=11.

Medecins Sans Frontieres. "Joint NGO Statement on TRIPS and Public Health WTO Deal on Medicines: A 'Gift' Bound in Red Tape." MSF Press Release, September 10, 2003. http://www.accessmed-msf.org/prod/publications.asp?scntid=1292003916443&contenttype=PARA&.

Medecins Sans Frontieres (International). *Official Website*. "About MSF." 2007. http://www.msf.org/msfinternational/aboutmsf/.

Merck & Co. *Official Website*. "The Merck MECTIZAN Donation Program." 2007. http://www.merck.com/cr/enabling_access/developing_world/mectizan/.

Miller, Judith, Stephen Engelberg, and William Broad. *Germs: Biological Weapons and America's Secret War*. New York: Simon and Schuster, 2001.

Morse, Edward L. *Modernization and the Transformation of International Relations*. New York: Free Press, 1976.

Morse, Stephen S., Barbara Hatch-Rosenberg, and Jack Woodall. "ProMED Global Monitoring of Emerging Diseases: Design for a Demonstration Program." Health Policy 38 (December, 1996): 135–153.

Moulin, Anne Marie. "The Pasteur Institutes between the Two World Wars: The Transformation of the International Sanitary Order." In *International Health Organizations and Movements 1918–1939*, edited by Paul Weindling, 244–265. Cambridge: Cambridge University Press, 1995.

Muraskin, William. 2002. "The Last Years of the CIV and the Birth of the GAVI." In *Public-Private Partnerships for Public Health*, edited by Michael R. Reich, 115–168. Cambridge, MA: Harvard Center for Population and Development Studies, 2002.

Murray, C. J. L. "Quantifying the Burden of Disease: The Technical Basis for Disability Adjusted Life Years." *Bulletin of the World Health Organization* 72: 3 (1994): 429–445. http://whqlibdoc.who.int/bulletin/1994/Vol72-No3/bulletin_1994_72(3)_429–445.pdf.

Murray, C. J. L. and A. D. Lopez. "Quantifying Disability: Data, Methods and Results." *Bulletin of the World Health Organization* 72: 3 (1994): 481–494. http://whqlibdoc.who.int/bulletin/1994/Vol72-No3/bulletin_1994_72(3)_481-494.pdf.

National Advisory Committee on SARS and Public Health. *Learning from SARS: Renewal of Public Health in Canada*. Ottawa: Health Canada, 2003.

National Science and Technology Council Committee on International Science, Engineering, and Technology (CISET) Working Group on Emerging and Re-emerging Infectious Diseases. *Infectious Diseases—A Global Health Threat*. Washington, DC: CISET, 1995.

Nikiforuk, Andrew. *The Fourth Horseman: a Short History of Epidemics, Plagues, Famine and Other Scourges.* Toronto: Viking Press, 2001.

The Nippon Foundation, *Official Website* "Supported Projects." 2006. http://www.nippon-foundation.or.jp/eng/projects/index.html.

Novartis Foundation for Sustainable Development. *Official Website.* "Leprosy Treatment and Care," 2007. http://www.novartisfoundation.com/en/projects/access_health/leprosy/index.htm.

O'Connell, Mary Ellen. "The Role of Soft Law in a Global Order." In *Commitment and Compliance: The Role of Non-binding Norms in the International Legal System,* edited by Dinah Shelton, 100–114. Oxford: Oxford University Press, 2000.

Oldstone, Michael B. A. *Viruses, Plagues, and History.* Oxford: Oxford University Press, 1998.

Olson, Kyle B. "Aum Shinrikyo: Once and Future Threat." *Emerging Infectious Diseases.* 5: 4 (1999): 513–516.

Orbinski, James and Barry Burciul. "Moving Beyond Charity for R&D for Neglected Diseases." In *The Power of Pills: Social, Ethical, and Legal Issues in Drug Development, Marketing & Pricing,* edited by Jillian Clare, Patricia Illingworth, and Udo Schuklenk, 117–124. Ann Arbor, MI: Pluto Press, 2006.

Organization for Economic Cooperation and Development (OECD). *Official Website.* "Aid Statistics—Donor Aid Charts" 2007. http://www.oecd.org/countrylist/0,3349,en_2649_34447_1783495_1_1_1_1,00.html.

———. *Official Website.* "Development Cooperation Directorate." 2007. http://www.oecd.org/searchResult/0,3400,en_2649_33721_1_1_1_1_1,00.html.

Organization for Economic Cooperation and Development (OECD) and World Health Organization (WHO). *Poverty and Health: DAC Guidelines and Reference Series.* Geneva: World Health Organization, 2003. http://whqlibdoc.who.int/publications/2003/9241562366.pdf.

Ostfield, Marc L. "Bioterrorism as a Foreign Policy Issue." *SAIS* 24 (Winter–Spring, 2004): 131–146. http://muse.jhu.edu/journals/sais_review/v024/24.1ostfield01.pdf.

Pan-American Health Organization (PAHO). *Official Website.* "History and Structure of the Pan American Health Organization." 2007. http://www.paho.org/English/PAHO/history.htm.

———. *Pro Salute Mundi: A History of the Pan American Health Organization.* Washington, DC: PAHO, 1992.

Pannenborg, Charles O. *A New International Health Order: An Inquiry into the International Relations of World Health and Medical Relations.* Boston: Brill, 1979.

Paris Declaration. *Paris Declaration on Aid Effectiveness: Ownership, Harmonization, Alignment, Results and Mutual Accountability.* Paris: High Level Forum on Aid Effectiveness, 2005.

People's Health Movement. *Official Website.* "About PHM." 2007. http://www.phmovement.org/en/about.

PhRMA. "Global Partnerships: Humanitarian Programs of the Pharmaceutical Industry in Developing Nations." 2003. http://world.phrma.org/global.partnership.2003.pdf.

"Poor Markets, Rich Rewards." *Economist*, September 30, 2004. http://www.
economist.com/displaystory.cfm?story_id=3253004.

President's Emergency Plan for AIDS Relief (PEPFAR). *Official Website.* "About
PEPFAR." 2006. http://www.pepfar.gov/about/.

Preston, Richard. *The Hot Zone: A Terrifying True Story.* New York: Random
House, 1995.

Price, Richard. "Transnational Civil Society and Advocacy in World Politics."
World Politics 55 (July, 2003): 579–606.

ProMed. *Official Website.* "About ProMed Mail" http://www.promedmail.org/
pls/promed/f?p=2400:1950:14756322966045941699::NO:::

"Publishing the anthrax genome." *Economist*, May 1, 2003.

Radelet, Steve. "Grants for the World's Poorest: How the World Bank Should
Distribute Its Funds." Center for Global Development. 2005. http://www.
cgdev.org/content/publications/detail/2681.

Radler, Toni, ed. "Christian Children's Fund 2003 Annual Report." 2007.
http://www.christianchildrensfund.org/uploadedFiles/Publications/Annual_
Report_2003.pdf.

Ranson, Kent, Robert Beaglehole, Carlos Correa, Zafar Mirza, Kent Buse, and
Nick Drager. "The Public Health Implications of Multilateral Trade
Agreements." In *Health Policy in a Globalizing World*, edited by Kelley Lee, Kent
Buse, and Suzanne Fustukian, 18–40. Cambridge: Cambridge University Press,
2002.

Reich, Michael. "Introduction: Public-Private Partnerships for Public Health." In
Public-Private Partnerships for Public Health, edited by Michael R. Reich, 1–16.
Cambridge, MA: Harvard Center for Population and Development Studies,
2002.

Resnik, David B. "Access to Medications and Global Justice." In *The Power of Pills:
Social, Ethical, and Legal Issues in Drug Development, Marketing & Pricing*, edited by
Jillian Clare, Patricia Illingworth, and Udo Schuklenk, 88–97. Ann Arbor, MI:
Pluto Press, 2006.

Reynolds, Gretchen. "The Flu Hunters." *New York Times Magazine*, November 7,
2004.

Richard, J. F. *High Noon: Twenty Global Problems, Twenty Years to Solve Them.* New
York: Basic Books, 2002.

"The Right Fix?" *Economist*, September 1, 2003.

Rockefeller Foundation. *Official Website.* "About Us." 2007. http://www.rockfound.
org/about_us/about_us.shtml.

———. *Official Website.* "The Rockefeller Foundation Timeline." 2006. http://www.
rockfound.org/about_us/history/timeline.shtml.

Rodier, Guenael R. M. "Why Was Toronto Included in the World Health
Organization's SARS-Related Travel Advisory?" *Journal of Canadian Medical
Association* 168: 11 (2003): 1434–1435.

Roodman, David. "An Index of Donor Performance." Washington, DC: Center
for Global Development, Working Paper 42. June 22, 2004. http://www.
cgdev.org/content/publications/detail/2747.

Rosenau, James N. "Governance, Order and Change in World Politics." In *Governance without Government: Order and Change in World Politics*, edited by James Rosenau, 1–29. Cambridge: Cambridge University Press, 1992.

———. *The Study of Global Interdependence.* London: Frances Pinter, 1980.

Ruggie, John G. "American Exceptionalism, Exemptionalism and Global Governance." In *American Exceptionalism and Human Rights*, edited by Michael Ignatieff, 304–338. Princeton, NJ: Princeton University Press, 2005.

———. "Multilateralism: The Anatomy of an Institution." In *Multilateralism Matters: The Theory and Praxis of an Institutional Form*, edited by John Gerard Ruggie, 3–50. New York: Columbia Univeristy Press, 1993.

Ryan, Michael P. *Knowledge Diplomacy: Global Competition and the Politics of Intellectual Property.* Washington, DC: Brookings Institution, 1998.

Sachs, Jeffrey, chair. "Macroeconomics and Health: Investing in Health for Economic Development." *Report of the Commission on Macroeconomics and Health.* Geneva: WHO, 2001.

Schepin, Oleg and Waldeermar Yermakov. *International Quarantine.* Madison, WI: International University Press, 1991.

Scherer, F. M. and Jayashree Watal. "Post-TRIPS Options of Access to Patented Medicines in Developing Nations." *Journal of International Economic Law* 5: 4 (2002): 913–939.

Sell, Susan, "Books, Drugs and Seeds: The Politics of Access." Paper Presented at the Annual Meeting of the International Studies Association, San Diego. March 22, 2006. http://www.allacademic.com/meta/p98118_index.html.

———. "Post-TRIPS Developments: The Tension between Commercial and Social Agendas in the Context of Intellectual Property." *Florida Journal of International Law* (Spring, 2002): 193–216.

Sell, Susan and Aseem Prakash. "Using Ideas Strategically: The Contest between Business and NGO Networks in Intellectual Property Rights." *International Studies Quarterly* 48 (2004): 143–175.

"A Shot of Transparency." *Economist*, August 12, 2006.

Siegfried, Andre, trans. *Routes of Contagion.* New York: Harcourt Press, 1965.

Simmons, P. J. and Chantal de Jonge Oudraat. *Managing Global Issues: Lessons Learned.* Washington, DC: Carnegie Endowment for International Peace, 2001.

Smith, R. D, R. Beaglehole, D. Woodward, and N. Drager, eds. *Global Public Goods for Health: Economic and Public Health Perspectives.* Oxford: Oxford University Press, 2003.

Solorzano, Armando. "Sowing the Seeds of Neo-imperialism: The Rockefeller Foundation's Yellow Fever Campaign." *International Journal of Health Service* 22: 3 (1992): 529–554.

Sridhar, Devi and Rajaie Batniji. "Global Health Institutions: Financing and Accountability." Global Economic Governance Programme, University of Oxford. 2006. www.globaleconomicgovernance.org/health/research.php.

Stebbins, Michael. "Is the U.S. Prepared for a Bioterrorist Attack?" *Technology for Training against Terror. Federation of American Scientists.* February 17, 2006. http://www.fas.org/main/content.jsp?formAction=297&contentId=343.

Stern, Alexandra Minna and Howard Markel. "International Efforts to Control Infectious Diseases, 1851 to the Present." *Journal of the American Medical Association* 292: 12 (2004): 1474–1479.

Sykes, Alan O. "TRIPS, Pharmaceuticals, Developing Countries and the Doha 'Solution.'" *Chicago Journal of International Law* 3: 1 (2002): 47–68.

Tam, John S. "Influenza A (H5N1) in Hong Kong: An Overview." *Vaccine* 20 (2002): S77–S81.

t'Hoen, Ellen. "TRIPS, Pharmaceutical Patents, and Access to Essential Medicines: A Long Way from Seattle to Doha." *Chicago Journal of International Law* 3: 1 (Spring, 2002): 27–46.

Thomas, Caroline. "Trade Policy, the Politics of Access to Drugs and Global Governance for Health." In *Health Impacts of Globalization*, edited by Kelley Lee, 177–191. London: Palgrave MacMillian, 2003.

Thomson, Theodore, trans. *International Sanitary Convention of Paris, 1903*. London: His Majesty's Stationery Office, 1904.

Thurman, Sandra. "The Shared Struggle against AIDS." *AIDS: The Threat to World Security* 5: 2 (July, 2000). http://usinfo.state.gov/journals/itgic/0700/ijge/gj01.htm.

Tucker, Jonathan B. *Scourge: The Once and Future Threat of Smallpox*. New York: Atlantic Monthly Press, 2001.

Tufts Center for the Study of Drug Development (CSDD). *Official Website*. "Tufts Center for the Study of Drug Development Pegs Cost of a New Prescription Medicine at $802 Million." 2001. http://csdd.tufts.edu/NewsEvents/RecentNews.asp?newsid=6.

Tussie, Diana. *The Multilateral Development Banks*. Ottawa: North-South Institute and Lynne Rienner Publishers, 1995.

United Nations. *Official Website: The Secretary General*. "Message on the Occasion of World AIDS Day." December 1, 2006. http://data.unaids.org/pub/PressStatement/2006/SG-worldaidsday2006.pdf.

———. *Official Website*. "UNDP Budget Estimates for the Biennium 2004–2005." 2003. http://www.undp.org/execbrd/pdf/dp03-28e.pdf.

United Nations Children's Fund (UNICEF). *Official Website*. "UNICEF in Emergencies." 2007. http://www.unicef.org/emerg/index_33296.html.

———. *Official Website*. "What We Do." 2007. http://www.unicef.org/whatwedo/index.html.

United Nations Children's Fund (UNICEF)/UNDP/World Bank/WHO Special Programme for Research and Training in Tropical Diseases (TDR). *Official Website*. "Strategy." September 10, 2007. http://www.who.int/tdr/about/strategy/default.htm.

United Nations Foundation. *Official Website*. "About Us." 2007. http://www.unfoundation.org/about/index.asp.

United Nations Millennium Project. *Official Website*. "About MDGs: What They Are." 2006. http://www.unmillenniumproject.org/goals/index.htm.

United States General Accounting Office (US-GAO). *Emerging Infectious Diseases: Asian SARS Outbreak Challenged International and National Responses*. Washington, DC: United States General Accounting Office, 2004.

United States Government. Presidential Documents. *Access to HIV/AIDS Pharmaceuticals and Medical Technologies.* Executive Order No 13155. May 10, 2000. http://frwebgate.access.gpo.gov/cgi-bin/getdoc.cgi?dbname=2000_register&docid=fr12my00-170.pdf.

Vance, James E. *Capturing the Horizon: The Historical Geography of Transportation since the Transportation Revolution of the Sixteenth Century.* New York: Harper and Row, 1986.

Vaughan, Megan. *Curing Their Ills: Colonial Power and African Illness.* Cambridge, MA: Polity, 1991.

Vick, Karl. "African AIDS Victims Losers of a Drug War: US Policy Keeps Prices Prohibitive." *Washington Post,* December 4, 1999, A01.

Watts, Sheldon. *Disease and Medicine in World History.* New York: Routledge, 2003.

———. *Epidemics and History: Disease, Power, and Imperialism.* New Haven, CT: Yale University Press, 1997.

Webby, Richard J. and Robert G. Webster. "Are We Ready for Pandemic Influenza?" In *Learning from SARS: Preparing for the Next Disease Outbreak,* edited by Stacey Knobler, Adel Mahmoud, Stanley Lemon, Alison Mack, Laura Sivitz, and Katherine Oberholtzer, 208–222. Washington, DC: National Academies Press, 2004.

Weekly Epidemiological Record. "Cholera." 56: 49 (1981): 385–392.

———. "Dracunculiasis Eradication Programme: Status during January–July 2004." 79: 38 (2004): 341–348.

———. "Functioning of the International Health Regulations from the Period 1 January to 31 December 1981." 57: 48 (1982): 369–376.

———. "Functioning of the International Health Regulations from the Period 1 January to 31 December 1981 (Continued from No 49)." 58: 50 (1983): 385–392.

———. "Functioning of the International Health Regulations from the Period 1 January to 31 December 1985." 61: 50 (1986): 385–392.

Wendt, Alexander. "Driving with the Rearview Mirror: On the Rational Science of Institutional Design." *International Organization* 55: 4 (2001): 1019–1050.

Westerhaus, Michael and Arachu Castro. "How Do Intellectual Property Law and International Trade Agreements Affect Access to Antiretroviral Therapy." *PLoS Medicine* 3: 8 (2006): 1230–1236.

Widdus, Roy. "Public-Private Partnerships for Health: Their Main Targets, Their Diversity, and Their Future Directions." *Bulletin of the World Health Organization* 79: 8 (2001): 713–720.

———. "Public-Private Partnerships for Health Require Thoughtful Evaluation." *Bulletin of the World Health Organization* 81: 4 (2003): 235.

Widdus, Roy and Katherine White. *Combating Diseases Associated with Poverty: Financing Strategies for Product Development and the Potential Role of Public-Private Partnerships. Workshop Report.* London: Initiative on Public Private Partnerships for Health, 2004.

William J. Clinton Foundation. *Official Website.* "HIV/AIDS Initiative." 2007. http://www.clintonfoundation.org/cf-pgm-hs-ai-home.htm.

Williams, Green. *The Plague Killers.* New York: Charles Scribner's Sons, 1969.

Winslow, Charles. *The Conquest of Epidemic Diseases*. Princeton, NJ: Princeton University Press, 1943.

Wogart, J. P. and G. Calcagnotto. "Brazil's Fight against AIDS and Its Implications for Global Health Governance." *World Health and Population* January (2006): 1–16.

Woodall, Jack. "Stalking the New Epidemic: Pro-MED Tracks Emerging Diseases." *Public Health Reports* 112: 1 (1997): 78.

Woods, Christopher, Adam M. Karpati, Thomas Grein, Noel McCarthy, Peter Gaturuku, Eric Muchiri, et al. "An Outbreak of Rift Valley Fever in Northeastern Kenya, 1997–1998." *Emerging Infectious Diseases* CDC 8: 2 (2002): 138–144.

World Bank. *Official Website*. "About Us." 2007. http://go.worldbank.org/3QT2P1GNH0.

———. *Official Website*. "The African Program for Riverblindness Control." 2007. http://www.worldbank.org/afr/gper/apoc.htm.

———. *Official Website*. "Communicable Diseases." 2004. http://go.worldbank.org/QAM90WR0A0.

———. *Official Website*. "Sector Strategy: Health Nutrition and Population." 2002. http://wbln0018.worldbank.org/HDNet/hddocs.nsf/c840b59b6982d2498525670c004def60/6fafece74ab8f0c6852568f00070542d?OpenDocument.

———. *World Bank Group: Working for a World Free of Poverty*. Washington, DC: World Bank Group, 2004.

———. *World Development Report: Investing in Health*. Washington, DC: World Bank, 1993.

World Health Organization. *Global Crises—Global Solutions: Managing Public Health Emergencies of International Concern Through the Revised International Health Regulations*. Geneva: WHO, 2002.

———. *Global Crises—Global Solutions: Managing Urgent International Public Health Events with the Revised International Health Regulations*. Geneva: WHO, 2000.

———. *Global Defense against the Infectious Disease Threat*. Geneva: WHO, 2002.

———. *Global Epidemics and Impact of Cholera*. Geneva: WHO, 2001. http://www.who.int/topics/cholera/impact/en/.

———. *International Health Regulations (Revised 1969)*. Geneva: WHO, 1969.

———. *International Health Regulations (Revised 1981)*. Geneva: WHO, 1983.

———. *International Health Regulations: Draft of the Proposed Revision*. Geneva: WHO, 2005.

———. *International Health Regulations: Provisional Draft*. Geneva: WHO, 1998.

———. *Public Health: Innovation and Intellectual Property Rights. Report of the Commission on Intellectual Property Rights, Innovation and Public Health*. Geneva: WHO, 2006.

———. *Severe Acute Respiratory Syndrome (SARS): Status of the Outbreak and Lessons for the Immediate Future*. WHO: Geneva, 2003.

———. *The World Health Report 1996: Fighting Disease, Fostering Development*. Geneva: WHO, 1996.

———. *The World Health Report 2002: Reducing Risks, Promoting Health Life*. Geneva: WHO, 2002.

————. *The World Health Report 2004: Changing History.* Geneva: WHO, 2004.

————. *Official Website.* "About WHO." 2007. http://www.who.int/about/en/.

————. *Official Website.* "African Program for Onchocerciasis Control." 2007. http://www.who.int/blindness/partnerships/APOC/en/.

————. *Official Website.* "Cholera." 2007. http://www.who.int/csr/disease/cholera/impactofcholera/en/.

————. *Official Website.* "Constitution of the World Health Organization," 45th Edition, Supplement, October 2006. http://www.who.int/governance/eb/who_constitution_en.pdf.

————. *Official Website.* "Disease Outbreak News." 2007. http://www.who.int/csr/don/archive/disease/en/.

————. *Official Website.* "Essential Drugs and Medicines." 2007. http://www.who.int/medicines/default.shtml.

————. *Official Website.* "Event Verification." 2007. http://www.who.int/csr/alertresponse/verification/en/.

————. *Official Website.* "Global Outbreak Alert & Response Network." 2007. www.who.int/csr/outbreaknetwork/en.

————. *Official Website.* "SARS Information Site." 2007. www.who.int/csr/sars/en.

————. *Official Website.* "What Are Essential Medicines?" 2004. http://www.who.int/medicines/rationale.shtml.

————. *Official Website.* "WHO Global Influenza Surveillance Network." 2007. http://www.who.int/csr/disease/influenza/surveillance/en/.

————. *Official Website.* "WHO Model List (Of Essential Medicines) 14th Edition." 2003. http://www.who.int/medicines/organization/par/edl/expcom14/eml14_en.pdf.

————. *Official Website.* "WHO Proposed Program Budget 2004–2005." 2002. http://www.who.int/gb/e/e_ppb2003.html.

————. *Official Website.* "WHO's Interaction with Civil Society and Nongovernmental Organizations." 2002. http://www.who.int/civilsociety/documents/en/RevreportE.pdf.

————. *Official Website.* "WHO-UNAIDS HIV Vaccine Initiative." 2007. http://www.who.int/vaccine_research/diseases/hiv/en/.

World Tourism Organization. *Official Website.* "Facts and Figures." 2007. http://www.world-tourism.org/facts/menu.html.

World Trade Organization. *Official Website.* "Agreement on Trade-Related Aspects of Intellectual Property Rights." 1994. (Text of the Agreement signed April 15, 1994, Marrakesh). http://www.wto.org/english/tratop_e/trips_e/trips_e.htm.

————. *Official Website.* "Declaration on the TRIPS Agreement and Public Health." November 20, 2001. http://www.wto.org/english/thewto_e/minist_e/min01_e/mindecl_trips_e.htm.

————. *Official Website.* "Implementation of paragraph 6 of the Doha Declaration on the TRIPS Agreement and public health." (Document: WT/L/540) September 1, 2003. http://www.wto.org/english/tratop_e/trips_e/implem_para6_e.htm.

————. *Official Website.* "WTO Structure." 2007. http://www.wto.org/english/thewto_e/whatis_e/tif_e/org2_e.htm.

World Trade Organization and World Health Organization. *WTO/WHO Joint Study: WTO Agreements and Public Health*. Geneva: WHO/WTO, 2002.

Young, Oran R. *Governance in World Affairs*. London: Cornell University Press, 1999.

———. *International Governance: Protecting the Environment in a Stateless Society*. Ithaca, NY: Cornell University Press, 1994.

Zacher, Mark W. "The Decaying Pillars of the Westphalian Temple: Implications for International Order and Governance." In *Governance Without Government*, edited by James Rosenau, 58–101. Cambridge: Cambridge University Press, 1992.

———. "Global Epidemiological Surveillance: International Cooperation to Monitor Infectious Diseases." In *Global Public Goods*, edited by Inge Kaul, Isabelle Grunberg, and Marc A Stern, 266–283. New York: Oxford University Press, 1999.

Zamora, Stephen. "Voting in International Economic Organizations." *American Journal of International Law* 74: 3 (1980): 566–608.

Zinsser, Hans. *Rats, Lice, and History*. New York: Black Dog and Leventhal Publishers, 1934.

INDEX